Reneé Gerlich's book *Out of the Fog* excavates layers of neoliberalism and misogyny as well as capitalism's hatred for the natural world. She shows us connections we needed to see years ago. Luckily, she also suggests how we might move through this calamitous state of affairs and reclaim that very human capability – love. I truly loved this book.
　—Janet Fraser, author of *Born Still: A Memoir of Grief*

Out of the Fog is an important book that skilfully orders the chaos characterizing today's political landscape.
　—Derrick Jensen, author of *A Language Older Than Words*

For women ready to move from confusion and paralysis into empowered action, Reneé Gerlich has written a remarkable work of radical feminist theory and praxis. *Out of the Fog* brilliantly exposes the history and power structures behind the perpetual crisis state and explains why marching, protesting, fundraising and online outrage fail to move us toward freedom and justice. Gerlich encourages women to fully embody their feminism and from this place of power go out and make a difference in the world.
　—Mary Lou Singleton, midwife and founder of Enchanted Family Medicine

Photo credit: D. Felidae

Renée Gerlich is a New Zealand-based writer whose work can be found on Feminist Current, Savage Minds, Uncommon Ground Media, and her blog, reneejg.net.

Renée has a background in art history and education and completed her Masters in Art History at Leiden University in the Netherlands. She was researcher for the 2016 documentary *The HeART of the Matter*, about the development and subsequent rollback of education reforms implemented by New Zealand's first Labour government, directed and produced by Luit and Jan Bieringa.

In 2021, Renée founded Dragon Cloud Press to publish *The Brief Complete Herstory*, an accessible, female-centred, short and illustrated history of the world from the Big Bang to neoliberalism, available at dragoncloudpress.com.

Other books by Renée Gerlich

The Brief Complete Herstory (2022)

OUT OF THE FOG

On politics, feminism and coming alive

Renée Gerlich

We respectfully acknowledge the wisdom of Aboriginal and Torres Strait Islander peoples and their custodianship of the lands and waterways. Spinifex offices are located on Djiru, Bunurong, Wadawurrung, Eora, and Noongar Country.

We also acknowledge the many women throughout history who have fought for women's freedom and the freedom of lesbians, often at the cost of their lives.

First published by Spinifex Press, 2022
Spinifex Press Pty Ltd
PO Box 5270, North Geelong, VIC 3215, Australia
PO Box 105, Mission Beach, QLD 4852, Australia
women@spinifexpress.com.au
www.spinifexpress.com.au

Copyright © Renée Gerlich, 2022

The moral right of the author has been asserted.

All rights reserved. Without limiting the rights under copyright reserved above, no part of this publication may be reproduced, stored in or introduced into a retrieval system, or transmitted, in any form or by any means (electronic, mechanical, photocopying, recording or otherwise) without prior written permission of both the copyright owner and the above publisher of the book.

Copying for educational purposes
Information in this book may be reproduced in whole or part for study or training purposes, subject to acknowledgement of the source and providing no commercial usage or sale of material occurs. Where copies of part or whole of the book are made under part VB of the Copyright Act, the law requires that prescribed procedures be followed. For information contact the Copyright Agency Limited.

Edited by Susan Hawthorne, Pauline Hopkins and Renate Klein
Index by Aviva Xue
Cover design by Deb Snibson, MAPG
Typesetting by Helen Christie, Blue Wren Books
Typeset in Albertina
Printed by McPherson's Printing Group

 A catalogue record for this book is available from the National Library of Australia

ISBN: 9781925950540 (paperback)
ISBN: 9781925950557 (ebook)

The text in this book has been printed on PEFC stock.

For the confused and longing

As the contradictions in the world of today grow deeper and more acute, the battle for people's minds and convictions is expanding in scope and complexity. This battle is being fought in all areas.
—Nawal El Saadawi

… our dysfunctional practices are calling out to us to awaken to the parallels between the numbing and abuse we express in our individual lives and that of our collective relationship to the life of our planet.
—Chellis Glendinning
with thanks to Brenda

The disconnect from the body of the earth really has to do with the disconnect from our bodies. The two are together. And the exploitation of the earth – as if it was something separate from us – has a lot to do with patriarchal domination. I mean, we talk about 'Mother Earth'. Look what we're doing to Mother. It's a Mother hatred, almost.
—Gabor Maté

Acknowledgements

First of all, I must thank Liz Miller for encouraging me to contribute to the anthology *Spinning and Weaving* (2021). I need to note that *Out of the Fog* follows the structure of my chapter in that book, and the two blog articles from which the chapter developed. Thank you Liz, for inviting me to be part of your anthology and for introducing me to Sonia Johnson's *Wildfire*! It was so uncanny to discover how much her experiences of feminism, her process of inquiry, and her conclusions reflected my own.

And now things get tricky. I am sure that writing acknowledgements is always tricky, for reasons particular to each author and their work. In this case, my manuscript went largely unseen before I submitted it to Spinifex Press, so I cannot keep my acknowledgements simple by limiting them to those who contributed to the text directly. Yet when I think about those who contributed to the text *indirectly*, the task of writing acknowledgements appears huge and unwieldy, since the book is inseparable from the context of my life.

Then there is the consideration that, since there is so much stigma on radical feminism today, many people I want to thank may not wish to be named or associated with my work, for fear of repercussions.

So: I will begin by thanking those people who brought books into my life without which *Out of the Fog* could not have been written, and I will use only first names unless I am confident the person I am acknowledging will not be negatively affected by me naming them in full. And I hope anyone who has not been mentioned here considers themselves spared rather than forgotten!

Out of the Fog: On politics, feminism and coming alive

Thank you Gerald Clevy (1972–2014) for introducing me to Aung Sun Suu Kyi, by way of your irrepressible spirit. To Christian for telling me to read Carol Henderson's *A Blaze of Colour*. And to Carol, and Luit Bieringa (1942–2022) and Jan, for the incredible gift of four years of working on *The HeART of the Matter*. Luit, such profound grief came over me when you passed.

I want to acknowledge another intellectual giant mentioned in this text, who passed away during the final stages of publication (and who I only met briefly): Moana Jackson (1945–2022). Jackson was a lawyer and spearhead of the prison abolition movement in Aotearoa New Zealand. My book has challenged that movement by suggesting that today's prison abolitionists seem more intent on promoting male sexual licence than resisting oppression.

Here I want to state that I do not consider Jackson to be an example of this trend. I wish to acknowledge Jackson as someone who never confused impunity with freedom, but saw the link between patriarchy, porn, colonisation, and prisons, and dreamt of an end to them all.

In his report on *The Māori and the Criminal Justice System*, Jackson criticises the pornography, sexist advertising, and objectification normalised in white society, saying that "they foster certain images about the violent resolution of conflict and sexist demeaning of women." He tackles "Western notions of machismo based on violent domination," and the replacement of "ancient respect of woman, her tapu," with "Western chauvinism" and "sexist definitions of a woman's place."

Next I want to say thank you to Pala, for introducing me to many radical thinkers like Jackson, to the legacy of your mother, Grace Molisa, to radical feminist literature, and later to Osho's *Love, Freedom and Aloneness*, and for changing my life.

Thank you to Emma for explaining the premise of Alice Miller's books, *The Drama of Being a Child* and *The Body Never Lies*, during a memorable walk through the wonderful city of Leiden. That conversation was a turning point that led me to other thinkers important in this book, like Gabor Maté.

Acknowledgements

Thank you Brenda, for introducing me to five writers who are vital to this work: Monica Sjöö and Barbara Mor, Charlotte Kasl, Chellis Glendinning (who provides an opening epigraph) and yourself. And thank you for much more: the rich friendship, deep, hard-earned wisdom, unparalleled hospitality and solace you've given me. You mean so much to me.

I also wish to thank those who have helped me improve my writing. For me, writing itself is not primary – coming out of the fog is primary. To that end, I ask questions and read, and to share the insights and analysis I gain from reading, I write. The writing is tricky. Thank you to Meghan Murphy and to Catherine, for feedback and advice that has helped me become a writer capable of producing a book. Thank you most of all to D. Felidae, for encouraging me toward a greater economy of language, and lending me your editing skills and listening ear as a talented editor, writer, and steadfast and marvellous friend.

I would like to thank more friends I met through my political life. I think that if inhumanity comes with a gift, it's that it brings humanity into starker relief, and so confronting transgenderism has allowed me to witness some of the beautiful qualities in people that I may have otherwise overlooked or undervalued: solidarity, compassion, constancy, sensitivity, sincerity, wisdom, wit, faith, curiosity, receptivity, commitment to questioning. Becoming a *persona non grata* has made these qualities all the more real and shining for me, when I encounter them. I hope that everyone who is forced to contend with the inhumanities of today has this experience too.

Thank you, Emily, my younger sister. Steph, for being unable to let a panicked a woman *also* feel alone. Chelsea, for your extraordinary courage. Tim, for the high value you place on critical thinking. Sunil, for long conversations that, for me, give meaning to the phrase 'free speech'!

Thank you Suzanne, for powerfully advising me not to worry about my rage, but instead address the powerlessness underneath.

Thank you to many Australian feminists: Susan Hawthorne and Renate Klein, who not only published this book, but took the idea seriously when it was not yet viable, and brought me over to Melbourne in 2019 just to keep me going. Thank you to Spider, and to Chris B., for guiding me through the practical struggles involved with receiving backlash. To Tashe, Heidi and Kylie for bringing me to women's lands, Mia for hearing my howl when it was time to leave, and to Dani Tauni for a beautiful trip to Brisbane and introducing me to Catharine MacKinnon's crucial essay *What is a White Woman Anyway?*

Thank you to Thistle Pettersen at Women's Liberation Radio News, and to the wonderful Julia Long, and Janet Fraser, for your sparkling and unconditional sisterhood. Also to Mary Lou Singleton, Janice Raymond, Jennifer Murnan and Derrick Jensen.

Thank you to my mother for your impossibly generous and unshakeable faith, the faith that fuels all of my writing, and to my father for being the most reliable person I could ever hope to know. To my brother, for our ever more honest and loving connection.

Lastly, thank you, to all who read my book and bibliography, for the effort of reading beyond my limited capacity with words and into the meanings I try to convey here.

If my past experiences are anything to go by, publishing this book will cause ripples that, however large or small, will change my life. I want to acknowledge those who may be affected by the ripples; those who will leave me, those who will stay to talk and listen, and those who will become new friends and teachers. I look forward to all that we will share, as we continue to come out of the fog.

Contents

Introduction	1
Chapter One: My Story	17
Chapter Two: Desire and Distortion	55
Chapter Three: Rebellion and Backlash	95
Chapter Four: Fatal Contradictions	147
Conclusion: Cassandra's Power	189
Bibliography	217
Index	231

Introduction

Over the last decade, various social movements have drawn our attention to a plethora of social problems: Black Lives Matter (BLM) was established in 2014 to protest racialised police brutality. The #MeToo phenomenon began in 2017, exposing rape and sexual predation. The 2018 March for Our Lives demanded an end to gun violence, and the climate strikes began the following year. Meanwhile, physician Gabor Maté's popular 2021 film *The Wisdom of Trauma* sheds light on epidemic levels of anxiety, depression, disconnection, addiction, and trauma; social worker Brené Brown's 2010 talk on vulnerability remains one of the most watched on ted.com.

From 2020, the world was confronted with a coronavirus pandemic and unprecedented government lockdowns followed by protests. The following year, the Taliban took over Afghanistan, and, as I write, the threat of World War Three looms after Russia's invasion of Ukraine.

These problems all deserve our attention, but they tend to be discussed as though they are separate, have no common denominator, and the solutions they require are at odds with one another. In particular, our perception of the state and its institutions – the government, military and police – seems to change depending on which social issue is highlighted. For example, while BLM activists remind us that the prison system functions as part of a racist 'war against the poor', the #MeToo movement asks that we listen to women and support rape victims to have perpetrators held to account and convicted.

In 2015, Brock Turner was on trial in Stanford, California, for raping a woman behind a dumpster. Chanel Miller's victim statement was published on the website *Buzzfeed* under the pseudonym Emily Doe, making the trial world news. The following year, Turner was given a six-month sentence, likely to be reduced to three months for good behaviour. After the sentencing, Miller wrote in her notebook, "*You are worth more than three months ... Your suffering means something. You are worth more than three months*" (italics in original).[1]

In her 2019 book, *Know My Name*, Miller describes how punishing the trial was for her, and how it felt to see televised footage of judge Rosemarie Aquilina sentencing Larry Nassar, former team doctor of the United States women's national gymnastics team, for up to 175 years in 2016. While Miller was given a short time limit for her victim statement, Aquilina made time for 169 victim statements from female gymnasts and athletes who saw Nassar for medical care over 30 years. "It had never occurred to me that the system itself could be wrong, could be changed or improved. Victims could ask for more. We could be treated better," Miller wrote.[2]

In 2017, approximately 60 women accused actor Bill Cosby of rape, drug-facilitated sexual assault, sexual battery, child sexual abuse, and sexual misconduct, and Donald Trump became POTUS despite enough sexual assault allegations to warrant a film called *16 Women and Donald Trump* – and prompt a federal lawsuit filed in June 2016 by a woman alleging Trump raped her when she was 13 years old. In 2018, 87 women accused former Hollywood producer Harvey Weinstein of assault. When Weinstein was arrested, charged, and sentenced to 23 years in prison, feminists could only say, *finally*.

But BLM activists support prison abolition. Co-founder Patrisse Cullors counts political activist Angela Davis among her mentors, and Davis' book *Are Prisons Obsolete?* (2003) explains that prison populations became overwhelmingly black after slavery abolition. It recounts how convicts were forced to provide free labour to companies through a lease system and concludes that

---

1 Miller, 2019, pp. 242–3.
2 Miller, 2019, p. 139.

racist oppression through prisons simply took the place of racist oppression through slavery.

Speaking to *Teen Vogue* about her work as a prison abolitionist, Cullors said, "I really wanted to talk about the impact state violence had on black people, on our bodies, on our spirits, and just the impact of law enforcement interactions on us."[3]

Gabor Maté, an expert on trauma and addiction, is also a critic of the prison system. In his book *In the Realm of Hungry Ghosts* (2013), he writes about Detective Sergeant Paul Gillespie, head of the Toronto Sex Crimes Unit, who rescued children from online pornographers and became traumatised from the footage himself, saying the children in the videos have "dead eyes," so that "you can tell that their spirit is broken." Maté asks,

> if that same policeman, instead of quitting the police force, had transferred to the drug squad, who do you think he'd be chasing in the streets? Those same kids 20 years later, because they're the ones who, according to all the statistics and all the studies, become the drug addicts. Essentially, what we're doing in this country, with our so-called justice system, is we're punishing people and jailing them for having been abused in the first place.[4]

When #MeToo is at the forefront of our attention, we want to see more judges like Rosemarie Aquilina. When it is BLM or *The Wisdom of Trauma* (2021), we loathe state violence and want prisons abolished – but when a mass shooting occurs, we want the state to lock up the killer and throw away the key. After the 2019 Christchurch massacre in New Zealand – in which a gunman killed 50 people in a mosque and Islamic centre – progressives praised those who handed in hunting rifles to the police, in support of stricter gun control. Concern about state violence was temporarily suspended, with one well-known BLM supporter and prison abolitionist tweeting the following about Prime Minister Jacinda Ardern's response:

---

3 *Teen Vogue*, 2019.
4 Maté, 2013.

As much as I appreciate Jacinda's overwhelming sympathy for the victims, and how she must work through her hurt for New Zealand itself, I'm not reassured until she promises the full weight of the New Zealand state and society will come down upon every single white supremacist.

The state cannot be both racist and violent *and* capable of stopping racism and violence with its "full weight."

Concern about state violence was revived again when George Floyd was murdered by a white officer in Minneapolis in May 2020 – activists certainly did not suggest handing in guns to police to curb violence in response to that. Indeed, as our attention shifts from one event, crisis, or social movement to another, our view of state institutions and our understanding of the major threats facing humanity seem to change accordingly. This causes us to act in ways that are inconsistent and contradictory, and the inconsistency is a feature of our day and age.

When the issue of climate change is highlighted, our understanding of the greatest threat to humanity changes again. Guns and violence are no longer the central problem – even though, as I will discuss in Chapter Four, the United States military is the biggest contributor to global fossil fuel emissions. Instead, the most problematic people are oil tycoons, and people who drive too much, overuse plastic, and 'deny the science' that shows we are living through the sixth mass extinction and must reduce our carbon dioxide emissions.

The March for Science campaign, represented in 600 cities worldwide, began in 2017 to "mobilise advocates around the world in support of evidence-based, science-informed public policies."[5] In April 2017, two Green Party representatives spoke at one of these marches in Wellington – but the Greens are not *always* 'for science'. Indeed, the Greens deny science altogether when it comes to questions of sex and identity. Their 'Documents with Dignity' policy proposed that New Zealand law should change to

---

5 <https://marchforscience.org/our-mission/>

allow people to self-select the sex marker on birth certificates and passports. This policy is based on the idea that identity trumps science, or even that biology is irrelevant and sex does not exist. In 2018, Julie Anne Genter, Green Party member and then Minister for Women, appeared on the television talk show *Q&A* to advocate for a man who wanted access to a women's gym, saying, "transwomen are women … feminism is about equality for everyone."[6] It is ironic enough that a Minister for Women representing a party that claims to advocate 'for science' would deny that 'female' is a real biological category – but Genter was heavily pregnant at the time. In the *Q&A* video, her body clearly testifies to what her words deny.

The human capacity for denial and contradiction is just as dazzling and dangerous when we apply it to human biology as it is when we apply it to the environment. The consequences of replacing sex with identity in law, healthcare, women's organisations, and public policy – as the Green Party suggests we should – are endless. Men will be able to access female-only public toilets, changing rooms, prisons, safehouses, organisations, and sports teams, and women would have no recognised right to stop them, or, as individuals, to request female doctors or counsellors. Statistics on many issues where sex plays a major role – such as health, violence, self-harm, and suicide – will become unreliable, and that will be reflected in responses to problems identified through misleading data.

Nevertheless, by 2021, a bill based on the Green Party's proposals became law, despite objections from women's groups. It allows for one-step sex self-identification, meaning that any man can change the sex marker on his birth certificate from an 'M' to an 'F' through a single administrative procedure. The same month, New Zealanders were living under the 'red' restrictions of the government's COVID-19 traffic light system. So, at the same time it became impossible to eat lunch in a café without a vaccine

---

6   1news, 2018.

pass, it became possible for men to declare themselves women and have their documentation changed accordingly, without question.

New Zealand's Labour government showed it was prepared to bring life-as-normal to a halt in order to protect the population from a virus, in the name of public health and science, despite the cost to individual freedom. At the same time, it would do *nothing* to protect women from the risk of sexual assault resulting from men's access to female-only spaces, and it would even fly in the face of science to give men that access, in the *name* of individual freedom.

Laws allowing for sex self-identification are fundamentally anti-science: they pretend that human reproductive biology is either irrelevant or does not exist. Regardless of what liberals may say about science when it comes to COVID-19, vaccination, or climate change, when it comes to sex, identity trumps biology, even if the non-existence of biology makes having a female identity meaningless and therefore pointless to claim. Trans activists often claim that science itself is a constructed and colonial paradigm that has been imposed on Indigenous peoples who once recognised a plethora of gender identities. Samoan fa'afafine and Native American 'two-spirit' people are used as proof that sex does not exist, and that a woman is simply anyone who claims to be a woman.

The 'progressive' social movements that have arisen over the past decade appeal to the human conscience: no one in their right mind wants to live in a brutally racist rape culture in which most people are depressed and killing ourselves, each other, and the planet. So, we listen to the spokespeople, attend the demonstrations, buy the t-shirts. Taking action helps us to alleviate feelings of despair and helplessness in the face of so much injustice.

But what does it cost us to suppress awareness of the contradictions between these movements? Are we less anxious, hypervigilant, and afraid of our own voices when we contradict ourselves, than when we do nothing? What if we become so passionate about prison abolition that we offend women trying to have rapists convicted? What if we become so adamant that all gun owners hand their weapons to police, that we offend BLM activists who work to raise awareness of police brutality? What if we become so vocal about hating science deniers that we offend someone who identifies as transgender and views science as oppressive?

Every news broadcast of a military strike, mass shooting, sexual assault, famine, flood, or bushfire conjures within us a deep need to act. But without knowing whether or how these problems connect, we cannot respond authentically. Feeling moved to act but powerless to do so, in an age that seems to be characterised by complexity, creates a tension in our lives that expresses itself both in hypervigilance and in the outsourcing of responsibility. We need to do something, *now* – but we need someone else to tell us *what*.

Governments take advantage of our guilt and need for direction by reinforcing the idea that the world will be saved through the micromanagement of citizens' behaviour. If only we would stop using plastic bags, being nasty to each other, and enjoying long showers – and if we would just learn to wash our hands and not sneeze into them – humanity might stand a chance. In 2018, the New Zealand government banned single-use plastic bags, and Wellington City is often plastered with posters stating things like, "shower as long as a 4-minute song."[7] At the same time, 'call out culture' is rife (in 2017, two women were prevented from opening a burrito stand in Portland (USA) because of accusations of racism and cultural appropriation) – so another poster campaign in Wellington, this time by the Human Rights Commission, attempts to control the effects by encouraging polite online conduct using the slogan, "dial it down."[8] "Dial it down a notch, Aotearoa," reads one poster, which elaborates:

> We're asking everyone to dial down the heat a notch, and keep conversations civil – online and in person. It's okay to

---

7   On August 20, 2018, New Zealand's Labour government banned single-use plastic bags, with retailers given six months to stop providing them or face fines of up to NZ$100,000. (Two years later, single-use face masks litter the pavements instead.)
8   Moreno, 2017.

be passionate about topics like COVID-19, but it's not okay to personally attack others.[9]

Now, there is nothing wrong with taking short showers, washing your hands for a round of *Happy Birthday*, sneezing into your elbow instead of your palms, or being polite with those your disagree with as a stand against the breakdown of civil discourse – and I celebrate the end of single-use plastic bags – but the overall dynamic that is established here is one of paternalism. The public is like a bunch of helpless, guilty, snot-nosed children making a mess that large institutions must clean up by directing us toward moral action and hygiene. Public institutions and political figures can pass irresponsible laws and fan the flames of fear while simultaneously telling the public to calm down, clean up, and grow up.

It is all too easy to fall prey to this paternalism when we ourselves experience a state of stress and pressure coupled with helplessness – having no idea what to do. Helplessness is what leads us to outsource responsibility to those we *do* perceive as having answers, placing our 'hopes' in one or other political party or charismatic leader, attending demonstrations and donating to causes. But the human heart is never satisfied with such substitutes for real responsibility. It is demoralising to go to work or school each day, feeling unsatisfied and guilty for everyday decisions we make, knowing deep down that if we could only set our own priorities, we could make a difference, but feeling that other people are better placed to do so.

I have felt these tensions from childhood. In the 1990s, images of emaciated children were broadcast on the news often, and as part of advertisements for charities like Save the Children Fund and World Vision. They shocked, baffled and haunted me. The first time I saw them, I assumed I was seeing evidence of a freak emergency that would subside now that the world knew what was happening through news broadcasts – but the images, and the poverty and famine *never ended*. I longed to understand how this

---

9 dialitdown.co.nz

could be possible so that I would know how to help. Living in a world in which children were allowed to starve, year upon year, was too painful to accept. I did the 40-hour famine annually into my early twenties and sent money and letters through World Vision to a boy in Honduras, not having any better ideas.

I eventually learned that mass starvation is not caused by large organisations not having enough money to fix the problem. By 2015, I had made the connection between oppression, violence and profit, and got involved in protesting corporate free trade and the arms industry, but the penny really dropped when I began reading feminist literature. I didn't read the popular, politically liberal varieties of feminism but the radical feminism born out of 1970s and 80s women's consciousness raising. One of the first texts I read was Kate Millett's *Sexual Politics* (1969), which explains that,

> our society, like all other historical civilisations, is a patriarchy. The fact is evident at once if one recalls that the military, industry, technology, universities, science, political office, and finance – in short, every avenue of power within the society, including the coercive force of the police, is entirely in male hands. As the essence of politics is power, such realisation cannot fail to carry impact.[10]

This male dominance is plainly visible, but I somehow hadn't 'seen' it, nor the problem it represents. Feminism taught me to reclaim this perception, and showed me how male dominance, the pattern of men's violence associated with it, my own suffering, and the suffering of humanity, are connected.

To address a common misconception with a standard disclaimer: the phrase 'men's violence' does not refer to a violent impulse 'innate' to men. It simply refers to the fact that most violence is committed by men, whether it takes place in the street, the home, the military, or in the name of law enforcement. As the environmental activist Jonah Mix wrote in an essay that has since been censored from *Medium*:

---

10   Millett, 1969/2000, p. 25.

Women commit perhaps one-tenth of all murders, and less than one-tenth of one percent of all mass shootings. When one removes from the pool of killers all women who struck back against abusive strangers and partners alike, only to be punished for their self-defense, the number drops further. To deny the specifically male nature of atrocity is to fool oneself.[11]

Equally, to point out the pattern of male violence is not to suggest that it is 'inherent' in men. If it were, we would hardly be able to change it. We would have little choice but to succumb, but it might not be a problem. Look at nature – when living beings are allowed to live exactly in accordance with their nature, they thrive. To live as nature intended is what it means to be healthy, and if men were *supposed* to be as violent as they are, if this violence were nature's design, then we, as a species, would not be suffering as a result – on the contrary, we would be revelling in the feelings that result from actualised potential.

We are not thriving. And whether the problem is climate change, gun violence, police brutality, rape, prisons, or widespread trauma and feelings of alienation and disconnection, men's violence and the patriarchal system that sustains it are in play. It is especially difficult to name this problem now that naming sex itself is taboo – patriarchy is a sex-based system and cannot be discussed wherever recognising biology is disallowed. Public discourse is doomed to remain more noisy, reactive and confusing than sincere, effective and clear as long as this is our situation.

Patriarchy is not a natural system but an imposed one. As I will explain in Chapter Two, it trains us to act against our nature, to be self-destructive. This training occurs through gender norms that teach boys to comply with masculine norms and see themselves as dominant, and girls to be feminine and submissive. As the spiritual teacher Krishnamurti wrote, "We have created society and that society has conditioned us."[12] Our conditioning causes us

---

11 Jonah Mix, from a *Medium* article that has since been removed by the platform.
12 Krishnamurti, 1972, p. 20.

Introduction

to replicate the very social patterns that make us suffer. The primary pattern is men's violence.

How can this conditioning have such a powerful hold that it overrides not only our deeper wisdom, but our more basic instinct to *survive* individually and collectively? This, too, is a question only feminism can answer. The most quintessential and unnatural act of violation that men carry out, and the one that is crucial to sustaining a patriarchal system of male dominance, is rape. By tying violation to the sexual response, rape teaches men to fetishise violence and domination, and it fuels all other forms. As Kate Millett wrote:

> What goes largely unexamined, often even unacknowledged (yet is institutionalised nonetheless) in our social order, is the birthright priority whereby males rule females. Through this system a most ingenious form of 'interior colonisation' has been achieved. It is one which tends moreover to be sturdier than any form of segregation, and more rigorous than class stratification, more uniform, certainly more enduring. However muted its present appearance may be, sexual dominion obtains [status] … as perhaps the most pervasive ideology of our culture and provides its most fundamental concept of power.[13]

For feminists, rape is the oil in the machine of human destructiveness. Institutionalised in prostitution, filmed in porn, and normalised in everything from media objectification and advertising to sexist 'banter' and sex role stereotypes, rape ties the act of violation to ejaculation, and that is the hook. The sexual payoff is what makes porn use so compulsive for men, and such an effective form of social conditioning.

Porn and patriarchy teach men to eroticise violence, and this is what enables men to become rapists and killers, even go to war. That is why humanity is caught in a web of destruction.

Feminists sometimes object to the word *rape* being used as a metaphor: the flesh-and-blood reality is that one in three women are raped in our lifetimes. To speak of rape metaphorically is to take the

---

[13] Millett, 1969/2000, p. 25.

visceral impact of rape on real women out of the equation, which is to give the word another meaning, and it is an insult to women that the full impact of the word *rape* can only be felt when we do this. When we talk about environmental destruction as the 'rape of the earth', we feel what that means. When a military invasion is described as the rape of one country by another, we feel what that means. When we analogise capitalism as rape – a system where we sell our labour to corporations and employers who 'fuck us over' – we feel what that means. When rape 'only' refers to male violence against women, we bristle (do we *really* need to talk about *that*?).

So, though some feminists resist using rape as an analogy for good reason, part of the insult of rape is precisely its abstract dimension: that it contradicts the greatest and deepest human impulse to love, that it is the quintessential act of desecration and an attempt at spiritual cannibalism. Rape selects the very origin of all humanity – the female sex – as its target, and subjects this target to an act that contradicts love like no other. If to love is to give and to be energised in the giving, to *fuck* something – excuse my language – is to take, to deplete in the taking, and yet to be gratified. The ultimate insult of rape is its revelation that it is possible for a human being to find gratification this way.

This is what hurts us about the state of humanity, and because we are socialised to accommodate rape, rape indeed expresses itself in numerous ways. When people say that humans are 'fucking up the planet', we mean that we are not living in harmony and gratitude with the living world, but taking from it, depleting it, and being gratified. It hurts us not only because we cannot survive that way, but because it is against our nature. When we use the word 'conquest' to describe both militarism and sex, it is because we are taught to approach both in the same way: pillage, deplete, triumph. Analogising environmental and military violation as rape is also appropriate because both are correlated with it literally: rape and prostitution are rife around 'man camps' like mines, resource extraction sites and army bases.

Introduction

Human beings are currently suffering epidemic levels of anxiety, depression, disconnection, and addiction, because of the state of our relationships with ourselves, each other and earth. The human heart is trying to speak to our conditioned minds about this the way that women try to speak to men about it: constantly, urgently, despite being largely ignored. Like the world's women, our hearts continue to keep us alive, day by day, minute by minute, yet we use that life sustenance to continue our trajectory of toxification. Rape is the toxin. If it was meant to be woven into the fabric of our sexuality, communities and life on earth, it would not hurt us physically and it would not hurt us spiritually and our hearts would not resist.

Many self-help authors who analyse today's epidemics of depression, anxiety and chronic stress tell us some version of the 'sabre tooth tiger' story about these problems. They say that we are anxious because the stress response, evolved in 'caveman' times to save us from grizzly bears and lions, lags behind the progress we have made building an industrial civilisation in which most of us no longer encounter lions and tigers in everyday life. Our bodies are such that we still get stressed as though our lives are wild when in fact they are thoroughly civilised, so silly billy humans sometimes react to a terse email as though it is a cobra poised to strike. We just need to retrain our backward nervous systems and encourage them to catch up with reality.

This explanation is wanting. It frames industrial civilisation as progressive, something human nature *should* catch up with, rather than resist (says who?). Meanwhile, war, rape and pornography have created a situation in which the biggest threat to human beings today, and certainly women and girls, are the *males of our own species*. Masculine socialisation makes this absurdly unnatural situation possible, by numbing the sensitivity of boys and men and creating an epidemic of sexual assault. Our nervous systems appear to be out of whack because they are responding to an absurd situation in which human beings have become predators unto ourselves. The threat we face is among and within us, and our bodies are responding accordingly.

One reason we fail to see this clearly is because of the false distinction we make between the 'public sphere' and 'private sphere'. In her book *Man's Dominion*, feminist author Sheila Jeffreys shows how patriarchy relies on the "public/private split common to political and legal theory and practice."[14] Cultures that are not patriarchal do not honour such a division, which is not to say that everyone has a right to meddle in everyone else's business. In women-friendly cultures, as discussed in Chapter Two, the activities that make up individual life, from child raising to food preparation and housing, are approached communally.

Under patriarchy, the private or domestic sphere is the realm of women. Women are expected to look after the home, raise children, and prepare food by themselves and as par for the course; or else we are only bedroom accessories. What happens in this private, domestic, 'female' realm is not considered of public or political importance. So, while #MeToo may have drawn attention to the rape epidemic, the wider political significance of it tends to go unacknowledged. We still think that what hurts us politically and what hurts us personally are two separate things, but they are not. What hurts human beings is the state of our relationships. So long as the issue of rape is seen as a women's issue or a matter of private trauma with low status in public discourse, we will not understand that the problem of rape is ubiquitous, and fail to make meaningful change. As Virginia Woolf wrote in her 1938 essay on militarism, *Three Guineas*, "The public and private worlds are inseparably connected … the tyrannies and servilities of one are the tyrannies and servilities of the other."[15]

Feminism is key to perceiving *how* the private and public realms connect, and to resolving the contradictions that exist between today's progressive movements. Women constitute *half* the human population – the half relegated to the so-called private sphere, the

---

14 Jeffreys, 2012, p. 9.
15 Woolf, 1938/2001, p. 240.

Introduction

half that knows the pain of living in a rape culture. Our feelings and experiences form patterns, and these are the basis of feminist analysis. Feminist analysis is what moves women's experience out of the private and into the public realm, but it is generally disallowed, because this process is so destabilising to the social order and status quo.

Nevertheless, understanding how our private heartbreak relates to our large-scale problems is the only way we can unravel the helplessness we feel, claim our voices, and take action in the way we deeply crave. We cannot do any of these things while living with the cognitive dissonance of competing ideas, priorities, solutions, and top-down paternalism.

Three of the authors I draw on in this book – Gabor Maté, clinical psychologist Harriet Lerner, and spiritual teacher Sadhguru – all explain the relationship between responsibility and freedom in the same way. They say that responsibility is not what we think it is: our layered burdens of moral obligation. None of us can 'fix' the world, nor is it our duty. Instead, we are each gifted the *ability to respond*. Having only one life, this response-ability we have is sacred, and not to be frittered away either on duty *or* avoidance.

The craving for a powerful and authentic voice that each of us carries is not conceited, unimportant, or based on some sort of saviour complex, though it can express itself in those ways. Each of us wants deeply to reclaim responsibility for the wellbeing of humankind, and we want our priorities in life to reflect this responsibility. This, in fact, is freedom.

To activate our response-ability *and* experience the freedom of expression we so desire, we need clarity. Clarity, responsibility, and freedom go together. I wrote this book because I believe that feminism – the kind that does not deny nature – offers us the clarity we seek in a world that looks increasingly confused. By questioning fundamental aspects of the social order from women's perspective, feminism gives us a way to see ourselves as a part of the totality of life and humanity, to understand our own suffering in context, and to name its root causes. With this clarity we can each reclaim the response-ability no politician, executive or spokesperson is qualified to claim on our behalf.

I wish you all the freedom this world can offer.

CHAPTER ONE

My Story

My being was overcome with an intense longing to return, to follow that ineffable call. I felt as though I were standing at a threshold obscured by a dense fog. If only I could dispel the fog, I would be able to see. See what? I did not know. But I was certain it would reveal my deepest longing.
—Thich Nhat Hanh, Fragrant Palm Leaves[16]

Our first task, as feminists, is to learn to see with our own eyes.
—Andrea Dworkin, Our Blood[17]

When my mother picked me up on my last day of kindergarten, I thanked my teacher.

"That's the first thing I've heard her say," she said, surprised.

"You mean today?" my mother asked.

"No, all year."

My parents immigrated to the Wellington region of New Zealand from the Netherlands in 1982, and I grew up in a small family of four, mystified by the strangers around us, including those I encountered each day at school. I watched the other children playing, unsure. Who are these people? Why do they do the things they do? What do they want from me?

In my early years of primary school in Paraparaumu, I went to a girls' dance class. In the photos of our 'beetles' performance, we are all on stage wearing brightly coloured, homemade cotton overalls and headbands with bug eyes bouncing on wire springs. The other girls are dancing. I am moving absentmindedly, my tongue searching the corner of my mouth, frozen between an awareness of

---

16 Nhat Hanh, 1966, p. 34.
17 Dworkin, 1976, p. 62.

two realities: my friends are dancing, but we are also being watched by a large group of people hard to see from the brightly lit stage.

As I grew up, I felt disconnected from a capacity for spontaneity and joy I perceived others to be naturally endowed with. I carried an almost constant feeling of watching life happen through some impenetrable fog, while harbouring an urgent desire to *feel* the world beyond. I wanted to understand the basis of my connection with the world, why I was stuck inside myself, and what I needed to do to be able to dance joyfully, laugh unselfconsciously, and fully feel my life.

I watched women who appeared to have that vitality. They were my role models, showing me what freedom would look and feel like when I was old enough to claim it. At my insistence, my mother hired *Grease* on VHS every time we went to the video store. I loved the opening scene, where the main characters, Sandy and Danny, run around on the beach and play in the waves together like two puppies. It seemed like a wonderful way to imagine what being adult and free would feel like. The day we hired the tape and this part of the reel was damaged, showing black and grey lines moving up and down the screen, I was inconsolable.

For the rest of *Grease,* Sandy and Danny are in high school, out of their casual beachwear. The school environment reveals some challenging differences between them: Danny is a rebel and the leader of the T-Birds 'greaser gang', and Sandy is a 'good girl' who wears pastel-coloured cardigans. Can they be together? The question is answered in the film's final theme park scene. Sandy approaches Danny as a transformed 'greaser girl', wearing skin-tight black leggings, heavy eyeliner, and lots of hairspray. She stubs a cigarette under her high heels before the couple go dirty dancing on a children's ride, singing *You're the One That I Want.*

This transformation is how Sandy 'came alive'. I took note. If I wanted to come alive and be my own woman someday and feel free like a puppy on a beach with my playmate, I would have to do things boys would not be caught dead doing, like wear hairspray, heels, and makeup, so that one of them would want me.

Was that it? I tried to figure it out, but it never made sense. By age 12, I looked for answers in a copy of Robert Graves' *Greek Myths* inherited from my oma, a painter. I presumed the Greek pantheon was a sort of metaphor for all the basic elements of the natural world, human psyche, and society, so I would read the stories and make maps and diagrams of the gods and goddesses, trying to decode the mythology, looking for whatever I needed to know to understand people and society and awaken to my life.

The absurdity, violence and inconsistencies in the stories left me frustrated. I connected with Athena, the goddess of arts, culture and wisdom associated with the owl – but what did it mean for me, a girl trying to understand the world and her place in it, that Athena was also a war goddess clad in armour, who was born from her father's head – her father being Zeus, the king of the gods and a serial rapist who deeply resented his wife, Hera?

My desire to understand the world was made more urgent by the images of African famines on television. I was disturbed to the core when I first saw those children with bones protruding and flies crawling over their faces. I can't have been older than four, but I immediately understood that vast networks of people needed to see those children and *not* feed them for the images to appear on television and reach me.

I assumed that the purpose of the news, and the reason why it was always so grim, was to broadcast the problems of the world to adults who went to work each day to address them. Pictures of starving children were being broadcast into my parents' living room to let my parents know, so that they could help. Since my father had a technical job and my mother looked after my brother and I, I thought it must be down to *me* to help – and that this was why activities like the annual 40 Hour Famine were targeted at children. There were children in Africa whose parents were prevented from feeding them. Global broadcasting networks could not help, my parents could not help, and so children like me had to do it.

The images never stopped. More disturbingly, they became a television 'meme' of the 1990s. How could a situation that looked to me like a freak emergency requiring immediate resolution, continue year upon year? Why did all the adults around me appear to simply continue with their lives unaffected, as if nothing was amiss? Such a world struck me as equally strange and terrifying, and I felt torn between the need to understand the cause of the suffering I could see so that I could respond, and the need to numb myself to it so that I could concentrate at school, do homework, and accomplish the things I was supposed to.

I perceived my hometown, Paraparaumu, as a place full of people who had largely chosen the latter option: numbing. The town's focal point is a large shopping mall with a trail of fast-food outlets along the highway; perpendicular to the highway is a long road leading to the beach lined with big box retail stores. To me it was a place where school education seemed to lead to work in retail, hairdressing, admin or construction. I saw little evidence of any global consciousness, creative community or critical discussion happening, and it seemed to me that people moved to Paraparaumu to raise children who left as soon as they could. I struggled to identify role models who could help me with my questions and feelings about the world or point the way to a large or meaningful life.

In my second year of high school, we started social studies classes. I was as eager as ever to learn. The year was divided into a series of 'Topics', two of which were World War Two and feudal Japan. I don't remember which came first. Our teacher, Mrs Surrell, would write screeds of text on a rolling blackboard before class and we were expected to sit and frantically copy, shaking out our writing hands periodically to stop the cramp. When Mrs Surrell gauged that we were done, she grabbed the handle of the blackboard and pulled it all the way down, revealing the rest of the text she'd prepared on the other side. Someone would inevitably groan.

I never took in a word of what I copied from that blackboard, not only because I was too focused on the act of transcription to worry about meaning, but also because I didn't have any frame of reference to help me interpret the text. I had no general sense of history and doing social studies through a series of units in random historic and geographic order felt like trying to follow directions to someone's house given in random order. It was bewildering.

I was also a skinny, blonde, Dutch girl who blushed easily, and this made me an irresistible target for sexual harassment. Being surrounded by teenage boys was terrifying for a girl who had not learned to take possession of her mind or body. Blushing easily was my response and a curse, because just knowing I did this automatically made the embarrassment compound on itself to the point that some days a boy would only have to look in my direction to turn me almost purple. This seemed to amuse them, and I monitored myself carefully to ensure I would not accidentally say or reveal anything they could leverage to make me the butt of some joke that would allow them to watch me redden and squirm.

I have never watched pornography, but they taught me about it. I hated those moments that some boy would ask me if I enjoyed 'teabagging', or whether I would like to 'spitroast' later. The fact I didn't know what these terms meant was a source of hilarity, and while I recall nothing about my fourth form unit on feudal Japan, I remember this education in porn vocabulary. The fog thickened around me as I navigated this sexualised torment. I felt childish for not being able to 'claim' my sexuality like Sandy in *Grease* – but I also didn't know how to do it in a way that was authentic and would not simply lead to more ridicule.

In my final year, I added art history to my school timetable, and it gave me something I craved: a digestible, overarching narrative of history. One that was malleable, beautiful, fascinating, and could connect me, in New Zealand in 2001, to people and places as far back and abroad as I wanted to go. I could learn the story while marvelling at all the creative wonders, from paintings and sculptures to architecture, that humanity has produced, and then amend, question, and add to the story throughout my life. This is what I wanted: not a story that claimed to be gospel, but an overall picture that I could relate to and use to constantly deepen my understanding of the world and my own life.

Art history was still dominated by men, of course, and I was a teenage girl. But unlike conventional history, it was not dominated by army uniforms, battles, weapons, and strategic and tactical questions that I simply could not connect with. I suspect that the boys in school who have an easier time with this form of history have been trained in childhood through video games and toy swords and soldiers and plastic guns that assume boys will have a lifelong interest in violence and the military. A childhood spent playing with dolls, dancing in beetle costumes, and reading the *Babysitters Club* doesn't prepare a kid to learn the history of men at war.

I loved art history so much that it dominated my life until my late twenties. I decided I wanted to be a museum curator and curate stories that would help people make sense of the world. When I enrolled at university, art history was my major.

I was still doing the 40 Hour Famine in my first year of uni, desperate for a way to help address the hunger and starvation in the world. I made monthly payments and corresponded with a boy in Honduras through World Vision, until my mother cancelled my membership while I was doing my Masters in the Netherlands in 2007. At that time, I was working three jobs and still struggling to manage my living costs.

Postmodernism and cultural relativism underpinned much of my university education, and these philosophical frameworks mixed uneasily with my conscience. Postmodernism seemed to be premised on the notion that since life is infinitely complex, ever changing, and incomprehensible, and since 'the world' is only knowable through unreliable, socially constructed ideas, there is no absolute truth, and therefore no right and wrong. Trying to answer big questions like, "what is the cause of suffering?" can only lead us to contrived answers that we try to impose on the world like little dictators.

I saw the truth in this proposition: of course life is incomprehensibly complex, ever changing, and impossible to capture in concepts. There was also something liberating in the idea that I was *not*, after all, responsible for all the poverty, famine, and starvation in the world. Yet it still seemed to me that the inordinate amounts of time and energy postmodern academics spent arguing that there was no such thing as truth could be better spent alleviating hunger. The idea that the world was too complex to grasp seemed both true *and* a cop out.

Meanwhile, my beautiful best friend, Kristina, seemed to carry such a heavy conscience that it weighed on her if she purchased anything that wasn't an organic cabbage. She bought only fair trade and second-hand clothes, nothing made in China. She suffered anorexia, and her conscience seemed to form part of its arsenal, reminding her that capitalism contaminates everything, including almost all food, if not with sugar and toxins, then with exploitation. Eat, partake, and be poisoned. Our sense of responsibility can paralyse us.

I was terrified of the prospect that life would pass me by before I could understand what to do with it.

After my undergraduate degree, I spent two years in the Netherlands studying for a master's degree in art history and museum studies, and to gain experience in the sector that I felt would give me an edge. I returned to New Zealand at the end of 2008, right as the global financial crisis (GFC) hit. The sudden shrinking of the art world left me searching in vain for a serious entry-level job, which prompted me to critically examine the priority I'd placed on my dream of becoming a curator. I considered how many hours of my life I had traded in for sentences on my CV. Was that going to work? If I'd spent a decade trying to build a career that never eventuated, would that spell failure? Did it mean I would have nothing to contribute to society – and would *that* mean I had no worth?

I cobbled jobs together, often dreaming of travelling again or living nomadically in a campervan. I decided to rekindle my high school French and used the website couchsurfing.com to look for French speakers in Wellington. That's how I met Gerald Clevy.

Gerald was a beautiful, bald, calm, sturdily-built man who connected more to his Spanish heritage than his French. He worked long hours as an animator at Weta Digital and harboured a spark of Catalonian anarchism that I loved. He told me that the one thing he missed most since moving to New Zealand from France was a decent political conversation. I had the same longing for different reasons, and felt ashamed not to have the political literacy to talk with him about the figures who fascinated him: Aung San Suu Kyi in Myanmar, Venezuelan president Hugo Chávez, and Bolivian president Evo Morales.

I looked up Suu Kyi and read her books, *Freedom from Fear* (1991) and *The Voice of Hope* (1997). Suu Kyi's commitment to 'socially engaged Buddhism' (a term associated with the Vietnamese monk and activist Thich Nhat Hanh) and to her country Myanmar, had a profound impact on me. Suu Kyi helped me see that no place on earth is irrelevant, and her voice cut through my feelings of needing to escape my hometown, Paraparaumu. She showed me that my contempt for it only contributed to the atmosphere I felt there. This simple shift brought me into my body. It lifted the fog, connected me with the humanity around me, and led me to a state that I can only describe as a *satori* experience that lasted until my birthday the following year, in June 2011.[18]

During this period, I changed in all sorts of ways: I saw myself and my response-ability in context; I saw myself as one human in seven billion. I wasn't irrationally anxious or afraid of anyone or anything, including institutions and authority figures, and didn't take anything personally. Usually a poor navigator who lost my bearings easily, my mind too clouded to take in my surrounds, with my newfound mental clarity I attuned to my physical environment and gained a sense of direction. I felt both decisive and open to change, and I was never in a state of waiting – five minutes at a bus stop was an opportunity to meditate. I would do this by remembering that if human beings are capable of peace, then peace

---

18 A *satori* is a temporary glimpse into awakening. I may be misusing the term here, and though I am also appalled at myself for the apparent claim to 'wokeness', I know no other word to convey how deeply and thoroughly the shift I experienced changed me, and my experience of life.

is always within me, and I would sit down, locate and activate this part of me, and allow it to swell with my breath. I had energy and a healthy lifestyle I found easy to maintain.

During my school education, my reports had so often relayed that I needed 'confidence', but longing for this mysterious quality only made me feel more deficient. Suu Kyi's engaged Buddhism helped me realise I didn't need any such thing, only for the fog – my fear, confusion, insecurity – to lift and expose the natural, alive peace underneath.

This peace is what first made me a protestor. At the end of 2010, I enrolled in teacher education. I thought a teaching diploma might help me find work in museums, but I commenced my studies with a full commitment to the responsibilities of teaching, and to learning how to address the needs of any child who might be in my classroom, should I end up with one. I wanted to learn how to give children with varied learning needs my full attention in a way that would help them find a voice and reap the benefits of literacy.

During our week-long campus orientation, I still felt utterly clear and present. The first day was lovely: it was summer, and there were lots of courtyards and grass areas to sit and meet new friends. When we all gathered in the campus marae, packed in like sardines, I was impressed when the faculty staff welcomed us to the programme one by one, with hongi.

The moment alarm bells first rang was during a lecture that formed part of our orientation. The lecturer was telling us that the year was going to be stressful. She said we would probably all break down at some point, and cry in her office. My immediate gut reaction was a firm, inner 'no'. I had enrolled to learn how to teach, and one thing I knew already was that this would require me to give children my full attention – and *that* would require a calm, attentive mind.

To me, what this lecturer communicated was not the inevitability of my impending 'breakdown', but that the course itself included elements that were antithetical to the real-life task of teaching. I felt calm, and I was enrolled in teacher education to gain knowledge about how to help kids become literate, *not* to be groomed into a culture of stress and burnout that would distract me from that very task. If maintaining a state of calm meant I could not meet all the course requirements, so be it. I would sooner hand in poor quality assignments than allow myself to be distracted with stress or so overcome with it that I would cry in someone's office.

As the programme continued, its problems became more apparent. A small group of friends and I discussed them, and shared feedback with staff. Someone nicknamed us the 'committee of dissent'. When we were brushed off and ignored, my sense of clarity transformed to action. I became an activist during my first semester of teacher training.

The catalyst was an educational psychology exam where much of the content required for study undermined the validity of the assessment itself. One prescribed text was an excerpt from Alfie Kohn's *Punished by Rewards* (1993), which argued that assessing qualitative information during heavily weighted, graded, closed-book exams is not conducive to learning.[19] Along with four friends from the committee of dissent, I wrote a submission to the faculty that read:

> There is an implicit irony in coming across such statements in compulsory readings as part of a course which is assessed with a 60%-weighted closed-book exam ... we are being asked to think critically and reflectively about issues relating to assessment and evaluation; at the same time, our learning is being assessed in a manner which we are taught is inimical to effective learning [...]

My politicisation was aided by Brazilian educator and liberation theorist Paulo Freire. A slide picturing Freire flashed by during one of our literacy lectures, but not so briefly that I couldn't catch his name and the title of his book, *Pedagogy of the Oppressed* (1970). I eagerly acquired my copy, and vividly remember reading it, as words that would echo through the next decade of my life etched themselves into my being.

---

19 Kohn, 1993, p. 203.

Freire opens his book by talking about "humanisation" or "becoming more fully human" as the central vocation of people. He writes about the ways that oppression dehumanises, including in its establishment of educational systems based on a "banking model," which sees students as passive receptacles for deposits made by teachers in positions of authority.

To Freire, true education was "the practice of freedom," carried out as we meet a "limit situation" with critical reflection. This reflection has the effect of undoing the "submersion" of consciousness into a mode of passive submission and socially conditioned identification with the interests of oppressors. Critical reflection illuminates and changes people's consciousness and the way they relate to a "limit situation." Relating differently, they act differently, and so transform the situation. To Freire, this is the only true purpose of education. There are no exceptions – no situations when the "banking" model can be deemed necessary, excusable, or better.[20]

Freire believed that education, along with any human endeavour or institution, should reflect and *follow* humanity, should arise *from* the human spirit, not be imposed *upon* it. At present, our society is comprised of systems and institutions that run according to their own protocols *in spite of* the best interests, needs and longings of human beings. This constitutes a "limit situation" that education *as the practice of freedom* must *transform*.

I agreed wholeheartedly with Paulo Freire. By the time I started teacher education, I had been through 13 years of compulsory education, four years of university, and a recession, always trying to gain knowledge for application 'later', when real life would begin. I had come to see that 'later' never comes; that no place on earth is a waiting room; that it makes no sense to delay responsibility for what you know is true; that there *is* no title or status or situation that suddenly makes it easy and appropriate to be responsible; that real life is now, and that there are no rewards for waiting.

---

20 Freire, 1970.

To me, Freire's ideas were especially applicable to teacher training, given that our cohort of primary school trainees consisted of over one hundred students who would, in theory, end up responsible for the education of around 30 children each per year, for maybe 30 years, assuming they were young and worked until retirement. I know this is a crude calculation, but if we account for each year of a child's education, that amounts to 90,000 years of schooling. To me, this meant that if there is *any* time when sound educational philosophies should be applied in earnest, it is in teacher training, where the groundwork is done for these invaluable years.

Many student teachers seem to assume that they will act on their principles once the conditions are more conducive. It is tempting to imagine that we can hold off practicing what we preach until we get our degree or our own classroom – but classroom teaching is highly bureaucratised. On discovering this, teachers may think that becoming syndicate leaders or principals will put them in a better position to prioritise relationships and values over job requirements, administration, and workload. Principals might dream of training other teachers to do what they wish they had done better. Everyone in the system imagines that someone else is better positioned to do what is needed.

It simply does not make sense to delay responsibility until we have the status we think we require to engage it – and gaining status does not amount to gaining autonomy. Teacher education proves this: almost all the staff on campus during my training claimed to be *hamstrung*, not empowered, by their job descriptions, superiors, time pressure, the programme itself and being part of a big bureaucracy. Many lamented the fact that the university had swallowed up what had previously been a perfectly wonderful teachers' college. Our lecturers, after long careers in education, still did not feel they had 'arrived'.

Students, on the other hand, are not beholden to job contracts. I believed this was to our advantage, and it made us best placed to activate both the university's role as society's 'critic and conscience', *and* the most recent ideas on best practice that we were exposed to. The power and responsibility of students lies in how well positioned they are to critically apply what they learn in the moment and truly engage in education as 'the practice of freedom'.

When faced with an educational psychology exam where the content undermined taking the exam, I felt that the real test was one of integrity. Did we, as students, really believe in the educational principles we were discussing on campus? Or did we believe in the protocol we were being asked to mindlessly follow? I felt that if I believed in the principles, which I did, I could not follow the protocol, i.e. sit the exam.

So instead of sitting the educational psychology exam as expected, I stayed up late the night before with four friends from the committee of dissent to write the "co-constructed examination submission," quoted from earlier. The first paragraph explained that "we believe the teaching career for which we are preparing begins in the present, as does our associated approach and attitude." We showed how the best ideas and values in the course materials conflicted with programme requirements and protocol,

> to the extent that we perceive non-participation in the EPSY 302 examination as an authorised and appropriate action ... Many students feel that the action of sitting the exam, though practical, directly contradicts content; and that meaningful, reflective and metacognitive understanding of its stated learning intentions would be better demonstrated through non-participation.

I felt that if the ideas and values taught on campus did not come to life there, then the diploma would more effectively train students in the art of rhetoric, resignation, and hypocrisy than teaching. On the day of the exam, I took my place in the lecture theatre and wrote a note on my paper saying that I would be handing the submission to the school office. I stayed in the room for the time needed to fulfil attendance requirements, then walked out to submit the paper, and waited for my friends in the campus marae (in the end, no one else wanted to risk an exam sit-out). After we gathered to debrief and let off steam, I went home.

My tutor and the head of school phoned me that afternoon. The submission, and my exam paper containing nothing but a brief note, had created a miniature crisis among staff who had to decide whether to kick me off the program because I had not completed the exam, or to keep me on because the submission demonstrated that I intended to *live* the values taught in the study material.

The head of school was a very warm-hearted assessment specialist who told me that he respected my stance and submission. He was also standing in temporarily for the *real* head of school who, I was told, was more conservative and would have booted me out immediately if he hadn't been on holiday. His substitute asked me to write a report about the teacher education program from a student perspective, for submission at the end of the year, and to sit an exam different to the one my peers had done, so that I could be kept on the program.

I accepted the deal and got to work on my submission, which became a programme redesign. To make it, I interviewed all the faculty staff I could, studied teacher education requirements and met with students and the Teachers Council. I showed the significant overlap in course content between our various papers, as well as how much extra time there would be without this overlap and what that would allow for. My submission was ignored by the faculty, and nearly cost me my diploma when I handed it in along with my final assignment, and my tutor objected and failed me. After several appeals – one of which resulted in a staff member amending the grade of my failed assignment so that it was within half a point of a pass – I won my diploma and graduated six months after my peers. I didn't mind missing out on the cap and gown.

In the meantime, I submitted my work to the organisers of the 2011 Festival for the Future. This annual gathering of "innovators, leaders and entrepreneurs" is now touted on the website as "New Zealand's largest social innovation summit," but 2011 was their first conference. I spoke about teacher education, and it took me from being an independent fledgling activist to one who was part of a wider community. I met people who had been involved in online education platforms, organic vegetable box delivery systems, 'conscious consumer' rating schemes, campaigns to change the legal system, and Occupy Wellington.

The worldwide Occupy movement was one of the events that led *Time* magazine to declare the 2011 Person of the Year as "The Protestor." Indeed, the Arab Spring, London riots, and Occupy movement which began at Zuccotti Park in the Wall Street district of New York City, marked the beginning of a decade of popular uprisings.

As Occupy went global, it exposed one of the core contradictions of capitalism: when a minority exploits a majority, that minority creates the conditions – the collective desperation, demoralisation, dispossession, powerlessness and rage – necessary for its own overthrow. Occupy aimed to build grassroots solidarity among the '99%' by creating new forms of assembly, awareness raising, decision making and direct action. There was an understanding that people's spiritual and material needs are inseparable, and people needed to be heard and involved in a process of tangible social transformation, as Freire taught.

Some of the people I met at the Festival for the Future started projects like Loomio, a social media tool designed to facilitate efficient voting, discussion and decision making in small assemblies like Occupy. Many festival attendees were involved at the intersection of digital technology and social enterprise. I was neither an entrepreneur nor Silicon Valley aspirant, but it was refreshing to meet so many people who were actively and vocally concerned about addressing inequality, wanting to talk and willing to work.

After my presentation, then-drama school director Christian Penny approached me to recommend a book called *A Blaze of Colour*.[21] Part biography and part social history, the book tells the

---

21 Henderson, 1998.

fascinating story of New Zealand's post-war departure from the Victorian rote-learning factory-line system (what Freire called "banking" education) in favour of arts-based education. The book showed me that New Zealand once had the beginnings of an education system to make Freire proud.

The story begins in the 1930s, during the emergence of the welfare state and revival of democratic socialist thinking. Within this intellectual climate, John Dewey developed a theory of education fully integrated with a democratic conception of society – perhaps the most significant since Plato. He sought to discover what an education system would look like if it were designed to support a democracy, and not systematically privilege children predisposed to middle class institutional norms. Even for those it advantaged, standardised education was not necessarily enabling meaningful personal development. Dewey argued that:

> Since growth is the characteristic of life, education is all one with growing; it has no end beyond itself. The criterion of the value of school education is the extent in which it creates a desire for continued growth and supplies means for making the desire effective in fact.[22]

Like Freire, Dewey stated that the value of a legitimate educational objective "lies in the fact that we can use it to change conditions."[23] For Dewey and his contemporaries, art and creativity were necessarily at the heart of such an education. "Art is the pattern evolved in a complex interplay of personal and societal processes of adjustment," wrote art historian Herbert Read, a major contributor to this post-war paradigm shift.[24] Read's book *Art and Alienation* opens with the lines:

> It has always seemed, even to Marxist critics, that art is an 'epiphenomenon', something that arises as a consequence of a prevailing economy. I believe that this is a basic error. The aesthetic

---

22   Dewey, 1916/2004, p. 51.
23   Dewey, 1916/2004, p. 100.
24   Read, 1967, p. 18.

activity is, on the contrary, a formative process with direct effect both on individual psychology and on social organisation.[25]

When the leader of New Zealand's second Labour government, Prime Minister Peter Fraser, asked the Director of Education, Clarence Beeby, to rewrite the Education Act, Beeby did so under the influence of thinkers like Dewey and Read. By 1944, he also established an Arts and Crafts branch within the Department of Education, with the intention of putting the idea of arts-based education into practice. Beeby appointed Gordon Tovey, a larger-than-life character who was previously head of art at Dunedin Technical College and also inspired by Read, as national supervisor for the Arts and Crafts branch.

A Blaze of Colour (1998) explores the work of Tovey and the Arts and Crafts branch. The author, Carol Henderson (Tovey's daughter) writes about how Beeby granted Tovey all the freedom necessary to coax Aotearoa's "drab and colourless" classrooms to life. By the time Tovey retired in 1977, Beeby looked with satisfaction on a country of classrooms "ablaze with colour, buzzing with activity and alive with crafts."[26]

Carol's book struck a deep chord with me. Since she happened to live in my suburb of Wellington, I visited her. We became friends, and I went to her place often to talk and investigate the archives she had used to write her book. The archives were so rich and plentiful I felt they needed to become a documentary, and when I said so, Carol showed me a documentary proposal written in the 1990s by filmmakers Jan and Luit Bieringa, also locals. When I contacted them, they said they were busy, but would consider reviving the documentary project if I could help secure some funding. I spent the next four years working with the Bieringas, writing funding proposals, doing research and compiling the script for a film that was finally released in 2016 with the title, *The HeART of the Matter*.

---

25   Read, 1967, p. 7.
26   Henderson, 1998, p. 233.

To put the script together, I spent hours in the archives indexing photographs, transcribing cassette recordings and interviews, reading books and taking notes from unpublished manuscripts. I was often moved to tears by beautiful historic footage showing children playing hand-painted drums, making theatre and mobiles, and reading rock pool poems after trips to the ocean, as part of a school education that was grounded in children's creativity and the local environment. That film, even the trailer, still makes me well up when I see it.[27] The footage was soul food.

While I was working on the film, though, I didn't experience the same state of ease and clarity I had at the beginning of teacher training. About halfway through the year, I got involved with Ivan, who was a loudmouth, but also creative and critically minded, and I was fond of him. While I was on my first seven-week teaching placement, he began to date another woman (whom he later married) and didn't tell me until I invited him to see me on my birthday, and he responded that his girlfriend wouldn't like it.

I felt disposed of, without tenderness or warning, by someone with whom I had shared both intimacy and camaraderie. The shock of it somehow dredged up a lifetime of confusion about intimacy and sex. It left me feeling depleted and emotionally frozen for much longer than this one man's disengagement warranted, and however inspired I was in my reading about arts, education, and social transformation, nothing I read addressed my confusion about intimacy, sexuality, and sexual betrayal. This seemed odd to me, since it is when human beings are sexually intimate that we are also most vulnerable, and so most prone to feeling dehumanised, depleted, and used. Is that not relevant to the question of social transformation, of humanisation?

It seemed to me that being open to intimacy meant to risk being rendered disposable. I did not know how to live with that while still

---

27   Trailer: <https://www.nzonscreen.com/title/heart-of-the-matter-2016>
     Film: <https://ondemand.nzfilm.co.nz/film/the-heart-of-the-matter/?fbclid=IwAR0ihLHoZ9Ev6EynEAhs1w60038SEw2TI1bY6IKq2lJxgwBnvug3WDu2cW4>

feeling energised by a deep connection to humankind who I was moved to act in solidarity with. There was nothing in Freire's book about this. I wished I could ask him, or someone, about it. Not knowing who to talk to or how, the implicit feeling of connectedness with humanity that had buoyed and centred me since reading Suu Kyi in 2010 simply collapsed. I stopped meditating, and the fog rolled back in as I fought for my teaching diploma.

I did a lot of my documentary research with the feeling that my inner brake and accelerator were on at the same time. The work was beautiful and implicitly motivating, but I was lugging around heavy, unresolved feelings about what people do to one another when they are closest. I felt so dismayed by what human beings do with the freedom of our private, intimate lives that it sucked out the energy I previously had for activism. Something in my heart was asking – who are these humans I've been so motivated to stick up for? Whoever we are in public, do our intimate lives reveal that so long as we have privacy and secrecy, we will just feed from each other like parasites? Since I could barely articulate, let alone answer these questions, they sat inside me like a weight.

At the end of 2012, I did a course in short fiction writing at Victoria University. Several of my stories – including 'Homeopathy', a story set at the Occupy Wellington camp in Civic Square – grappled with the problem of a political left full of people who, when we are most intimate with each other, when it causes the most heartache, undermine the very human intimacy and connection we claim to seek in the world by treating one another with insensitivity and detachment. In 'Homeopathy' I wrote:

> I want to tell this now to Ana. If we are *all one*, all connected like she says, we are all shards in a broken pane. I want to shake her and say we do *matter* to each other here, in this square of people, crucifying themselves for the world. Not primordially. Not politically. Not abstractly.[28]

---

28   Gerlich, 2013, pp. 12–13.

In another story, 'Ceasefire', I imagined a series of historic uprisings and revolutions populated by vampires hungry enough for life to fight oppressors for it, but also to suck it out of each other through sexual cruelty. A classmate scrawled in the margins of one of my stories, "MORE ANGST, MORE ANGST!" Much later, I would read Betty Friedan's *The Feminine Mystique* (1963), in which Friedan laments how women all over the world suffer in isolation from a "problem that has no name."[29] I was one of those women, and it indeed made me anxious and melancholic. But I was about to learn the problem's name.

In 2013, I met Pala Molisa, who was lecturing at Victoria University. His parents, Grace and Sela, had been instrumental in Vanuatu's independence movement. Grace was a poet, the Secretary to Vanuatu's first prime minister post-independence, and a feminist who challenged the sexism of the independence movement. Pala's teaching was critically informed and drew not only on figures like Freire, but on the radical feminist literature of his mother's generation, which I had never encountered.

Pala and I began a relationship that lasted more than five years, and with him I deepened my engagement with leftist activism and read feminist books voraciously.

In 2015, we were arrested twice during demonstrations against corporate free trade and militarism. The New Zealand government was discussing plans to sign the Trans Pacific Partnership Agreement (TPPA), which would allow corporations to sue governments for passing laws or regulations that could obstruct profit (think of the graphic health warnings placed on cigarette packets to deter buyers). The Ministry of Foreign Affairs and Trade (MFAT) refused to release the full text of the agreement. A group called Show Us Ya Text challenged the lack of transparency and consultation by conducting a nationwide 'search' for the text, starting at the Auckland MFAT offices. They took giant magnifying glasses, making a show of hunting around the building for the TPPA.

---

29   Friedan, 1963.

In September, Pala and I joined the search as it moved to Wellington. The campaign was well organised, and we spent a few days planning and rehearsing to encounter the police line we knew would be blocking the entrance to MFAT on our arrival. Spokesperson Lizzie Sullivan told the media, "We've come down here because we've asked the Government countless times to release the text of the TPP and they have not obliged, so we're conducting a citizens-initiated search and seizure to attempt to enter the building and retrieve the text ourselves."[30]

We needed to make a scene out of 'trying to enter' the building, but not be arrested for assaulting police (a serious offence). The solution was to line up in two adjacent rows and approach the police line in pairs, declaring our intention to break through it. We then made a show of chest-bumping the police and wriggling between them with our hands by our sides, making for some rather comical footage. After a minute or two of this dramatic wriggling and being pushed back by officers, we went to the back of the queue as the next pair went ahead. Our group included a police liaison who gave us a warning whenever an officer told him that we could be construed as crossing the line from performative bumping to assault.

It was a tense morning, but the police refused either to budge or to arrest us, and we had come to make headlines. So, we sat down on the road and 26 of us were finally arrested for blocking a carriageway. We spent several hours in the holding cells on Victoria Street before charges were dropped.

Two months later, Pala and I were back in the holding cells. For several years, Wellington had played host to an international weapons conference sponsored by the world's largest nuclear arms manufacturer, Lockheed Martin, and hosted by the New Zealand Defence Industry Association. Peace Action Wellington (PAW) organised a blockade to prevent conference participants, including local Ministry of Defence representatives and delegates from Serco,

---

30 Radio New Zealand, 2015.

Lockheed, and General Dynamics, from entering the venue. In a press release, PAW member Valerie Morse stated:

> Companies that profit from war and murder have no place in a civilised society. We don't want the companies responsible for the murder of thousands of innocent people around the world to feel comfortable holding a large arms fair to showcase their wares. Theirs is the business of death and destruction for profit ...
>
> These companies are not simply neutral bystanders selling a product – they actively lobby governments to go to war. Lockheed Martin is the seventh largest individual spender on political lobbying in the United States.[31]

Morse hated both the military and the police and was appalled when I mentioned to her that Show Us Ya Text had a police liaison among its ranks. To PAW, the police and military were the "Army of the rich! Enemy of the poor!" to cite one of the slogans we chanted into our megaphones.

Pala was the first protestor to be arrested. Several police officers grabbed him and pushed him over to the police van. While other arrestees on that day and during the TPPA protests – including me – would drop to the ground while being arrested, to show non-compliance and force police to drag us, Pala never did such things. He remained dignified and upright. I watched several officers push him over to the van and then up against it, as if he were resisting or was somehow dangerous, and it made me livid.

Without thinking, I broke from the blockade and stormed over to the police van calling Pala's name and yelling at the police for arresting a man because he is black. I did not think any of us deserved to be arrested that day, but if they were going to pick someone, there were many boisterous activists around and I did not believe that Pala was picked off and handled like a loaded gun for being one of them. I decided that I would be arrested next and gave my backpack to a friend before storming back into the blockade and reclaiming the megaphone. My face was painted with red tears, an

---

31 Peace Action Wellington (PAW), 2015.

expression of the grief and rage I carried, growing up in a world in which some people lived in famine and war that others could profit from or choose to ignore. After my tirade I knew I'd be next in the van. I was arrested for trespassing, Pala for disorderly behaviour.

Taking part in these actions taught me more about how suffering is sustained in the world. My teaching diploma taught me about the stagnancy of institutions, but leftist activists showed me how institutions are invested in *maintaining* the status quo, maintaining oppression. The state requires an obedient citizenry to rule; the arms trade requires war to profit; capitalism requires a working class, structural unemployment, and the plundering of resources from so-called third world countries to function. Human suffering is not accidental, it is profitable. This is why I never learned about it in school, instead always wondering why it felt like my sense of responsibility and my need for an education were at odds.

Perhaps the fog around me represented my inability to be seen and heard in a world I could not comprehend. The more I learned about the culture I lived in, the more it lifted, allowing me to see both the world and myself. The small personal library of feminist books I was accruing helped a great deal, and Pala and I talked constantly about power, freedom, sex, race and the left.

Reading feminist literature helped me put words to what I saw *and* could not see: that men dominate every sphere of society – state, military, corporate and domestic – both in numbers and in principle. Such a society *teaches men* to dominate, and women to submit, as sex objects and domestic servants. This hierarchy is ultimately sustained and expressed by the act of rape, the quintessential act of violation. It is the act that teaches men to fetishise violence, which enables them to kill in war. It is promoted through pornography and culturally pervasive gender norms that imagine men as aggressive and women as submissive. It is protected by the association between women, sex and the 'private sphere'.

Understanding patriarchy helped me grasp how human nature can be essentially good, even while violence, hunger and illiteracy persist. It taught me why governments, media and universities cannot solve these problems. It helped me to see how social conditioning works, how it hooks boys and men. Feminism explained the sexual intimidation and confusion I'd experienced in high school, why the history I'd learned in school was so unrelatable, and the Greek myths too. It explained why I feared intimacy and couldn't reconcile my need for it with my need for respect, camaraderie, and solidarity.

It is no wonder that anxiety, disconnection, and depression are so widespread. Even liberally minded, bestselling authors like Brené Brown identify gender socialisation as the primary cause of the feelings of shame that plague humanity. In her bestselling book *Daring Greatly* (2015), Brown writes,

> shame is universal, but the messages and expectations that drive shame are organised by gender. These feminine and masculine norms are the foundation of shame triggers, and here's why: If women want to play by the rules, they need to be sweet, thin, and pretty, stay quiet, be perfect moms and wives, and not own their power. One move outside of these expectations and BAM! the shame web closes in. Men, on the other hand, need to stop feeling, start earning, put everyone in their place, and climb their way to the top or die trying. Push open the lid of your box to grab a breath of air, or slide that curtain back a bit to see what's going on, and BAM! shame cuts you down to size.[32]

In another bestseller, Glennon Doyle's *Untamed,* gender is also identified as our primary problem. Doyle writes:

> In a culture as unbalanced as ours – in which a few hoard billions while others starve, in which wars are fought for oil, in which children are shot and killed while gun manufacturers and politicians collect the blood money – mercy, humanity and vulnerability cannot be tolerated. Mercy and empathy are great threats to an unjust society.
>
> So how does power squash the expression of these traits? In a misogynistic culture, all that is needed is to label them feminine.

---

32 Brown, 2015, p. 107.

> Then we can forever discount them in women and forever shame them out of men.[33]

Brown says that the number one requirement for men is "do not be perceived as weak."[34] Doyle, and feminists like Andrea Dworkin, Lierre Keith and Cynthia Enloe put it differently – the requirement is not so much that men should not be perceived as weak, but that they should not be perceived to be *like women*. In Enloe's words, "[t]o prove one's manhood is imagined to be to prove (to oneself and to other men and women) that one is not 'a woman'."[35] As Keith says, for a boy on the school playground "no insult is worse than some version of 'girl'."[36] Gender allocates human qualities to each sex and stigmatises those associated with women. Men are not supposed to empathise with women, and this is the basis of sexual objectification. Objectification means rendering groups of people subhuman – a precondition for violence.

This is what confused me so much as a kid: the idea that I was meant to learn how to *please* males by doing things they would never do, like wear lipstick, uncomfortable shoes, and skin-tight clothing. My closest friendships with other girls and then women were based on what we enjoyed together and had in common, whereas my closest connections with men were supposed to be based on me doing things that they would consider humiliating. Why? My own feelings of shame, anxiety, defectiveness, and disconnection lessened significantly as I learnt how the system works, and that it is hard to understand because it *is* nonsensical. Shame relies on an inclination to personalise, and an illusion of isolation that feminism destroys. As second wave feminist Andrea Dworkin said:

> If it's done to you because you're a woman, it's not done to you because you're Andrea or Susan or Felicity. It's done to you because you're a woman. And somebody noticed that you are a woman and somebody decided to hurt you because they wanted

---

33 Doyle, 2020, p. 165.
34 Brown, 2015, p. 92.
35 Enloe, 1983, p. 13.
36 Keith, 2011, p. 82.

to hurt a woman. Not you in particular – a woman, any woman. You also. And you're not free of it. The question is, how are you ever going to be free of it?[37]

While men are encouraged to bond through masculinity, sexual conquest, misogynist banter, and other boys-will-be-boys behaviour, the experience and ever-present threat of rape alienates women in a fundamental way. Feminism breaks that isolation by naming the problem and lifting the shame. When even two women come together, knowing that they have three things in common – their humanity, their sex, and their oppression – they are doing just what the world needs most. Feminism is Freire's liberation philosophy applied to women and patriarchy.

Indeed, feminist writer bell hooks challenged Freire for omitting sexual politics and feminism from his exploration of oppression and humanisation. Her book *Teaching to Transgress* (1994) includes a chapter titled 'Paulo Freire' and her thoughts on his work are not only a valuable reflection on the relationship between feminism and Freire, but between feminism and any perspective that is valuable to women without being feminist itself (many such texts are cited in this work). Hooks wrote:

> Freire constructs a phallocentric paradigm of liberation – wherein freedom and the experience of patriarchal manhood are always linked as though they are one and the same. For me this is always a source of anguish as it represents a blind spot in the vision of men who have profound insight. And yet, I never wish to see a critique of this blind spot overshadow anyone's (and feminists' in particular) capacity to learn from the insights.[38]

Hooks formed a personal friendship with Freire that began when he visited the university where she studied and taught. He held a lecture and workshop that hooks had trouble registering for since other participants saw her as disruptive, and tried to prevent her attendance. After managing to attend the workshop by taking

---

37 Dworkin, 2002.
38 hooks, 1994, p. 49.

the place of someone who dropped out at the last minute, hooks indeed took the opportunity to question Freire ("with courtesy") about the male bias in his work. When other attendees became uncomfortable and tried to silence her, "Paulo intervened to say that these questions were crucial and he addressed them. Truthfully, I loved him at this moment for exemplifying by his actions the principles of his work."[39]

I relate very much to this story. When I began to read feminist literature, it not only opened my eyes to my own life, it taught me to explore the real implications wherever women are ignored, omitted, misrepresented, or erased.

I learned to carry out such investigations right at the time that transgender ideology went mainstream. New Zealand's annual state and corporate funded Pride Parades commenced in 2013, with heavy emphasis on transgenderism. In the anthology *Female Erasure* (2016), Jennifer Bilek and Mary Ceallaigh point out that in 2013 transgenderism barely registered on our cultural radar, but by 2014, there'd been a 400 per cent spike in pro-transgender media coverage. The public has been under increasing pressure to support the rights of 'transwomen' ever since, or else be considered complicit in violence and suicide.[40]

The story this movement tells is very inconsistent, but it is essentially that some people are 'born in the wrong body', or wrongly 'assigned' a sex at birth by ignorant doctors who believe in biology (one would think that the process of childbirth itself offered quite indisputable proof). These people might claim to be the opposite sex, to have a unique gender identity, or be 'nonbinary'. Living in a society that believes there are only two sexes is, they argue, oppressive for them, to the point that many choose suicide. Men who claim to be women also assert that they suffer more violence than other groups.[41]

---

39   hooks, 1994, p. 55.
40   Bilek and Ceallaigh, 2016, pp. 138–170.
41   This claim is hard for transactivists to substantiate with data, since transgenderism relies on obfuscation. There are two other aspects to this claim that liberals do not

The truth is that sex *is* real, and there are only two sexes – male and female – not a spectrum. Sex cannot be changed. Moreover, people do not have gender identities, they have a sex, a personality, and trauma.

In a patriarchal society, denying sex and promoting gender not only has huge implications for women, it also functions to prevent women from breaking down the invisible barrier between the private sphere to which we are relegated, and the public sphere in which social patterns are identified, analysed and addressed. Furthermore, the rapid spread of any kind of pseudoscience is always a red flag for the general population.

While trans activists profess to be motivated by the desire to end violence and suicide, their work does not so much *draw attention* to the statistics as *politicise* them in a very particular way. At present, data on violence and suicide is organised by sex, and it shows a pattern of men's violence including murder and suicide that the factors of dysphoria and transgenderism can indeed amplify. It also shows that one in three women are raped in our lifetimes, and we are more likely than men to engage in self-harm without killing. Transactivists muddy the data with ideology, for instance by insisting that male violence and suicide be recorded as *female* when it is committed by a man who says he is female. This does not help.

Transgenderism does not stand on any solid premise but a mantra: "transwomen are women." To support this mantra, trans advocates switch between contradictory claims: that biological sex is changeable through willpower or surgery; that biological sex is a spectrum rather than a binary, and that biological sex is not real at all, but a fabrication of western science. These are not solid, evidence-based grounds for an argument that could help end

---

like to consider: 1) how high rates of violence against men who identify as women might be correlated with prostitution and point to the violence of prostitution, and 2) how no type or degree of male violence can ever serve as evidence that human beings can change sex, that men should be allowed into female only spaces, or that pseudoscience should be allowed to enter law.

violence, but weak justifications to redefine womanhood so that men can claim it.

Transactivists switch between these three propositions depending on who they are advocating for at the time. Imagine a man who claims that he will not be able to tolerate life if he does not receive state funded genital surgery to help him imitate a biological 'female'. This man relies on the claim that *sex can be changed*. He is physically male but says that he is psychologically 'female', and needs his body to look biologically female so that the two can align.

Heterosexual men who claim to be lesbian, and have no plans to remove their penises, need to argue something different: that sex is a meaningless notion and only 'gender identity' is real. A 'woman' could have a penis *and* be perfectly happy, if it weren't for the social stigma caused by the common misconception that sex is real and that a woman must have a vagina. Another argument is posed by people claiming to be 'nonbinary'. They say that sex is a spectrum – while simultaneously arguing that there is something special about existing in the middle rather than the polar extremes.

Seeing this contradictory pseudoscience gain traction alarmed me. Many of the activists I knew and had worked with, who once stood against capitalism and with the silent majority at Occupy, supported this new style of state and corporate-funded 'activism'. This put us at odds. I had come to understand rape as the quintessential human problem, and solidarity between women as the answer. I saw that making the recognition of sex taboo not only puts women in danger, it prevents solidarity between women. Not being able to name sex or women's oppression means it will once again become 'the problem that has no name'.

Making sex taboo prevents the establishment of female only spaces. In her 2019 talk 'Male-Pattern Violence, Women's Trauma and the Need for Women's Safe Spaces', Stephanie Hughes explains why, in a rape culture, female-only recovery centres are necessary.[42]

---

42   Hughes, 2019.

She points out that women who run female-only rape crisis shelters and refuge houses have always known that it is not possible to calm the autonomic nervous system, and allow women to come out of a state of fear and stress, without taking them out of an environment where violence and re-traumatisation is possible. Hughes said that women can remain fearful for up to 12 months after one specific act of violence, and this fear can involve startling easily, reacting irritably to small provocations, poor sleep, nightmares, flashbacks, and panic and anxiety attacks. Women are more likely than men to feel this ongoing fear, because the threat of rape is ongoing. Culturally, we diagnose women with post-traumatic stress disorder instead of committing to eliminating rape culture. The least we can offer is female-only crisis and refuge centres, but today, these centres are being dismantled on the premise that biology is bigotry.

In 2016, I was having coffee with my friend Jane, a Women's Refuge volunteer, when this topic arose. I can't remember how our conversation led me to utter the line, "but – men can't get pregnant," but I do remember that it made Jane upset to the point that she told me those words constituted violence, and our conversation ground to a halt. I got out of my chair and told her that if she felt I was being violent, I had better go. We hugged, and I gave her a kiss on the cheek, said I'd see her soon, and left. I haven't seen her for years.

I soon learned that face-to-face conversations on this topic tended to be exhausting, circular, and futile, with trans advocates denying the basic facts of life, intentionally misinterpreting feminist arguments, switching between justifications, and accusing women of violence and bigotry in the meantime. They don't persist with this behaviour because the arguments they use are logical or convincing. What is important is simply a man's right to claim female identity *if he wants to*. This right must be defended at any intellectual or emotional cost.

Behaving this way requires a person to ignore the proof their own bodies, and the bodies of those they know most intimately, offer them: that sex is real. They must go blind to the facts graphically presented to them between their legs in the shower every morning.

I have learned that if someone cannot be convinced by what their own bodies state more clearly, graphically, and perfectly than I could, I have no reason to believe they will listen to me.

It was in 2015 that I decided to explore the nature and origins of transgenderism through writing. The feminist perspective needed to be explored and expressed. I wanted to do this, and thought it may help that I had worked as a freelance writer since 2012, but it didn't. No New Zealand media outlet has ever been interested in my work.

It is par for the course for publications like *Stuff*, *The Herald* and *The Spinoff* to publish stories about the importance of celebrating nonbinary identities and the 'bravery' of 'transwomen' like Gavin 'Laurel' Hubbard, representing New Zealand in women's weightlifting. I had critical articles on gender identity rejected by *Stuff* ("Unfortunately it's not something that Stuff Nation is interested in publishing on our site at this time"); *The Herald* ("I don't have room for this one, sorry"), and the *Wireless* ("the format you're suggesting isn't ... strong for getting a broader audience to pay attention").

People can say what they like about the quality of my writing or pitches, but if balance and critical thinking are central premises of journalism, New Zealand journalists were not achieving either. Articles celebrating transgenderism tend to frame all dissent as 'bigotry' and feminists are cast as micro-managers who, driven by an irrational phobia of boogeymen, get over-involved in other people's business, including their toileting habits and the contents of their underwear. I wanted to talk about our real concerns.

So, I started a blog. In July 2016, I wrote an article called 'When the shoe won't fit: transgenderism's sticking points'. I followed it up in October with an open letter to RainbowYouth and InsideOut, two of New Zealand's most prominent trans lobbies. Both pieces were comprehensive and covered the issues of medical experimentation, particularly on gay and lesbian youth, male violence, and the dangers of ideology. If anything, I expected them to be ignored, at least initially. The internet is a big place, my blog was new and nothing flash, and I was not someone whose voice was known or sought after. Writing allowed me to organise and share my thoughts fully, without interruption, and in a way that people could process in their own time, but I hadn't considered how I might promote my work.

The promotion was done for me. I will never forget that 2016 was the year of Pokémon Go, an online game that uses players' smartphone cameras and GPS trackers. It guides players to 'PokéStops' where they can 'catch' Pokémon figures that appear in the view of their phone cameras as if they were there in real life.[43] So people walked around the city, hunched over their phones on the hunt for Pokémon, being shepherded to landmarks and Starbucks cafés by this app. Some of the activists I knew played this game, and their enthusiasm on discovering my blog felt disturbingly like the enthusiasm of gamers spotting Pokémon and excitedly announcing, "I caught one!"

In the United States and elsewhere, feminists like myself were being hounded as 'TERFs' – 'trans exclusionary radical feminists.' If I assumed I had no readership, I soon gained one, since my blog was the only place in New Zealand where transgenderism was being thoroughly and substantively challenged. In August 2016, I went to WoLF (Women's Liberation Front) Festival in California to meet other women talking about the same issues. I met author Lierre Keith, broadcaster Thistle Pettersen, midwife Mary Lou Singleton, and many others.

Soon after returning, I registered for a stall at the 2016 Wellington Zinefest. I had several handmade books or 'zines' – one on peace struggle since the peasant revolts, one on West Papua, and one on feminism from the time of Sojourner Truth. I was banned from attending. When I went along anyway and put a picnic blanket on the grass outside the venue (Wellington High School), three activists came to heckle me for several hours, including an Amnesty International and a UniQ spokesperson (UniQ is Victoria

---

43   Zuboff, 2019, pp. 308–318.

University's 'queer' association). They seemed to want to 'occupy' my picnic blanket.

I approached the Human Rights Commission (HRC) about the unprecedented ban. They acted as a carrier pigeon, sending letters back and forth between myself and the Zinefest committee, who told the HRC they had considered calling security to have my picnic blanket removed. They seemed to feel generous for having 'allowed' me to sit peacefully on the grass outside the school hall.

Then said committee, along with RainbowYouth, InsideOut, the New Zealand Prostitutes Collective (NZPC) – and members of PAW, who I had protested the arms trade with – contributed to a 120-signature strong online pact, launched by NZPC's community liaison. People I had considered friends and allies signed it. The coordinator of a group for freedom in Palestine sent me a tonne of private messages telling me that "you are harming people" and "I am trying to get you to stop doing really dangerous unnecessary things which will cause death poverty pain violence by the state." A policy advisor to Women's Refuge suggested 'swarming' my blog on social media, to shut it down.

It was not long before I could fill an entire ringbinder with evidence of harassment clearly fuelled by a few individuals. I approached NetSafe, an organisation that claims to "keep people safe online." They told me they required proof that the bullying had done me harm by asking me a long list of personal questions about my sleep, eating habits, the state of my relationships, and whether I was self-harming. Without this proof, they refused to intervene. It seemed their help was conditional on me becoming somehow visibly broken, and I thought it strange that an organisation purporting to help victims of harassment would ultimately make the same demand on me as my harassers. They both wanted me to show signs of breakdown.

In 2017, I signed up for a six-day intensive Women's Refuge training course after being asked to participate. I lasted about four and a half days. Women's Refuge is in the process of being liberalised, so my group were given some original feminist training documents and some new, updated ones.

We received the 'Power and Control Wheel', which outlines the various ways that men attempt to control women in the home. The wheel was developed in 1984 by the Domestic Abuse Intervention Project in Minnesota that developed programs both for violent men and battered women. Through months of focus groups listening to "heart-wrenching stories of violence, terror and survival," the most common abusive tactics used against these women were compiled into the wheel.[44] The tactics include minimising, denial, blame, intimidation, blackmail, coercion and threats, and economic and emotional abuse. One corner of the wheel identifies "using male privilege" as a method of power and control that can include "treating her like a servant," "making all the big decisions," "acting like the master of the castle," and "being the one to define men's and women's roles."

During my training, we were also given the 'Gay, Lesbian, Bisexual and Trans' version of this wheel. It refers to "using looks, actions, gestures to reinforce homophobic, biphobic or transphobic control" as an intimidation tactic, and "questioning if you are a 'real' lesbian, 'real' man, 'real' woman, 'real' femme, 'real' butch, etc," as a form of emotional abuse. Since the two wheels contradicted, I had questions. It was too hard to stomach having to talk about male privilege and lesbian visibility during the course while having to swallow the idea that men should be allowed to use the refuge as women, indeed as lesbians, without question, because questions would constitute 'abuse'.

I was as tactful as possible in the circumstances about seeking clarification. The day I was told that I couldn't ask any more questions because I had already asked two, I excused myself and went home. On the way I stopped to lie in the grass and watch some skylarks. I didn't return to finish the course.

---

44 Domestic Abuse Intervention Project.

In 2018, I did an interview on Wellington's Access Radio, and the station manager sent a warning email to the broadcaster who had invited me on, saying, "Some of Renée Gerlich's views could be seen as an attack on minority groups or as hate speech." The broadcaster was 'allowed' to interview me on the condition that he first read me the broadcasting standards. We then did the interview, in which I discussed why prostitution amounts to exploitation of women, a perspective I see as the very opposite of 'attack'.

The same year, Radio New Zealand 'lost' an interview with me, saying that, "It appears to have simply dropped out of the system." When I wrote an article on gender identity for the left-wing outlet *Scoop*, the editor subsequently deleted it without notifying me, and then passed it on to two Green Party politicians: Minister for Women, Julie Anne Genter, and spokesperson for 'rainbow issues' Jan Logie. When I alerted the Media Council, they ruled that this did not constitute censorship and there were "no grounds to proceed."[45]

Since New Zealand was celebrating 125 years of women's suffrage, I made some posters including suffragist quotes that mentioned sex, such as Susan B. Anthony saying, "No self-respecting woman should wish or work for the success of a party that ignores her sex." Each poster included the tagline, "Suffragists fought for the female sex. Stop rewriting history." The posters went up around Wellington city and were torn down by activists. The postering company, Phantom Billstickers, cancelled my campaign and blacklisted me as a customer – something they had not done before.[46] I asked a lawyer whether businesses were allowed to discriminate in this way, and he informed me that when it comes to commerce, anti-discrimination laws are undermined by those which state that both business and customer have a right to engage, or not, in any given transaction (or 'contract').

---

45 Media Council, 2018.
46 Gerlich, 2018.

On my own, I didn't have a legal leg to stand on. There was no law, organisation or advocate on my side, and my isolation was very emboldening to anyone who wanted to either censor or harass me. Indeed, women's isolation sustains patriarchy, it is just that this isolation is normally implicit and structural. When women become consciously aware of how male dominance works, we become feminists, and those with a vested interest in our silence and alienation become equally explicit about their expectations. Misogyny is the insistence that women *remain* submissive, vulnerable to violation and harassment, ignorant of sexism as a social pattern and not a personal insult, ashamed, and silent.

On June 21, 2021, I was denied a pinwheel scone because of my writing. I stood in line as the owner of a small café in Paekakariki frothed milk at the coffee machine. She looked up, saw me, and announced that I was making her "feel awkward." Confused, I asked her to repeat herself. When I understood what was happening, I took out my phone to record the exchange. It went like this:

> Café Owner (CO): I'm really shaky just having you stand there.
> Me: Okay.
> CO: I'm not gonna serve you.
> Me: You're not going to serve me?
> CO: No, I'm not gonna serve you. Making me so angry.
> Me: It's making you angry just …
> CO: Just having your presence in my café, yeah.
> Me: Okay.
> CO: Yeah, I just really disagree with your whole, everything about your attitude on trans.
> Me: So, um – we've never met before and I just …
> CO: I know! But I know exactly who you are.
> Me: I just walked in off the street hoping to get something for breakfast?

I left empty-handed.

The following year, the same café began promoting itself as 'inclusive', because of welcoming customers who do not carry vaccine passes. A sign on the door read, "All welcome, vaxed and unvaxed – our business does not discriminate." Such are the political contradictions we live with today.

These experiences have taught me a great deal about human psychology, trauma, and the political landscape. This book is a record of what I have learned from my ongoing search for a way out of the fog: the personal, the social, the political, the spiritual. It forms part of my ongoing effort to come alive, whether this society is prepared to accommodate such efforts or not.

CHAPTER TWO

Desire and Distortion

It is okay if we don't go to the moon, there is no real need to go there ... But one thing is absolutely necessary – of ultimate concern – and that is that we come to know and understand sex rightly so we can succeed in giving birth to a new humanity.
—Osho, Sex Matters[47]

The fundamental patriarchal re-write of life is to swap out creation for control and then pawn off control as creative rather than destructive.
—Vajra Ma, From a Hidden Stream[48]

When I started to write about transgenderism and cop the backlash, friends and family were confused about my choice of topic. *Why transgenderism?* They felt it was 'fringe'. Now, the more common initial response I receive involves people telling me about their 'trans' or 'non-binary' friend, sibling, niece, classmate or cousin. In five years, the topic has moved from being widely regarded as offbeat and unrelatable, to something that is a personal or family matter for many people.

The question of 'why transgenderism?' is really a question of 'why *sex?*' Politics is about public concerns, and public matters include things like elections, economics, taxation, immigration, foreign policy, military spending, law, education, housing, welfare, healthcare. But ... *transgenderism?* Men in wigs? Aren't people's sexual identities and orientations, even their fetishes and the surgical procedures they want carried out on their bodies, *private* matters? You seem like a nice girl who minds her own business.

---

47 Osho, 2002a, p. 92.
48 Ma, 2016, p. 20.

Why are you trying to talk about other people's personal and sexual choices and … well, *genitals* … in *public*?

The thing is, transgenderism is an ideology, and as such, it is public, not private. Yes, it revolves around sex – and genitals – and sex and genitals are basic to our common experience. All of us exist because of a sex act, and all of us have genitals. So, when we redefine what these things are in law, science, health, and education, it affects everyone. When that redefinition occurs in a rape culture, it affects women most of all, because women require sex-specific spaces for safety and recovery.

To advocate for female-only spaces, women need to be able to publicly state what they *are*. This necessarily involves referring to females, girls, and women as a group defined by sex, exclusive by nature. Transgenderism makes this controversial because its proponents argue that human beings are not sexually dimorphic, which means reframing natural law as feminist dogma. From this perspective, the reality that *males cannot be female* is not seen as a neutral, natural fact, but a nasty women's rule, a mean girls' taunt, a witch's curse. Resisting this astounding projection, and the implications it has for the status of women, is the main reason that feminists normally take on this hairball of a topic.

There is also a deeper reading of the question 'why *sex?*', in which it is not just a confounded, 'why make private matters public?' but an inquiry into why one of the most twisted ideologies confronting us today is *sexual* in nature. 'Why are so many people so prepared to deny and distort the realities of *sex* specifically?' 'What is it about *sex* that can activate the human capacity for denial in a way nothing else can?' Imagine if, instead of sex, it was the weather that was being denied and misrepresented. Suddenly, each night on the 6 o'clock news, weather forecasters began to declare that it was winter when it was in fact summer. Imagine them telling us that there would be plenty of snow for skiing this week, when it was over 30 degrees centigrade and everyone was either sunbathing or putting their heads in the fridge to escape the heat. Nobody would nod along with that – so why sex? Why are we so prepared to accept strange, reversed narratives about sex that we would not accept about other everyday observable realities of life?

This question prompts us to remember that, while *sex* normally refers to male and female anatomical parts, genital intercourse, reproduction, and an animal drive to procreate advantageously, that is not its full meaning for us. In human life, sex denotes a world of energy, feeling, longing, attraction, love, excitement, anticipation, delight, disappointment, and trauma that is not reducible to organ function and breeding. What's more, the intangible aspects of sex, like *attraction*, are not about seeking out partners we think will help us produce genetically superior offspring. Attraction is about who we are, who we want to become, the life we long for, and the kind of world we want to live in. Those longings also form the basis of our unconscious and conscious identities and creative expression.

Considered together, these aspects of being human – our sexed bodies, reproduction, desire, longing, creativity, evolution – constitute *eros*. So the question of 'why *sex*?' has now become, '*what is eros?*' and to my mind, that is one of the most important questions that can be asked in this day and age. As Audre Lorde writes in her essay 'Uses of the Erotic: The Erotic as Power', the Greek word *eros* refers to the personification of love, creative power, and harmony.[49] Consider that none of us individually manufactured our own desire, longing, and creativity, that these are aspects of our humanity, and that human beings were not in charge of our own evolution – we evolved through the movement of life itself. Then we can begin to understand *eros* as energy, as 'lifeforce'. As the spiritual mystic Osho wrote in *Sex Matters*:

> If we look closely into nature, we will find that there is only one process, only one wholehearted process going on. And that process is one of continuous creation, of procreation, of continuous resurrection of life in newer and newer forms.[50]

---

49   Lorde, 1984, pp. 53–9.
50   Osho, 2002a, p. 36.

To elaborate on this very simply, I will relay an answer I once wrote on a questionnaire asking participants to imagine our own 'Planet', a planet on which everything exists just as we envisage it. There were many questions about the planet's terrain, the architecture, and how people would spend their time. Three of the questions concerned sex specifically: "Do the people form monogamous bonds or marriages? If not, what type of relationships do you see between people?" and, "What is sex like on your planet?" I combined these answers into one, and wrote:

> Sexual relationships are about discovery. The chemistry between two people is so unique that each intimacy is respected as its own revelation. Flirting is fun because it is a celebration of the unique chemistry between two people. When flirtation becomes physical intimacy, this is one of the greatest joys. This joy, this kind of celebration of self and other, leads sexual partners to feel immense gratitude for one another. This means that sex is something deep and intrinsic to the joy, respect, confidence, and reverence for life that underpins and sustains the whole planet.

This is a personal take, but it says something about how sex is not only how we all originate; it is one of the most intimate, intense, and multisensory forms of communion we can engage in. On a cumulative and cultural level, this "sharing of joy," in Lorde's words, really could represent a creative wellspring among human beings. Intuitively, instinctively, deeply, *we know this*. We want to be seen and loved at the deepest core of our being – and there is nothing we can do about it, because the desire is bigger than we are,

> [a]nd that deep and irreplaceable knowledge of my capacity for joy comes to demand from all of my life that it be lived within the knowledge that such satisfaction is possible, and does not have to be called *marriage,* or *god,* or *an afterlife.*
>
> This is one reason why the erotic is so feared, and so often relegated to the bedroom alone, when it is recognised at all. For once we begin to feel deeply all the aspects of our lives, we begin to demand from ourselves and from our life-pursuits that they

feel in accordance with that joy which we know ourselves to be capable of.[51]

When people who carry the desire for shared joy, and the desire to be seen and loved in all dimensions, build a culture that treats everything like something to consume and profit from, including sex, it hurts us at the core of our humanity – because this way of living represents a devolution away from the potential that human sexuality and consciousness truly represent. As organic beings who exist inseparably from the movement of life as a whole, attempting to function in a society that views even sex as transactional is so antithetical to our nature that it fosters trauma that is not only personal but inherited, intergenerational, and cultural. We are not meant to be cut off from feeling, from eros, from joy. We also *cannot* be.

Distortion

Freire, Lorde and Osho all recognised that, since eros is a 'lifeforce' that cannot be destroyed, social control requires that it must be distorted instead. As Lorde wrote, "to perpetuate itself, every oppression must corrupt or distort those various sources of power … that can provide energy for change."[52] In Freire's words, "Dehumanisation, which marks not only those whose humanity has been stolen, but also (though in a different way) those who have stolen it, is a *distortion* of the vocation of becoming more fully human."[53] In *Nineteen Eighty-Four*, George Orwell put it so:

> How could the fear, the hatred and the lunatic credulity which the Party needed in its members be kept at the right pitch, except by bottling down some powerful force? The sex impulse was dangerous to the Party, and the Party turned it to account.[54]

---

51 Lorde, 1984, p. 57.
52 Lorde, 1984, p. 53.
53 Freire, 1970, p. 26.
54 Orwell, 1949/1989, p. 140.

We may insist that sex and trauma are private matters, but popular culture begs to differ. In film, theatre, television, and music, we constantly – even obsessively – retell and relate to stories about heartbreak and sex. Our collective creative expression is *shaped* by the way we suffer because we treat sex like something to consume rather than something to respect or revere, just as it is shaped by our longing for a life beyond the conventional. Our longings, creativity and sexuality are connected, and the societal forces that direct our lives down socially prescribed and predictable routes thwart them all. Popular culture reflects this, which is why Herbert Read argued that art is not an 'epiphenomenon', but something 'formative' both individually and socially. Lorde expressed the same thing by saying that "poetry is not a luxury." She also pointed out that in a rape culture, the quintessential distortion of *eros* is through pornography:

> The erotic has often been misnamed by men and used against women ... For this reason, we have often turned away from the exploration and consideration of the erotic as a source of power and information, confusing it with its opposite, the pornographic. But pornography is a direct denial of the power of the erotic, for it represents the suppression of true feeling. Pornography emphasises sensation without feeling.[55]

Pornography posing as eroticism: this is an example of distortion, or what Derrick Jensen calls 'toxic mimicry', which is:

> Something that the system does to everything ... takes the form and perverts the content of the thing. And one of the prototypical examples I use with this would be rape, which takes the *form* of – you could either say lovemaking, or you could say reproduction – the ultimate creative act – and perverts the content entirely into an act of domination and violation.[56]

This phenomenon is a "feature not a bug" of the social order.[57] The reason it works is that for each distortion we are baited with, there

---

55 Lorde, 1984, p. 54.
56 Jensen, 2022.
57 Jensen, 2022.

is a corresponding longing in the human heart. Since we can no longer remember how to meet that longing authentically, we are predisposed to accepting substitutes. This dynamic is pervasive: "Propaganda and advertising have always been designed to appeal to unacknowledged fears and yearnings."[58]

Naomi Wolf's classic text *The Beauty Myth* (1991) conveys this well. In a chapter titled 'Religion', Wolf offers a plethora of examples of cosmetic companies like Estée Lauder, Elizabeth Arden, Clarins and L'Oréal, targeting women's deepest longings by making claims about their products that relate to them. Balms and oils "soothe," "comfort," "calm," offer "intensive nourishment," and "Special Care," "Intensive Care," (Johnson & Johnson), "Loving Care" (Clairol), or "Natural Care" (Clarins). A face cream might act as "an invisible shield," a "protective barrier," or a "buffer," against "the stresses and strains of today's lifestyle."[59] The language is seductive because of the longing to which it appeals.

In Osho's view, sex repression is fundamental to the functioning of this system of distortion:

> Sex energy is life energy … And the politician and the priest are not interested in you, they are interested in channelling your energy into other directions. So there is a certain mechanism behind it – it has to be understood.
>
> Sex repression, tabooing sex, is the very foundation of human slavery … Man [sic] cannot really be free unless his [sic] sex energy is allowed natural growth.[60]

Sex repression has always been basic to patriarchal religious beliefs and institutions because it functions in this way – to distort, since it cannot destroy, *eros*. In patriarchal societies, the repression of sex means the oppression of women and the redirection of human energy away from life-affirming activities and toward external power, profit – and rape, prostitution, and pornography. These

---

58 Zuboff, 2019, p. 283.
59 Wolf, 1991, pp. 114–5.
60 Osho, 2001, pp. 109–10.

distortions are ongoing and cyclical because of the trauma they generate.

We now live in a time when the very numbing of sexuality through pornography, and the denial and manipulation of biology through transgenderism, are being presented to us as the kind of sexual freedom that Osho called for in the quote above, and that we all seek – but these movements appropriate, distort, and commercialise the idea of sexual liberation, leaving many casualties in their wake. Though transgenderism appears exhibitionist and flagrantly 'free', genuine inquiry into its nature and historic roots reveals that it reaffirms the basic rule of sex repression, updating it for today's social and political climate.

To understand transgenderism and all it reveals, we first need to understand the spiritual, psychological, and political significance of sex, repression, distortion, and trauma. When we do so, we will also uncover the ideas and contradictions responsible for human suffering, and for our social and political dysfunction. Indeed, the advent of transgenderism is a warning to us all that if we refuse to consider the pain we feel as more than fodder for entertainment, we are headed somewhere *truly* dystopian.

Evolution

If there was one quality that we could attribute to all of life itself, it would be *sensitivity*. Life is sensitive, down to the molecule: it detects, feels, and responds. Perhaps this quality comes from water, the substance on which all life depends. Water has the mysterious capacity to take on the qualities – like colours and flavours – of whatever it makes contact with. It has a kind of sensitivity, 'memory' or ability to store information.

Indeed, life on earth began in what authors Monica Sjöö and Barbara Mor called "a very female sea."[61] In the amniotic fluid of the sea, single cell organisms evolved with this miraculous

---

61   Sjöö and Mor, 1987, p. 2.

quality of sensitivity. As the herbalist Stephen Buhner writes in *The Secret Teachings of Plants*:

> When a cell forms, one of its major parts is its exterior or plasma membrane. This plasma membrane is a primary sensory organ for all cells. It possesses thousands of receptors across its surface, designed to detect perturbations, influxes of chemical, electric, magnetic, hormonal, pressure, and mechanical impulses, among other things ... The cell membrane mediates the responses of the cell to all of these influxes ...[62]

Eventually, multi-celled creatures like sea sponges and jellyfish evolved, then fish. Animals started moving onto land about 400 million years ago.

In Sjöö and Mor's *Great Cosmic Mother* (1987) and marine biologist Rachel Carson's *The Sea Around Us* (1951), the question of evolution is inseparable from the question of reproduction: life creating new life. Carson explains that as animals moved onto land, the life-giving conditions of the sea were replicated inside their bodies, so that "each of us begins his [sic] individual life in a miniature ocean within his mother's womb."[63] Our bodies carry about the same proportion of water as the earth's surface – 70 per cent – and our blood combines the elements sodium, potassium, and calcium in almost the same proportions as sea water. Charles Darwin himself argued that the menstrual cycle had its origin in the ocean and lunar tides.

Sjöö and Mor explain how the menstrual cycle and other changes to the female body were central to hominisation (the evolution of human beings from primates). Most female mammals reproduce through oestrus: they bleed as the lining of their uterus thickens to prepare for a fertilised egg. Women bleed when we are *not* fertile, and we are potentially fertile at any other time. During hominisation, this freed human sexuality from being solely about reproduction. And women have a clitoris: "the only organ in the

---

62 Buhner, 2004, p. 52.
63 Carson, 1951/2014, p. 20.

human body whose purpose is exclusively that of erotic stimulation and release."[64]

These changes to the female body were central to the evolution of human consciousness. Sjöö and Mor write:

> The change from rear to frontal sex, we can imagine, created an enormous change in relations between the sexes; frontal sex means a prolonged and enhanced lovemaking period, and what might be called the personalisation of sex. The emotion-evoking role of face-to-face intercourse in the development of human self-consciousness has yet to be evaluated (she turned around and looked him [or her] in the eye: and there was light!).[65]

Sex means total attention: the beauty of sex lies in this paradox of two people seeing themselves being seen. When attention is mutual and total, and each person gives themselves to the experience of perceiving the other, there are no longer two distinct individuals so much as two beings melting into this miraculous phenomenon of awareness. "We feel ourselves unique lovers, and at the same time uniquely in communion with all loving. We merge in love until there is neither the one nor the other."[66]

In his books *Love, Freedom and Aloneness* (2001) and *Sex Matters* (2002) Osho argues that this experience was the beginning of spirituality. He writes:

> My own understanding is that man had his first glimpses of awakening, of meditation, in moments of lovemaking – nowhere else. It was only in moments of lovemaking that human beings realised for the first time that so much bliss is possible.[67]

Osho argued that the first spiritual practitioners were people who attained *samadhi*, or an experience of 'oneness', through sex. "Sex has been the very source of religion, and the sexual experience has been the first experience of *samadhi*." Osho explains:

---

64 Sjöö and Mor, 1987, p. 5.
65 Sjöö and Mor, 1987, p. 10.
66 Giles, 1982, p. 11.
67 Osho, 2002a, p. 21.

They watched, meditated, and saw one thing: sex is only a psychological triggering of a certain process that can be triggered without sex too, which can be triggered just by meditation. There is no need to go into sex. Once they had known that the process could be triggered by other means also – by Yoga methods, by Tao methods, by Tantra methods, by Sufi methods – once they knew that the same state could be attained, of no ego, no mind, no time, without going into sex, they had found the key.[68]

Osho adds that, "From this grew the systems of yoga and of no-mind that gave birth to meditation."[69]

Today, sex is often considered a basic, instinctual need and bodily function, like eating or defecating. Moreover, this 'need' is considered more pronounced in men, who are not only bigger and stronger than women but allegedly 'innately' sexually aggressive. These ideas are not *true* – they are attempts to explain why rape is one of the most common, everyday forms of violation on the planet. They are attempts to accommodate the idea that rape is inevitable, despite this being a spiritually deadening notion. Rape does not arise from our humanity. It is the quintessential act of dehumanisation, a direct attack on the capacity for loving consciousness, communion, and the creation of new life that makes us human.

The work of Sjöö and Mor and Osho offer a different take on sex and need. Sex is not necessary to survive; a person can live a long and healthy life without sexual intercourse. Sexuality is not a survival instinct, or a merely procreative one or a matter of pleasure seeking. It is not secondary, either. If anything, sex is *more basic* to us than these instincts: it is because of a sexual act that you and I came into being. Our approach to sex shapes our collective evolution.

As we grow, the movement of our lives is informed by *eros*, or desire: by what attracts and holds meaning for us, and what burning questions seek resolution inside us. Eros does not arise *from* life, it *is* the basic energy *of* life. This energy situates us in a timeless, creative

---

68 Osho, 2002a, p. 275.
69 Osho, 2002a, p. 21.

movement toward loving consciousness that underlies the story of evolution and humanity. When this impulse is threatened or halted, it affects our survival instincts: we may stop eating, or lose our will to live. Freire discusses *eros* in the language of "humanisation," and writes:

> While both humanisation and dehumanisation are real alternatives, only the first is the people's vocation. This vocation is constantly negated, yet it is affirmed by that very negation. It is thwarted by injustice, exploitation, oppression, and the violence of the oppressors; it is affirmed by the yearning of the oppressed for freedom and justice, and by their struggle to recover their lost humanity.[70]

What human beings do with *eros*, this impulse toward humanisation, defines us, and our approach to sexuality is primary. What sexuality truly requires of human beings is what *humanity* requires of us, and the way we approach sex is the way we shape humanity. Sex and humanisation cannot be separated, and the fundamental question we need to ask is: is the way we treat life, and sexuality, making us more exquisitely alive, loving, and sensitive, or is it deadening, making us dissociated and numb?

Dualism

In his book *The Seat of the Soul* (1990), Gary Zukav introduces the terms *authentic power* and *external power*, and distinguishes them. Authentic power is another term for *eros*, and "has its roots in the deepest source of our being."[71] It is what John Dewey meant when he wrote that "growth is the characteristic of life," as quoted in Chapter One; it is the aliveness and vitality I want to reconnect with whenever I feel trapped in the 'fog', and it is what Freire means by *humanisation*. In contrast, external power is what feminists often call *power over*. Zukav writes:

---

70 Freire, 1970, p. 25.
71 Zukav, 1990, p. 26.

> External power can be acquired or lost, as in the stock market or an election. It can be bought or stolen, transferred or inherited. It is thought of as something that can be gotten from someone else, or somewhere else. One person's gain of external power is perceived as another person's loss.
>
> ... Competition for external power lies at the heart of all violence.[72]

External power refers to anything outside of us that we may reach for any time we feel cut off from authentic power, including attention from others, social status or indicators thereof, money – or *control* over other people through manipulation or violence.[73] External power itself is not *bad,* in Zukav's framing – what is dangerous is to seek it as a substitute for authentic power. Since we can never truly possess what is external to us, and since our deepest longings are not *for* such possession, the very effort to 'acquire' power cannot satisfy, and inevitably leads to frustration, competition, and violence. This is the moral of many a fable and film: that what we seek *outside* us is actually *inside*. And our deepest longings do not represent a desire to possess and accumulate, as we may think – but to remove those obstacles and hindrances that block our "very being."[74]

If authentic power is not only natural to us, but ultimately who and what we *are*, then how did we become cut off from it? And why do we continue to trade authentic power for external substitutes none of us are satisfied with?

Feminist authors, archaeologists and historians offer us answers. Our species of *homo sapiens sapiens* has existed for about 100,000 years. For most of that time, we have lived in cultures deeply connected to the earth and to natural systems – it could not have been otherwise. According to writers like Monica Sjöö and Barbara Mor, this involved us living in cultures where women

---

72 Zukav, 1990, pp. 23–5.
73 For more discussion of different forms of power and tactics used to accumulate power, see Hawthorne, 2002/2022, pp. 69–93.
74 Osho, 2001, p. 77.

were honoured, and children grew up learning to take care of their mothers' homelands. This could be a summary of what a matriarchy is: a culture where children grow up learning to care for their mothers' homelands.

There are two main elements to a matriarchal culture: being matrilineal, and matrilocal. The word matrilineal means "a lineage through the mother." In such a culture, people trace their family lineage through their mother's line, rather than being named after their fathers. A *matrilocal* culture is one in which women and children are recognised as having ancestral connections and birthright to their mothers' lands. Children inherit birthright to land through their mothers' connection to it. Such cultures have many myths and creation stories that involve a life-giving Great Mother who reflects the fact that human beings are bound to each other and to life through blood ties. She is often associated with a local mountain, river, or lake.

In her essay 'Tao as the Great Mother and the Influence of Motherly Love in the Shaping of Chinese Philosophy', Ellen Chen argues that the *Tao* – one of the earliest works of Chinese philosophy, written around 500 BCE (and a favourite text of the contemporary spiritual teacher Eckhart Tolle) – is "rooted in the worship of the Mother-goddess."[75] Lao Tzu states, "There was something undefined and complete, coming into existence before Heaven and Earth … It may be regarded as the Mother of all things."[76] The *Tao* says that, "If we choose to avoid mistakes and desire to have a wise guide throughout life, we should study the wisdom of Mother Nature's ways … She is the ultimate source of all that exists …"[77] Lao Tzu warns what happens when we neglect to do this:

> When man interferes with the Tao,
> the sky becomes filthy,
> the earth becomes depleted,

---

[75] Chen, 1974.
[76] Tzu/Legge, 1997, p. 21.
[77] Chen, 1974.

Chapter Two: Desire and Distortion

the equilibrium crumbles,
creatures become extinct.[78]

In her books *When God Was a Woman* and *Ancient Mirrors of Womanhood*, feminist historian Merlin Stone reflects on the image of the Great Mother around the world. Such a comparative study thwarts any attempt to come up with some ultimate, universal concept of the Mother or idea of the 'feminine'. While one culture might associate the Mother with the moon, for another, the sun is female. What Stone *does* say is that wherever she is found, this goddess tends to be both *gentle* and *fierce*. She says that western scholars tend to consider this a paradox – but it is not. Imagine a mother swan floating on a river with her cygnets: you are observing the most gentle scene, until you try to approach the cygnets.[79]

Sjöö and Mor refer to the Great Mother as "she who gives us all to each other as food."[80] Imagine the many-armed Indian goddess Kali, extending one hand in offering while another holds a severed head. *Kāla* also means 'time' – that which births and consumes everything – and shares its etymology with the word *calendar*. Here we find another association with women: women created the first calendars by tracking their menstrual cycles against the cycles of the moon.[81] The words Kali, *kāla*, and calendar connect time, women, the moon and "she who gives us all to each other as food."[82]

Gerda Lerner's *Creation of Patriarchy* explains that the patriarchal system we know today usurped earlier matriarchal cultures in a process involving several key phases. In the first, children started being named after their fathers, and matrilineal systems became patrilineal. As men claimed ownership of children, cultures became patrilocal, and women were married off to live in male-run households, instead of remaining on their mothers' lands.[83]

---

78 Tzu/Mitchell, 2015, p. 39.
79 Stone, 1976; 1984.
80 Sjöö and Mor, 1987, p. 180.
81 Sjöö and Mor, 1987, p. 191.
82 Harding, 1993, p. 59.
83 Lerner, 1986.

This was the beginning of the 'private sphere', and, I would argue, of the private *ego*, the "illusion of ... a separate self," divorced from unconditional belonging to land and community and forced into self-interest.[84] Indeed, Sadhguru writes:

> Never is the body allowed to forget its origins. When it is allowed to forget, it often starts making fanciful demands. When it is constantly reminded, it knows its place. This contact with the earth is a vital reconnection of the body with its physical source. This restores stability to the system for rejuvenation greatly.[85]

The early patriarchs required justifications for fracturing, replacing, and destroying the ancient ways of life that people knew and loved; they needed their own arguments and logic to replace spiritual traditions that honoured women. New ideas and religions were required, ones that could support a hierarchy in which men ruled over women. These religions could not be mere fabrications, otherwise people would not connect with them. They had to connect with humanity, with *eros*. So, the new religions took old beliefs and customs, and distorted them to fit a patriarchal power system. Contrary to popular belief that war is inevitable and part of human nature, the earliest known weapons of warfare were fashioned after these early patriarchal developments took place.[86]

Sjöö and Mor write that even with the dualistic formula, "it must have been an awkward job for patriarchs," trying to figure out how to turn the mother of all life into a father in their stories. They had to explain how a man brought life to earth, even though men cannot create either children or food for children from their bodies like women can. "The father is not of the same all-containing, all-infusing, shaping and nourishing substance, and so the relation between humans and the Father God becomes abstract and alienated, distant and moralistic."[87]

---

84 Osho, 2001, p. 36.
85 Sadhguru, 2016a, p. 111.
86 Foster, 2013, p. 118.
87 Sjöö and Mor, 1987, p. 231.

Chapter Two: Desire and Distortion

In her book *Invisible Women of Prehistory* (2013), Judy Foster explains that the invention of philosophical dualism enabled the distortion of eros and the creation of the patriarchal religions that justify hierarchies of external power. While matriarchal spiritual traditions are integrated and holistic, patriarchal religions are fragmented and hierarchical. For example, in the *Tao*, science, art, law, education, philosophy, and spirituality are all implied by the same practice: the study of Mother Nature. But in the west today, we consider these to be distinct fields of study and specialisation. These divisions arise out of a more primary separation from Mother Nature in favour of a system that must control and manipulate, rather than observe and honour, her.

In western culture, *law* in the sense of 'natural law' and *law* as in the legal system are two very different things. Natural laws, like gravity, are *laws* precisely because they cannot be changed; while *legislation* is created by lawmakers. Among the Minangkabau of Indonesia, matriarchal 'mother law' or *adat ibu* is not a system that has been created to maintain social order and good behaviour among the citizenry.[88] Mother law is a law of nature that people must observe, lest we fall on our faces in much the same way we do if we ignore or dishonour the law of gravity, or cause and effect. Natural and cultural law are not perceived as wholly distinct.

The same could be said of nature, law, and education. In the anthology *Societies of Peace,* Olokinwinapi says that a slogan of the Kuna people in Panama is, "We do not need schools. The mother is our teacher in Indigenous America."[89] This statement implies a connection between science, nature, law, education, and social participation. As John Dewey said, "education is all one with growing; it has no end beyond itself."[90] When we needlessly fragment these aspects of life, we do the same with the process of *living*.

---

88   Usria Dhavida, in Göttner-Abendroth, 2009, pp. 228–9.
89   Antje Olowaili, in Göttner-Abendroth, 2009, p. 84.
90   Dewey, 1916/2004, p. 62.

Foster explains how dualism fragmented these previously holistic and integrated traditions. It is not a philosophy in and of itself so much as a formula that can be applied either to observable realities or existing philosophies. It begins with complementary principles, pairs, or opposites – such as sky and earth, light and dark, high and low, male and female, mind and body, concept and material, white and black, production and reproduction, freedom and necessity, thinking and feeling, conscious and unconscious, reason and nature – and it declares all the former concepts in these couplets *superior* and morally correct, and the latter *inferior* and corrupt.[91] Everything inferior is associated with sin (and evil, demons, and the Devil), and with women (since we are down there too) and "outside the realm of reason, goodness and value."[92] Dualism is the distortion of difference, complements or opposites, into hierarchies of value. It also provided the groundwork and rationale for slavery based on race and class, by deeming some people closer to 'God' than others by virtue of their skin colour.

History reveals how dualism distorted older belief systems from about 4,000 to 6,000 years ago, and feminist writers like Merlin Stone, Marilyn French and Marija Gimbutas have shown how mythology reflects the gradual subjugation of women, often through wars between the sexes that result in male gods – especially gods of the sky, thunder, or underworld – claiming women's powers.

French writes that in early Sumerian myths, "goddesses created everything, and Siduri, one of the most prominent, reigned in paradise. Later, a sun god usurped her realms, goddesses were demoted, and, by the later epic of the legendary king Gilgamesh, Siduri was a barmaid."[93]

Gimbutas' book *The Living Goddesses* (2001) shows how the goddesses of the Greek pantheon are much older than the patriarchal classical myths we know today.[94] Athena and the owl, who so

---

91 Foster, 2013.
92 Foster, 2013, p. 150.
93 French, 2008, p. 97.
94 Gimbutas, 2001.

appealed to me; Artemis and the bear, Hecate and the frog – these goddesses speak to us because they once formed part of an older, matriarchal spiritual tradition in which wisdom emerged from the observation of nature and its cycles. Gimbutas elucidates how, after the Indo-European invasions, these goddesses became the props of a patriarchal story in which Zeus reigns supreme and bore Athena from his head, clad for battle.

Eventually, Judeo-Christian myth declared that God made Adam first, and that Eve was created from his rib. Jesus was supposed to have been born when his heavenly father God, who creates all life, impregnated a chaste and sexless woman named Mary with the aid of the holy spirit. As Sjöö and Mor write, "This is our grotesque situation today. *An anti-sexual God is now worshipped as the creator of life.*" [95]

Nineteenth century feminist Matilda Joslyn Gage explained that under Christianity, both women and sex – and women *as* sex – are believed to contaminate the soul and man's divine relation to God. Eve caused the fall of mankind by tempting Adam with 'forbidden fruit' in the Garden of Eden. Because of this 'feminine' evil, women, and intercourse with women, were considered polluted, and more animal than human, but necessary for procreation. In Sjöö and Mor's words, "Christian religious doctrine exists to punish us for a 'bestiality' which it has itself created." [96] The church decided that God's ceremonial witnessing of a marriage, and church control over the contract, was required to make it 'clean' and to lessen the evil, and it gradually criminalised marriage without priestly sanction. If a man and woman lived together unmarried, they were perceived to be 'living in sin' – sex is 'sin.'

The dualistic, patriarchal conception of men and women views us not as two *sexes* but as two *classes*, one dominant and the other subordinate. Applying it to biological sex results in what we call 'gender': a cultural concept of masculine dominance and

---

95   Sjöö and Mor, 1987, p. 234.
96   Sjöö and Mor, 1987, p. 291.

feminine submissiveness. The cultural myth that rape is inevitable is embedded in these concepts. As Dworkin wrote:

> In this male supremacist society, men are defined as one order of being over and against women who are defined as another, opposite, entirely different order of being. Men are defined as aggressive, dominant, powerful. Women are defined as passive, submissive, powerless. Given these polar gender definitions, it is the very nature of men to aggress sexually against women. Rape occurs when a man, who is dominant by definition, takes a woman who, according to men and all the organs of their culture, was put on this earth for his use and gratification. Rape, then, is the logical consequence of a system of definitions of what is normative. Rape is no excess, no aberration, no accident, no mistake – it embodies sexuality as the culture defines it. As long as these definitions remain intact – that is, as long as men are defined as sexual aggressors and women are defined as passive receptors lacking integrity – men who are exemplars of the norm will rape women.[97]

Through understanding dualism we can also see what happened to the simultaneous gentleness and fierceness of the Great Mother: they are fragmented. First, dualistic distortion transformed 'God' from a mother into a man, and from an intelligent lifeforce existing within us, into a punitive representative of man-made law and external power. Accordingly, for women, gentleness is elevated, something women should aspire to, almost out of apology for our femaleness, and to demonstrate that we do not mean to threaten male power – while fierceness is stigmatised. This fragmentation and imbalance means that the gentleness that is held up for women as a 'feminine' ideal also becomes artificial, a social performance. Women's gentleness is not celebrated, but distorted into an instruction to become "passive, submissive, powerless."

In Christian myth, the Virgin Mary becomes a mother after she utters the words, "do unto me according to thy word." She is a model

---

97 Dworkin, 1976, pp. 45–6.

woman because of her surrender. In spiritual terms, surrendering one's body to god is like surrendering it to life, *the Tao,* or the cycles of nature – a beautiful act, antithetical to the effort to manipulate, destroy, and control. As Lao Tzu says, "Because she has let go of herself / she is perfectly fulfilled."[98] Yet within a patriarchal power structure, surrender becomes distorted, because it is not Mother Nature whose power and laws we are to honour and celebrate, and to whom we must concede ultimate control, but men, and male gods and rulers. The symbol of the Virgin Mary is what remains of the Great Mother when she is stripped of her capacity for fierceness and self-assertion and *only* allowed to surrender, to men, with a smile.

In society, these kinds of feminine symbols function to justify and promote men's dominance over women. Specifically, they justify laws that treat women as men's property. As Dworkin wrote, "law is an instrument of religion" and the earliest legal codes emphasised the sexual regulation of women.[99] This was true all the way up to William Blackstone's codification of British common law in 1770, which developed from church law and provided the basis for today's legal system. Common law made marriage a covenant with God, so women could not divorce. A woman fleeing from a violent or abusive husband could be hunted down, jailed, or whipped, or returned to her husband by the police, as a runaway slave.

The culture that we live in today is still one in which men who control land, property, finance, and politics, create the conditions of acceptance. If we want a roof over our heads, we need to pay what landlords require; if we want an income, we need to comply with the expectations of employers. These expectations and conditions are not based on natural law or justice, but the interests of those at the top of the social order. All of us are subject to the conditions of the culture we live in, and so were our parents. We are also taught to

---

98 Tzu/Mitchell, 2015, p. 7.
99 Dworkin, 1983, p. 78.

meet social expectations through more than a decade of schooling within an education system more devoted to showing us how to satisfy the requirements of authority figures, and be ranked and graded by them, than how to express what we can learn and observe through the study of Mother Nature.

Dualism is at the core of the social norms that each of us are subjected to and conditioned to comply with from childhood. As Dworkin writes, "[the] position of the mother, in particular, in a male supremacist society, is absolutely untenable." Something that clearly affects us all.[100]

Domestication

I had a spontaneous realisation about *eros* one day when I was walking around Brisbane, Australia, and stopped to admire a striking, deep red orange hibiscus. It evoked in me a feeling like desire – that's why many people pick flowers – and I realised how beautiful the feeling is, and how stigmatised. We tend to feel guilty for desire, and to assume it is 'spiritual' to transcend it. We think the Buddhists don't want us to want. We think that our wanting reveals we are not grateful for what we already have, as God and our families and teachers and partners wish us to be.

When I looked at this flower and saw the generous way that it was opening out to me, I realised what a disservice we are doing each other with these guilt-inducing notions. To be *wanted* is what everybody longs for most deeply. *Desire* is different from *need* precisely because it implies total freedom and lack of dependency. It is our freely given affirmation of the life around us, our inner 'yes', and it is what life most delights in because it is delicious, and the basis of our existence. As I looked at that hibiscus flower, I felt how true desire is not an expression of greed, but the celebration of life.

As we grow up, it is this desire, this *"yes* within ourselves," that is directed toward socially acceptable ends and shaped into

---

100 Dworkin, 1976, p. 57.

Chapter Two: Desire and Distortion

socially acceptable forms.[101] If desire is like a current or a stream – inseparable from the oceans and waters of earth and sky – the culturally prescribed *identifications* we are conditioned to accept which follow the dualistic template, function to dam and re-route the stream. The stream does not dry up, but its shape is distorted. Instead of moving toward the sea, the water is re-routed to a chlorinated, concrete swimming pool. Desire cannot be dealt with any other way because it cannot be destroyed. Life wants to live.

If the pool represents socially approved forms of consumption, status, accumulation, and possession, the damming of the stream creates an insatiable hunger within us that we channel toward this pool with urgency. We learn that we 'want' a career, we 'want' money, we 'want' to be physically desirable in specific ways, we 'want' one special someone to love us as though we are descended from heaven. We learn that all this will require us to be seen as 'good' or 'successful' by particular people. We learn that if we are successful, we will be rewarded with the love, happiness, wealth, and joy that exist at our destination, the swimming pool.

Only – love, happiness, wealth, and joy are not rewards. They are qualities of a free-flowing stream, expressions of authentic power; of *eros*. When we seek them as rewards, we can never be satisfied, even when we reach the pool – because we needed to *dam up* this undercurrent of eros, our inner 'yes', to get there.

Why are human beings predisposed to such self-destructive social conditioning? Because of our childhood dependency. During hominisation, our species evolved to stand upright, female bodies changed, our brains became larger, and babies started being born at an earlier stage of development. While a horse or dog can walk almost as soon as it is born, human infants are characterised by a long period of total dependency. Three-quarters of our brain growth and almost 90 per cent of brain development take place after we are born, mostly in the first three years of life. In other words, the 'fourth trimester' of pregnancy occurs outside the womb.

---

101 Lorde, 1984, p. 57.

During this time, we cannot survive by ourselves. We need to be fed, kept warm, cleaned, and toileted. We also cannot regulate our own nervous systems: we need to be entertained and stimulated, and when stressed, we need to be soothed. *Connection* is of primary importance to us. A threat to our connection with our caregivers is a threat to our lives, and abandonment is fatal.

It seems safe to presume that if children grew up learning to look after their mothers' homelands – within a community who knew them well, on land they had a birth right to live on, and with parents who had the support to raise children without undue stress – we would grow out of the sense that abandonment is lethal at roughly the same time that this was no longer physiologically true for us. But in a patriarchal culture, just about every aspect of life comes with conditions: making sure you are warm, dry, fed, clothed, and sheltered requires meeting those conditions. Our parents help to teach us what those conditions are, so that we can take care of ourselves successfully. As we grow, our fear of abandonment is confirmed and consolidated rather than gradually shed. This leads us to employ our sensitivity for the purpose of self-protective hypervigilance, rather than an ever-refining attunement to the natural world and one another.[102]

Our nervous systems learn their patterns and habits of emotional regulation *in relationship* with our caregivers, and as we accept the conditions we are presented with. We allow our stream to fall into the grooves and channels already shaped around us, and we also create our own dams anywhere we have seen signs of potential rejection and become wounded and hurt. Wherever a stone is thrown into the stream, it leaves us feeling shame (which Brené Brown defines as "fear of disconnection") about who we really

---

[102] Art theorist Herbert Read lamented the "atrophy of sensibility" in art and education and connected it to violence and to the transformation of the human being into an "automaton" (1967, p. 21). For contrast, I highly recommend the book *Songspirals: Sharing Women's Wisdom of Country through Songlines* (2019) by a Gay'wu Group of Women. It offers a beautiful illustration of life and culture among people with exquisitely refined capacity for attunement.

are. We build a dam where the stone landed, so that part will not be wounded again. This dam represents a dissociation not only from aspects of ourselves, but also other people who may make us look guilty by association.

These dams also represent the beliefs we cultivate about why we are unloveable, what face we must show the world, and what is good and bad, right and wrong. While they may seem all the more private for being unconscious, these beliefs are in fact culturally patterned and meant to help us adapt to the social order. They represent a redirection of our life energies away from *eros* and toward the interests of those in charge, those from whom we need approval. This is what identification is, and identification shapes our outlook, direction, and the way we think and behave. In Freire's words:

> The oppressed suffer from the duality which has established itself in their innermost being. They discover that without freedom they cannot exist authentically. Yet, although they desire authentic existence, they fear it. They are at one at the same time themselves and the oppressor whose consciousness they have internalised.[103]

The impact and the prevalence of lifelong repression for the sake of acceptance is the subject of Gabor Maté's book *When the Body Says No,* which integrates an analysis of gender. He shows how habits of shame, 'niceness', the inability to say no, and the repression of anger, are correlated not only with long-term stress, anxiety, and depression, but with illness such as multiple sclerosis, cancers and rheumatoid and autoimmune disease. This is because,

> repression – dissociating emotions from awareness and relegating them to the unconscious realm – disorganizes and confuses our physiological defences so that in some people these defences go awry, becoming the destroyers of health rather than its protectors.[104]

---

103 Freire, 1970, p. 30. Don Miguel Ruiz also offers a very clear and simple explanation of "domestication" in his *Four Agreements* (1997).
104 Maté, 2019, p. 7.

The upper layer of this system of repression, stress and addiction, particularly for women, is 'niceness', since the whole point is to *please*. Niceness is the mask that other people see. Maté says that "Rage and anguish exist under the veneer of niceness, no matter how sincerely a person mistakes the facade for her true self."[105] Addressing the rage, Maté writes:

> Why do we have anger? In the animal world, anger is not a 'negative emotion'. An animal experiences anger when some essential need is either threatened or frustrated.
>
> ... A cornered animal turns to face his pursuer with a fierce display of rage. Anger may save his life, either by intimidating the hunter or by enabling the prey to resist successfully.
>
> ... For anger to be deployed appropriately, the organism has to distinguish between threat and non-threat. The fundamental differentiation to be made is between self and non-self. If I don't know where my own boundaries begin and end, I cannot know when something potentially dangerous is intruding on them. The necessary distinctions between what is familiar or foreign, and what is benign or potentially harmful, require an accurate appraisal of self and non-self. Anger represents both a recognition of the foreign and dangerous and a response to it.[106]

Maté proposes – in a way that echoes Freire, but from the perspective of a physician – that when we internalise societal expectations that run contrary to our own desire for authentic existence, this means *internalising* what our bodies recognise as a *threat*. In an otherwise healthy world, if we were to meet such a threat, we would take the simplest course of action to remove it from our environment: we might walk past it, run, or scare it off. In an oppressive society, being compelled to internalise the demands of an otherwise external threat means that the stress mechanism cannot switch off, and it means bottling anger, which confuses the immune system. It creates an inner war.

---

105 Maté, 2019, p. 49.
106 Maté, 2019, p. 174.

Chapter Two: Desire and Distortion

Joe Dispenza, author of *Becoming Supernatural*, explains that this combination of repression and long-term stress can make people chemically addicted to their own stress hormones. Our understanding of what it means to feel 'awake' and 'alive' becomes synonymous with a degree of stress. Our stress mechanism is triggered easily by all sorts of things that remind us of the 'threat', and this in turn kicks off what Dispenza calls the "thinking-feeling loop," a familiar pattern of thoughts and emotions that we recognise as *ourselves*. The cycle is so perpetual that stress becomes the way we know we're switched 'on'.[107] We become accustomed to how it feels to be a stream constantly bumping into dams while heading to a swimming pool, rather than a free-flowing current moving to the sea.

Maté is an expert on addiction, and for him, addictions develop as a way of coping with this combination of repression, emotional numbing, and chronic stress. Addictions are the outlets we find for our stream that substitute for our longing to meet the ocean. We develop addictions that help us switch the stress *off* and relax (like social media scrolling, television, alcohol), as well as to give us a kick so that we can feel *alive* – thrilled, euphoric, anything but numb. Many of the world's major industries are based on these addictions and coping mechanisms, as Sjöö and Mor point out:

> The bulk of patriarchal industries – drugs, alcohol, entertainment media, fashion and cosmetics, pornography, the tourist business, polyester-suited politics, drive-in religious sermons, interstate freeway systems, you name it – exist and profit solely by selling momentary diversions to multitudes of 'quietly desperate people', seeking anaesthetic escape from the pain of personal alienation.[108]

Despite its negative effects, this pattern of internalisation, repression, numbing, stress, and addiction becomes our comfort zone, even what we recognise as our *self*. That is because, from our earliest years, it was programmed into our nervous system and became

---

107 Dispenza, 2017.
108 Sjöö and Mor, 1987, p. 29.

the way that we find regulation or homeostasis. Psychologist Nicole LePera who specialises in codependency, explores how this operates in her book *How to Do the Work*.[109]

LePera explains that the subconscious mind operates with a *homeostatic impulse*. Through this impulse, it regulates physiological functions like heart rate and body temperature by keeping them within a particular range. Our subconscious does the same thing with our thoughts, feelings and behaviours: keeps them within the familiar range we recognise as our 'comfort zone'. Our everyday patterns of repression and compensation are part of this program, which is organised around our identifications – the people or groups we need to have approval from, *or else I will be helpless and alone, which will either kill me or make life unbearable.*

There is a feeling that many writers, healers, and spiritual teachers identify as sitting right in the middle of this comfort zone we create, whereby we hide ourselves to please others, and become accustomed to unhealthy levels of stress. These days it is popularly called 'disconnection'. Karl Marx called it 'alienation'. In *Trauma and Recovery* (1992), Judith Herman calls it 'helplessness'.[110] In *Daring Greatly* (2015), Brené Brown calls it 'vulnerability'. It is the experience of the person inside us who is repressed, stuck, invisible, and somehow cannot reach life, or other people, through the fog. It is also the feeling that if she emerges and is rejected, that rejection will spell death.

Repression means that we simultaneously try to *avoid* aloneness by meeting the expectations of others to stay connected, while we *exacerbate* isolation because nobody can see who we truly are, and we constantly remind ourselves not to reveal the truth. This is why the 'comfort zones' we develop are both protective and damaging, and why we insist on maintaining them. To threaten any aspect of this system of repression and compensation is to threaten the homeostasis and balance, to risk exposing what should

---

109 LePera, 2021.
110 Herman, 1992.

be repressed, *and* to finally risk rejection and abandonment. This feels just as life-threatening as it did when we were infants, because a patriarchal culture does not allow people to gradually mature out of childhood dependency. It leverages our dependency instead, to promote conformity.

Meanwhile, our desire to be and feel alive, seen and heard – to feel one with the ocean – has gone nowhere. Our addictions don't help, "since secondary sources can never satisfy primary needs."[111] As Freire and Lorde pointed out, oppression does not destroy our aliveness, or *eros*, but turns this lifeforce into a longing, a yearning.

Gender

In her book *Unmaking War Remaking Men* (2011), Kathleen Barry asks the question:

> How in the madness of war do so many human beings throughout the world – who share an unconditional love of life, who are connected to each other through the life force that urges us away from death to spontaneously want to save another's life and to protect one's own – come to accept war as inevitable? … How do we hold in our hearts, against our shared human consciousness, the conviction that men will be killed in combat and that it must be that way?[112]

Barry discusses how men and boys come to internalise the principle of their own expendability, as they are fed war movies, shoot-em-up video games, violent sports, and plastic guns, right from childhood. In response to her questions, she says, "The answer to them is stunningly, frighteningly simple: masculinity."[113]

Barry says boys receive the message from a young age that men's lives are expendable, and this creates an angry 'smoldering' in men that is the very source of rage that the military will 'tap'

---

111 Glendinning, 1994, p. 99.
112 Barry, 2011, p. 7.
113 Barry, 2011, p. 10.

to prepare them for combat. The army employs humiliation to reshape trainees' basic human needs to connect with others, to "produce in them the desire to belong to a team effort to kill." The military "counts on the cowardice," she says, that is tangled up with this rage that masculinity seals away. Those who refuse to shoot know they are leaving the burden with their buddies, Barry says – and the reward for the loss of soul that comes with destruction is masculinity: becoming one of the boys.

It is not just violent video games that boys are exposed to from childhood, but pornography. The two are linked: online and video games are often pornified, as feminist author Gail Dines explains in *Pornland*, using the example of Grand Theft Auto.[114] Moreover, pornographers know how to lure boys from gaming to pornography using clickbait and Malware.[115] Porn is the major tool for teaching the fetishisation of violence and domination, including to children, because it includes a very efficient reward mechanism: it ties the act of violation to orgasm. This does two things: it reduces a person's sexual response to something mechanical and insensitive, and cultivates a compensatory addiction to whatever provokes that sex response. Porn is dehumanising, the ultimate distortion of *eros* – as I learned in high school.

Pornographers can maximise profit by getting consumers hooked young, and according to Dines, the average age that boys begin to watch pornography is 11 years old.[116] Both the porn industry and patriarchy itself are sustained by this phenomenon: boys having their sexuality co-opted before they have a chance to grapple with the nature of what it is, and how they might wish to express it for themselves. Men come to see *women* as the ones responsible for taking their humanity from them, and so women remain the primary target of male rage.

Because porn is addictive, the industry also operates according to the habituation principle: over time, consumers need a stronger

---

114 Dines, 2010, p. 50, p. 62.
115 Root and Melnykov, 2018.
116 Dines, 2010, p. xi.

Chapter Two: Desire and Distortion

and stronger dose to get the same 'hit'. In pornography, this amounts to ever increasing degradation and brutality. While the real potential of human sexuality is for a full-bodied experience of loving awareness, the gradual and infinite refinement of sensitivity, ecstasy and *samadhi,* the distortion of this in pornography is the antithesis.

Apparently, the 'spitroasting' and 'teabagging' I learned about in high school are now considered tame. Now there is 'rosebudding', which involves men raping women anally until they suffer rectal prolapse. Other abuses that are now typical include two men penetrating a woman vaginally, at the same time; or three or more men penetrating a woman vaginally, anally, and orally, all at once. 'Gagging' – in which a man thrusts his penis down a woman's throat until she chokes – is another one.

None of this arises out of female (or human) desire. Pornography records and promotes *rape*: the act of a man who is enslaved by his own sex response but disconnected from his humanity and sensitivity; from the drive toward loving consciousness that is part of our evolution; from his capacity for emotional intimacy, and from his ability to celebrate life.

Generations of behavioural psychologists have experimented with ways to take advantage of the human propensity to override our own free will, best interests, capacity for empathy, or better judgement, to follow instructions or the crowd. Naomi Klein's book *The Shock Doctrine* (discussed in Chapter Three), explores how, over the last half century, putting populations in a state of 'shock' has been crucial to imposing the legal reforms, political narratives, land confiscation and rollback of rights that characterise neoliberalism worldwide. Rape is the original 'shock': the definitive way to override the desire and will of another. Rape enables men to terrorise and control women, in private and as a class.

Rape hurts in a way that goes beyond other forms of physical assault because it is an attempt to injure more than our physical bodies. An attack on female sexuality is an attack on women's freedom, and therefore humanity's. Rape opposes all that human sexuality represents: sensitivity, intimacy, *eros*. Epidemic rape generates collective trauma.

When a rapist makes his intention clear, he inflicts terror, to which women's nervous systems often respond with dissociation, the means by which our bodies protect us from conscious experience of an event too painful to bear.[117] The victim experiences herself as drifting or floating away from her body – sometimes seeing herself as if from above, looking down – while memories of the event are stored in the subconscious (or body).

Actress Rose McGowan describes the experience of dissociation, and its connection to the 'triggering' of memories stored in the body in her memoir, *Brave* (2018). McGowan was sexually assaulted early in her career, on a movie set. When she spoke up about the event later, the director denied it had happened. McGowan writes:

> Don't gaslight me, motherfucker. My vagina remembers. My body remembers … The body has memory that is even more accurate than the mind. Women know when they have been violated emotionally, physically, or verbally … Our bodies shake, they burn, they do all kinds of things when they remember. Our muscles remember. Even when we are drunk we know the difference between welcome and unwelcome – the body always feels it during and after.[118]

McGowan's book also revealed that she was raped by Harvey Weinstein, and described the dissociation she experienced in the moments after he released her from his hotel room. She describes how and why this state was useful to Weinstein, writing:

> My whole body is shaking. I try to find my clothes. I'm in total shock, and moving somewhat mechanically. I'm still hovering up above, not quite in my body. And I'm trying to put my clothes on and make sense of what has just happened. It's like a race you can't keep up with. My life has been re-routed. I just got hijacked.[119]

---

117 Herman, 1992, p. 42; Glendinning, 1994, p. 62.
118 McGowan, 2018, p. 102.
119 McGowan, 2018, p. 123.

Chapter Two: Desire and Distortion

This word, *hijacked*, makes it clear why rape is such an effective means of social control. When rape occurs, there may be two people in a room, but one of them appears to have made himself more than half the equation by compelling the other to leave her body to make room for him. Terror and dissociation create an apparent identification of interests: *his* emotional state is of supreme importance to both parties. He wants something, and since he has cornered her, she needs him placated. Her safety and freedom are in this moment bound up with his inner state. When he is calm, she can be safe. Terror has made his requirements paramount. This is what we mean when we say that rape is about dominance, about control.

In a rape *culture,* in which the act of rape is consistent with social norms, women who have experienced dissociation never get the message that it is safe to *recover* conscious experience of the here and now. In *Know My Name* (2019), Chanel Miller writes about entering the court system after rape, and the way that her dissociation from her body at the time represented Turner's opportunity to 'hijack' and 'write the script' in court. Turner claimed that Miller had enjoyed being assaulted behind the dumpster, and that he had even sought her consent – that she had said, "uh huh." At first, Miller found this preposterous and called her defence attorney in disbelief:

> But as she [Miller's defence attorney] spoke, her reasoning hit me with horrifying clarity: his only way out is through you. It was like watching wolves being clipped off their leashes while someone whispered in your ear that meat has been sewn into your pockets. The only chance he had of being acquitted was to prove that to his knowledge, the sexual act had been consensual. He'd force moans in my mouth, assign lecherous behaviour, to shift the blame onto me.[120]

In a patriarchal culture, the whole world appears to belong to men, who dominate women collectively, just as they do individually in a rape scenario. In her online talk 'The Sexy Lie', Caroline Heldman

---

120 Miller, 2019, p. 46.

discusses the objectification of women in mainstream media, questioning the popular justification that 'sex sells'. Heldman points out that sex, by definition, is mutual – but 96 per cent of objectifying media depicts women. "If sex sold, why wouldn't we see half naked men everywhere in advertising?" Heldman asks. Because it's not sex that is being sold, she says: it's something else.

"To men, they're being sold this idea constantly that they are sexual subjects. They are in the driver's seat," Heldman explains. "It makes men feel powerful to see images of objectified women everywhere" – and to be able to buy and sell access to women in prostitution and strip clubs. On the flip side, Heldman says: "women are being sold this idea that this is how we get our value; and this is the way to become the ideal sex object."[121]

This measure of value is at the core of 'feminine' socialisation, which teaches girls and women to comply with men's demands – not only for approval, but because girls' and women's safety is only possible when men are satisfied. When men are happy, we can relax. The culture calls women's prioritisation of men's needs 'selflessness', 'kindness', and 'love' – but many feminists and therapists call this *distortion* of love, *codependency*. In Women, Sex and Addiction (1987), Charlotte Kasl explains the cost to women when she says:

> Codependency is difficult to describe because it is often about what a person does *not* do, which is basically to live her life. She doesn't follow the path of her own interests or let her passions flow through her. She is afraid of strong feelings and power. If the addict overindulges in sensory pleasures, the codependent starves herself of them. Or if she does indulge, she immediately feels guilty and can't enjoy them because at her core she feels undeserving.[122]

Codependency is a contested term because many people see it as pathologising or victim blaming, but the point is not to blame

---

121 Heldman, 2013.
122 Kasl, 1987, p. 34.

Chapter Two: Desire and Distortion

women for our conditioning – it is to identify and recognise the effects of that conditioning. Brenda Cheyne puts it this way:

> Caring for others is a basic human activity. However, when it extends to rescue, control and not dealing with your own pain, it's a survival system.
>
> Until I became aware, I continued to have relationships with males who were extremely needy. But they were always putting me down. Everything was always my fault. Looking back, I was safe because few of my needs were met. My work was caring for others and my private life was trying to make him feel better. That never worked because no matter how I cared for him, he'd always become abusive. I couldn't make it better. I eventually learned after much heartache to care for myself and saw the trap. His abusive behaviour was the problem. I now understand that healing and valuing myself go together.[123]

Dale Spender discusses the work that women do to "protect men's egos" and keep men comfortable in *Reflecting Men At Twice Their Natural Size* (1989, written with Sally Cline). Her research involved recording conversations between women and men, and analysing the proportion of time that men occupy in conversations as compared to women; who gets to determine the topics discussed; who interrupts who (men make approximately 99 per cent of interruptions), and what happens if women attempt to talk for an equal share of time. Spender notes the way that women often "smile – rather than scowl – when interrupted by men." Discussing her tapes, Spender says that,

> again and again they have revealed that in conversation with men it is almost unknown for any woman to talk for more than one third of the time. This is in itself quite astonishing; what is more astonishing, however, is that women consistently report that they had a fair share of the conversation, even if their 'share' was less than 20%.

---

123 Cheyne, 2003, p. 82.

> When I first began to amass these findings, they represented something of a challenge to me. I set up conversations with men (which were taped) and I determined to talk for 50% of the time. Even when the disapproval started, I persevered. I have believed myself to be aggressive, rude, inconsiderate, domineering and unpleasant, as I have tried to get an equal share. And before the tapes were analysed I was prepared to claim that it felt as though I had talked for 50% of the time …
>
> Yet never had I talked for more than 42% of the time.[124]

Spender also examined patterns of behaviour in the household, and notes that "it is not uncommon to find men saying that they don't like to see women doing domestic chores. It makes them feel uneasy." In response, "To preserve the peace she may try to get through it all while he is not around."

Discussing heterosexual marriage, Gabor Maté says:

> The less powerful partner in any relationship will absorb a disproportionate amount of the shared anxiety – which is the reason that so many more women than men are treated for, say, anxiety and depression. (The issue here is not *strength* but power. That is, who is serving whose needs?) It is not that these women are more psychologically unbalanced than their husbands, even though the latter may seem to function at higher levels. What is unbalanced is the relationship, so that the women are absorbing the husband's stresses and anxieties while also having to contain their own …
>
> The partner who must suppress more of his or her own needs for the sake of the relationship is more likely to develop physical illness as well – hence the greater incidence, for example, of autoimmune disease and of non-smoking-related cancers among women.[125]

Insofar as women seek acceptance in return for our efforts, we are perpetually disappointed, since the feminine role assigned to women is based on "a double bind: whichever way they turn there

---

124 Cline and Spender, 1989, p. 9.
125 Maté, 2019, pp. 195–6.

Chapter Two: Desire and Distortion

is disapproval."[126] Naomi Wolf examined this double bind in *The Beauty Myth*, by examining sex discrimination and harassment cases in the United States, the outcomes of which undermine one another. She writes that, "United States law developed to protect the interests of the power structure by setting up a legal maze in which the beauty myth blocks each path so that no woman can 'look right' and win."[127] According to her findings, the law will defend a male employer who insists on 'feminine' workplace standards and dress codes, and also defend that employer if he claims that a woman's feminine dress in the workplace provoked him to sexually harrass or assault her. Wolf says that, "With these rulings, a woman's beauty became at once her job and her fault."[128]

Wolf offers ample illustrations to make her point. She describes how in a Hopkins v Price-Waterhouse case, a woman called Hopkins was denied a partnership despite bringing in the most business of any employee. She was told she "needed to learn to 'walk more femininely, talk more femininely, dress more femininely' and 'wear makeup'." In another case, a woman by the name of St Cross lost her job because she was too "old" and too "ugly." Craft lost hers because she was too "old," too "ugly," "unfeminine," and didn't dress right. The case Tamini v Howard Johnson Company, Inc, proved that "you can lose your job if you don't wear make-up."[129]

Do these cases prove that the law will treat a woman fairly in employment disputes if she dresses 'femininely'? On the contrary: policewoman Nancy Fahdl was fired because she looked "'too much like a lady." Michelle Vinson, who took a sex discrimination case against Meritor Savings Bank in 1986,

> was young and 'beautiful' and carefully dressed. The district court ruled that her appearance counted against her ... 'provocative' dress could ... decide whether her harassment was 'welcome' ...

---

126 Hawthorne, 1976/2019, p. 36.
127 Wolf, 1991, p. 38.
128 Wolf, 1991, p. 38.
129 Wolf, 1991, p. 39.

> Her beauty in her clothes was admitted as evidence to prove that she welcomed rape from her employer.[130]

In the ultimate expression of this contradictory standard, the Diaz v Coleman case, "a dress code of short skirts was set by an employer who allegedly sexually harassed his female employees because they complied with it," writes Wolf.[131] What is at stake in each case like this is not only a set of misogynist rules that women alone are expected to comply with – but male power and capacity to dictate and redefine the rules, narratives, and stories we live by at will.

In her essay 'The Sexual Politics of Fear and Courage', Andrea Dworkin explains this in another way. She writes:

> A man can be a hero if he climbs a mountain, or plays football, or pilots an airplane. A man can be a hero if he writes a book, or composes a piece of music, or directs a play. A man can be a hero if he is a scientist, or a soldier, or a drug addict, or a disc jockey, or a crummy mediocre politician. A man can be a hero because he suffers and despairs; or because he thinks logically and analytically; or because he is 'sensitive'; or because he is cruel. Wealth establishes a man as a hero, and so does poverty. Virtually any circumstance in a man's life will make him a hero to some group of people and has a mythic rendering in the culture – in literature, art, theatre, or the daily newspapers.
>
> It is precisely this mythic dimension of all male activity which reifies the gender class system so that male supremacy is unchallengeable and unchangeable …
>
> This goes right to the core of female invisibility in this culture. No matter what we do, we are not seen. Our acts are not witnessed, not observed, not experienced, not recorded, not affirmed.[132]

Our gendered conditioning installs an identification with masculinity within men, and an identification with men inside of women. For girls, this means receiving mixed messages, as Egyptian feminist Nawal El Saadawi recalls:

---

130 Wolf, 1991, pp. 21–57.
131 Wolf, 1991, p. 39.
132 Dworkin, 1976, p .53.

Chapter Two: Desire and Distortion

> Everything my mother said seemed to be contradictory. How come that she should always be warning me about sex and men, and yet always be so careful about my appearance and clothes, with the sole aim of making me more desirable to them?[133]

The invisibilisation of women and repression of sex results not only in this kind of contradiction and "obscurantism",[134] but ideologies as bizarre as transgenderism. Sadhguru explains this according to the yogic philosophy of mind. He says that "the fundamental nature of the intellect is to discriminate," to distinguish *x* from *y* and *a* from *b*. "This discriminatory quality is very important for survival. If you want to break a stone, you have to discriminate between the stone and your finger, otherwise you will break your finger."[135] Our conditioned identifications distort this capacity, because:

> The way you're identified, that is the way your intellect will function. Now, if you say: 'I belong to this nation', your intellect will function just to protect that identity. If you say, 'I belong to this religion', or race, or caste, or creed, or gender, or whatever – accordingly, your intellect functions, because intellect is essentially ... a survival process. If you identify with something, intellect will constantly go around ... trying to protect that identity.
>
> In the yogic system we consider the *ahaṅkāra* [or *ahaṃkāra*], or the identity that you take on, far more important than the nature of the intellect itself, because intellect is a slave of the identity that you have taken. Once you take a certain identity, intellect will function in a specific way, only towards that. And what is right for [according to] you, what is wrong for you, everything is dependent on how you're identified.[136]

In Osho's words, "the mind is ... society's agent within you."[137] The reason why it is so difficult to break out of our conditioned

---

133 El Saadawi, 1980/2015, p. 95.
134 El Saadawi, 1980/2015, p. 90.
135 Sadhguru, 2016b.
136 Sadhguru, 2020. I have read Sadhguru's book *Inner Engineering* and *Karma*, taken his Inner Engineering course and read an entry about yogic philosophy of mind on his website, and still feel this explanation is his clearest.
137 Osho, 2002a, p. 15.

roles – and the reason why people can come to believe and irrationally defend absurdities like 'biological sex does not exist' – is not because it is all so convincing. This system of gender does not operate through persuasive reasoning, but through the power of identification rooted in *pain* – the stones, rocks and boulders thrown into the stream (which in yogic philosophy, create *saṃskāra*). Gender lodges itself into us through a culturally normalised rape epidemic, and through our childhood stress and vulnerability.

In a patriarchal culture, the effect of both epidemic rape and social conditioning is to establish a social pattern of dissociation and repression designed to keep men contented. This orientation toward emotionally appeasing men at any cost is called *male identification* – and since our identifications are established out of fear for our survival, the human intellect follows identification "like an obedient courtier."[138] This is why male identification or bias leads to all sorts of distortions and contradictions in our capacity to observe and discern. Politically, our selective vision and distorted longings express themselves both in sex denialism *and* compensatory sexual fixation; in resentment toward feminists as moral 'prudes', and in wilful ignorance of the form of epidemic violence most deeply embedded in society and socialisation and most essential to sustaining our collective, destructive behaviour: rape. The conversations we are prevented from having as a result are personal, political, spiritual, and emotional all at once. As Osho wrote, "Unless sex gains a spiritual dimension, a spiritual status, a new humanity can never be born."[139]

---

138 The similie "like an obedient courtier" comes from my friend Sunil Williams.
139 Osho, 2002a, p. 89.

CHAPTER THREE

Rebellion and Backlash

If you really love a man you will be considerate of his true need but you will not show unnecessary concern for his foolish, stupid fantasies.
—Osho, Love, Freedom, Aloneness [140]

I mean that there is a relationship between the way that women are raped and your socialization to rape and the war machine that grinds you up and spits you out ... Because you're turned into little soldier boys from the day you are born and everything that you learn about how to avoid the humanity of women becomes part of the militarism of the country in which you live and the world in which you live. It is also part of the economy that you frequently claim to protest.
—Andrea Dworkin, I Want a Twenty-Four-Hour Truce During Which There Is No Rape [141]

Feminism collapses the dualistic morality of patriarchy. It does this by prioritising women's experiences and longings, and encouraging women to face the fears associated with breaking the rule of male identification, courageously reclaim authentic power, and act in our own interests. As Freire's work shows, loyalty to the oppressed is not a form of artificial bias or *identification* in the same way that investment in external power is; rather, rejecting the stigmatisation of oppressed voices is necessary to *correct* the distortions of the mind created by oppression, and a prerequisite to achieving humanisation and liberation for all. "This, then," Freire wrote,

---

140 Osho, 2001, p. 4.
141 Dworkin, 1988, p. 165.

"is the great humanistic and historical task of the oppressed: to liberate themselves and their oppressors as well."[142]

For both Maté and Freire, the work of healing, and liberation, is the process of 'ejecting' the internalised oppressor from the mind. 'Consciousness raising' is the feminist term for this process as it applies to the internalised 'male gaze'. It involves gaining awareness of patriarchy as a system, set of norms, and pattern of social conditioning. As we come to clearly perceive the cultural patterns that once affected us subliminally, we see that we are *not* alone or defective, but that these are conditioned beliefs we share with others. We see that 'The Man' doesn't deserve our unwavering allegiance, and other women could use our support. The process unravels the distortions of patriarchy within our own being, allowing for a new lease of energy.

Countermoves

Consciousness raising is not easy, because acting from authentic power to break culturally prescribed identifications involves meeting fear within ourselves, and resistance in our relationships and the wider culture. Indeed, we can learn a lot about the current political and cultural climate by understanding that the resistance women meet as we learn to shed conditioned behaviour works much the same whether it arises in the nervous system, the domestic sphere, the courtroom, or in politics.

Nicole LePera defines 'mental resistance' as "the internal thoughts or chatter that we all experience that prevent us from … doing something we set an intention to do, we mean to do, we want to do" and explains that this internal chatter is not simply a psychological, but physiological, phenomenon. Our nervous systems attempt to keep us within a safe, familiar and predictable range of thinking, feeling, and behaving in the interests of

---

142 Freire, 1970, p. 26.

'homeostasis'.[143] As Audre Lorde writes, "[t]he fear that we cannot grow beyond whatever distortions we may find within ourselves keeps us docile and loyal and obedient, externally defined, and leads us to accept many facets of our oppression as women."[144]

If we persist with the effort to break old patterns, then on top of our own fear and 'mental resistance', we meet resistance from others. Harriet Lerner's *The Dance of Anger* (1989, a book that changed my life) refers to this interpersonal form of resistance in the language of "countermoves" or "Change back!" reactions. She explains why those closest to us can often be the most resistant to the changes we make in our own interest, and says countermoves often involve the attempt to evoke guilt: "[w]e may be accused of coldness, disloyalty, selfishness, or disregard for others." These reactions can extend to demands reaching "almost absurd proportions, in a powerful effort to protect … from the strong anxiety that standing on one's own can provoke in parties who are close to each other."[145]

In the political sphere, Paulo Freire describes how countermoves can come from ourselves, our opponents and comrades alike. As he writes,

> the oppressed, who have adapted to the structure of domination in which they are immersed, and have become resigned to it, are inhibited from waging the struggle for freedom so long as they feel incapable of running the risks it requires. Moreover, their struggle for freedom threatens not only the oppressor, but also their own oppressed comrades who are fearful of still greater repression.[146]

The process of learning about "countermoves" and backlash was central to my own politicisation. When I began to write a feminist blog, I had to develop strategies to deal with the reactions I received, which included harassment, organised bullying, doxxing,

---

143 LePera, 2019.
144 Lorde, 1984, p. 58.
145 Lerner, 1989, p. 79.
146 Freire, 1970, p. 29.

and accusations of hate, white supremacy, and responsibility for murder and suicide. I needed to learn not to default to a conditioned response of shame and self-doubt, without discounting any valid criticism that might enter the mix. I did this by asking myself the question, "Is this an okay way to treat a woman?" when people reacted to my work. When I felt the answer was no, I would follow it up with another – how do I want women to change their responses to this sort of thing, so that the culture changes? I thought about what sort of responses to misogyny I wanted there to be in order to make more space for women.

I wanted women to stop letting anger eat us up from inside while we ask what's 'wrong' with us, and why we feel bad, and how we can fix ourselves, and be nicer. I wanted to see us name abuse for what it is, rather than excusing it. I wanted us to seek accountability so that it's not so easy for men to harass us. So, I made it my aim to name sexist behaviour for what it was, set boundaries around it and seek accountability. I came to see anger as my body's way of alerting me to my boundaries, inviting me to restore them. I saw its clear expression as being part of what it means to stand up for women's humanity. I was interested in *humanisation*, not representing a feminist 'cause' in a way that others might consider appealing.

During the Women's Liberation Movement of the 1970s and 80s, countless women walked a similar path. They came together in consciousness-raising groups to break the rule of silence, repression and 'coping', and speak about their heartbreaks. This practice gave women not only the relief of understanding, but the opportunity to transmute pain into power as they supported one another to break out of the socially imposed roles they were identifying as oppressive. Women gave up feminine grooming rituals and the 'corset', left abusive husbands and boyfriends, promoted lesbian visibility, and some went separatist to dedicate their lives to women.[147] They made art, music, theatre, and political action invigorated with a newfound preparedness to confront the reality of women's lives and expand

---

147 See Hawthorne, 1976/2019.

the possibilities. They started rape crisis shelters, feminist presses and periodicals, theatre groups, bands, women's lands, and Reclaim the Night marches.

'The personal is political' was a catch-cry of feminist consciousness raising. Through it, women learned to name social patterns: of feminine conditioning, male violence and patriarchal power and control tactics in private and public. In the 1980s, while setting up safehouses and rape crisis centres, women developed the 'Power and Control Wheel' mentioned in Chapter One. They saw that tactics like gaslighting did not only happen in private but also in public, where the law, institutional policy, and every major religion and tradition told some version of the story of 'feminine evil'. They rewrote history to tell the story of how this happened and what came before. And then the backlash came.

Hijacking

The term *gaslighting* comes from a 1938 play and 1944 film by Patrick Hamilton, *Gas Light*, about a newly married couple. Gregory and Paula meet in Italy and fall so madly in love that they decide to marry after only a fortnight – at least, that is the story Paula believes. In truth, Gregory knows more about Paula's past than she realises, and wants access to her inheritance. To prevent her from finding out, Gregory starts to comment on Paula's poor memory and tendency to lose things (that he has in fact hidden). After they move in together, Gregory dims the gaslights in their house at night while making noise in the attic, then convinces Paula that she imagines the sounds and the lights dimming. He causes Paula to question her own sanity, and stops her from leaving the house since she is 'ill'. *Gaslighting* refers to the tactic of 'hijacking' someone's reality, to use Rose McGowan's phrase.

Gaslighting is a perpetrator's attempt to secure external power by controlling the story of what is happening – particularly after an act of abuse – without having to provide any evidence, logic, or moral justification for why their version of events should prevail. On the contrary, an abuser's defensiveness generally involves lies, contradictions, aggression, and cruelty. Its purpose is to cultivate a perception of his own behaviour as 'normal', and therefore 'reasonable', while rendering his victim contemptible and beneath and beyond the reach of reason, justice, or support. As his actions are normalised, he is humanised. Meanwhile, the victim is symbolically *de*humanised in ways that cause and exacerbate real suffering and isolation. It helps if the original abuse has left her disoriented and in shock.

In *Know My Name* (2019), Chanel Miller observed the difference in how the defence attorney at Brock Turner's rape trial questioned Turner versus how he interrogated her. Turner was asked questions about things like whether 'grinding' and drinking at parties was common and whether everybody did it. Considering these lines of questioning, Miller wrote:

> In each line, I found *common, common, a part of, everybody, everybody*. This pattern was not an accident. He was leading Brock back into the herd, where he could blend into the comfort of community. Compare this to when he had questioned me: *You did a lot of partying. You've had blackouts before*. It was *you* and *you*, the lens fixed so close I was stripped of surrounding. For Brock, his goal was to integrate, for me it was to isolate.[148]

The acronym DARVO – deny, attack, reverse victim and offender – specifies some gaslighting tactics. The first thing women normally face when we break silence about abuse is denial in its barefaced form: 'Gregory didn't dim the gaslights.' 'The abuse didn't happen.' When there is too much evidence, a new tactic is required: the victim's story needs to be minimised, rather than denied. (In *Gas Light*, Gregory tells Paula, "I was only trifling.") The victim should also be aggressively discouraged from speaking. The last aspect of DARVO is to reverse the positions of victim and offender, and this reversal tends to focus on how the perpetrator's reputation is affected by the accusations being levelled against him: "I'm very

---

148 Miller, 2019, p. 271.

sorry, but I'm afraid my wife's illness has returned." As Freire writes, "For the oppressors ... it is always the oppressed ... who are disaffected, who are 'violent', 'barbaric', 'wicked', or 'ferocious' when they react to the violence of the oppressors."[149]

As part of this reversal, a perpetrator of rape has to paint a convincing picture of a woman who 'wanted it' – the assault – in the first place.[150] One common strategy for achieving this in rape trials is the 'rough sex defence'. In December 2018, British backpacker Grace Millane was murdered in New Zealand by a man who strangled her following a Tinder date. He then searched online for information about disposing of bodies and watched pornography. He disposed of Millane's body and other evidence and created a "labyrinth of storytelling and lies," in the words of crown solicitor Brian Dickey, to cover his tracks.

In November 2019, the murderer, Jesse Kempson, was convicted after a three-week trial at the Auckland High Court, and sentenced to life imprisonment with a minimum non-parole period of 17 years. Defence lawyer Ian Brookie argued that Millane died because of a sexual "misadventure." He alleged that Millane had an interest in bondage and sado-masochism, and she had asked the man to choke her.

The UK-based campaign We Can't Consent To This keeps a tally of cases where British women are killed by men who claim it happened during violent, yet consensual sex. Campaign founder Fiona Mackenzie responded to the trial of Millane's murderer, saying this "rough sex defence" is the "ultimate victim blaming." Mackenzie explained that:

> [H]e gets to tell her story, he gets to tell the story of what she was like and how she asked for it.
>
> Families not only lose their loved one but these men [those who use such a defence] steal the public perception of them and destroy their reputation. It's appalling.[151]

---

149 Freire, 1970, p. 38.
150 I have explored these dynamics in more detail in Gerlich, 2020.
151 Radio New Zealand, 2019.

Liberals

Events that take place in the public sphere can often follow the same patterns we see in our private lives. Many people are mystified by the big questions of politics, economics, and concepts such as neoliberalism, postmodernism, or structural adjustment. But when we understand that securing external power involves the same DARVO tactics whether in the public or private sphere, we can start to demystify complex political trends.

The witch hunts of the fifteenth and sixteenth centuries are an obvious example of how misogynist gaslighting and abuse tactics take place on a collective, public scale. They were premised on the myth of feminine evil central to dualistic philosophy, which is, after all, the ultimate gaslight – the way that 'he gets to tell the story'. 'His' story has been circulating for five thousand years, shaping our external power systems, cultural myths, norms, and the gender roles we – and the media, entertainment and porn industries, schools, and history books – teach children to accept.

The classic dualistic model is associated with patriarchal religions, political conservativism, and the idea of a punitive 'sky god' patriarch with the divine right to exercise absolute power, a right that can be transferred to popes and kings. Men have resisted this form of absolute rule throughout the centuries, but they have tended to do so without objecting to the rape and sexual oppression fundamental to it. The history of liberalism is the history of men attempting to resist the tyranny of undiluted patriarchy without relinquishing the male privilege it offers them, and it is men's reluctance to openly reject sexual violation and exploitation that has led to many of the absurd ideologies and contradictions that dominate politics today.

As Lierre Keith writes in her brilliant essay 'Liberals and Radicals', "[w]e need to understand the contradictory legacy of liberalism to understand the left today."[152] A good starting point

---

152 Keith, 2011, p. 65.

for this is the Protestant Reformation, started when Martin Luther famously nailed his *Ninety-five Theses* to the door of the Wittenberg Castle church in Germany, 1517. Luther was a monk, priest and professor of theology who rejected the practice of indulgences and the absolute rule of the pope – but he was not against all forms of authority and domination. During the Peasant Revolt of 1500, he called for the punishment of "thieving, murderous gangs of peasants."[153] Luther supported the witchcraze, declaring, "I would have no compassion on the witches! I would burn them all."[154] He glorified women's pain, reasoning that the more pain a woman suffered in childbirth, the more she would love her child – and yet neither the acknowledgement of women's pain nor children's need for love inspired him to soften the statement about women, "Let them bear children to death. They are created for that."[155]

The Reformation did not aim to dismantle the hierarchies of oppression that patriarchal religions exist to justify – rather, Protestantism helped create the philosophical basis for capitalism by freeing male merchant capitalists from the absolute rule of the church. As Keith writes, "God was still operable, he'd just switched allegiance from the old inherited powers to the rising mercantile class."[156]

In England, the Reformation allowed the Tudors to split from Rome, seize church property, privatise common lands (also known as the 'enclosure movement'), and drive Indigenous Irish farmers off the northern province of Ulster in Ireland in order to open the area for Protestant settlers under English protection.[157] The common lands had been used by peasants for centuries to graze milch cows, collect water, forage edible and medicinal plants, and gather wood for construction and making fires for cooking and heating. When the Tudors enclosed these lands, peasants were evicted, and much

---

153 Sjöö and Mor, 1987, p. 319.
154 Sjöö and Mor, 1987.
155 Raymond, 1993, p. xix ; Federici, 2018, p. 30.
156 Keith, 2011, p. 63.
157 Pankhurst, 2015, p. 22.

of the land was used to graze sheep for wool production in the growing textile industry.

Having no access to land for subsistence or the church for assistance, people were desperate. The double assault hit women, particularly older women, hardest, and left them dependent "on the charity of the better-off at a time when communal bonds were disintegrating and a new morality was taking hold that criminalised begging and looked down upon charity, the reputed path to eternal salvation in the medieval world."[158]

In her book *Witches, Witch-Hunting and Women* (2018), Silvia Federici shows how the enclosure of the commons was linked with the witch hunts in England. Between the fifteenth and eighteenth centuries, thousands of women throughout Europe were arrested, interrogated, tortured, and/or burned alive as 'witches'. In England, the witch trials began in the sixteenth century and peaked in the seventeenth, in tandem with the enclosure of the commons.[159] Federici argues that "[t]he 'rationalisation' of the natural world – the precondition for a more regimented work discipline and for the scientific revolution – passed through the destruction of the 'witch'."

Women could be branded 'witches' for resisting their impoverishment, and participating in protests by pulling up fences surrounding the commons.[160] Yet Federici stresses that women were not only punished for their desperation, or their resistance, but their mere existence, since the threat women pose to capitalism is implicit as well as explicit. Therefore, women could be labelled 'witches' for any reason: because they were 'difficult' wives, or unmarried, widowed, or lesbian; because they were poor and begging, or wealthy and propertied (in which case the church confiscated their property); because they were dangerously attractive; because they took care of other women as healers or midwives.[161] According

---

158 Federici, 2018, p. 25.
159 Federici, 2018, p. 17.
160 Federici, 2018, pp. 19–20, p. 28, p. 31.
161 Gage, 1893/1980; Dworkin, 1974, 1976; Daly, 1978; Achterberg, 1990; Dashu, 1998; Federici, 2018.

to Andrea Dworkin, it was as midwives, especially, that learned women really offended the church. She writes:

> The witches used drugs like belladonna and aconite, organic amphetamines, and hallucinogenics. They also pioneered the development of analgesics. They performed abortions, provided all medical help for births, were consulted in cases of impotence which they treated with herbs and hypnotism, and were the first practitioners of euthanasia.[162]

Capitalism simply cannot contend with either women or sex: both defy the imperative of rationalisation and commodification, and both challenge the very notion of individual self-interest. Capitalism cannot account for "[e]ros, sexual attraction, which has always been suspect in the eyes of political elites, as an uncontrollable force."[163] It cannot account for bodies that bleed in rhythm with the cycles of the moon; for voluntary intimacy that does not involve any transaction; for the creative act of intercourse in which two people come together and make three, the equation from which a whole world of human life is born; for the way that a human being grows in a woman's womb; for how a mother's body naturally prepares to nourish and feed her child, with no invoice to follow; for *belonging* free of possessive *ownership*. Through a capitalist lens, this *is* all inexplicable witchcraft, and though women constitute half the world's population, we are still an inconceivable anomaly, our contribution indeed impossible to account for on any balance sheet. Federici writes:

> As a mode of production positing 'industry' as the main source of ... accumulation, capitalism could not take hold without forging a new type of individual and a new social discipline boosting the productive capacity of labor. This involved a historic battle against anything posing a limit to the full exploitation of the laborer,

---

162 Dworkin, 1974, p. 139.
163 Federici, 2018, p. 29.

starting with the web of relations that tied the individuals to the natural world, to other people, and to their own bodies.[164]

Women were stripped, completely shaved and pricked with long needles all over their bodies by men searching for the 'Devil's mark', during sexualised and fetishised routines that form an important part of the history of pornography, and in which women were forced to confess to grotesque sex with devils.[165] "The most sadistic tortures ever invented were inflicted on the body of the woman accused, which provided an ideal laboratory for the development of the science of pain and torture."[166]

After the witch hunts ended, men had succeeded in taking over the practice of controlling women's health, and gynaecology was established as a technological, mechanised field in which men appointed themselves experts and authorities on women's anatomy, sexual health and reproductive decision making.[167] The witchcraze also forced women to "submit to the patriarchal control of the nuclear family," and provided the 'shock',

> from which emerged the new model of femininity to which women had to conform to be socially accepted in the developing capitalist society: sexless, obedient, submissive, resigned to subordination to the male world, accepting as natural the confinement to a sphere of activities that in capitalism has been completely devalued.[168]

According to those who carried out this abuse, they were doing 'God's work'. After the Tudor period, under the same pretence,

> the African slaves, the expropriated peasants of Africa and Latin America, and the massacred populations of North America became the kin of the sixteenth- and seventeenth-century European witches, who, like them, saw their common lands taken

---

164 Federici, 2018, p. 27.
165 Federici, 2018, p. 32; Dashu, 1998.
166 Federici, 2018, p. 32.
167 Daly, 1978.
168 Federici, 2018, p. 11, p. 32.

away, experienced hunger by the move to cash crops, and saw their resistance persecuted as a sign of a diabolical pact.[169]

Britain established its first North American colony in Virginia in 1607, and the core group of frontier settlers in North America were the Ulster-Scots, or Scots-Irish. These were Protestants from Scotland who had been recruited by the British as settlers in the aforementioned Irish province of Ulster. The Ulster-Scots took a form of Protestantism called Calvinism (named after John Calvin from Geneva), with them to North America. Later, a Scotsman named John Locke, the 'grandfather of liberalism', secularised this ideology into classical liberalism.[170]

Locke wrote his *Second Treatise on Government* in 1689, while the American settlers were rebelling against the British monarchy and setting up a parliamentary government. Locke employed the language of equality, autonomy, and rights to challenge church rule and the 'divine right' of kings. He stated that since "all mankind" is "equal and independent, no one ought to harm another in his life, health, liberty or possessions," while he himself maintained investments in the slave trade.[171] As Lierre Keith writes:

> Classical liberalism from Locke forward has a contradiction at its centre. It believes in human sovereignty as a natural or inalienable right, but only against the power of a monarchy or other civic tyranny. By loosening the ethical constraints that had existed on the wealthy, classical liberalism turned the powerless over to the economically powerful, simply swapping the monarchs for the merchant-barons.[172]

By 1776, the same year *The Wealth of Nations* was published, a committee of five 'founding fathers', including the first two US presidents Thomas Jefferson and John Adams, drew on Locke's ideas to draft the *Declaration of Independence*. Critical historian

---

169 Federici, 2018, p. 12.
170 Dunbar-Ortiz, 2014, pp. 51–4.
171 Zinn, 1999, p. 73.
172 Keith, 2011, p. 67.

Howard Zinn explains that the *Declaration* was never intended to be universally applicable. By 1760, there had been 18 uprisings aimed at overthrowing colonial governments in the United States. There had also been 40 riots, and six black rebellions from South Carolina to New York. Zinn writes that "[e]specially in Philadelphia … the consciousness of the lower middle classes grew to the point where it must have caused some hard thinking, even among leaders of the Revolution."[173]

The wealthy elite feared that different despised groups – the Indians, the slaves, the poor whites – might join forces. So, laws were passed that prohibited free blacks from travelling in Indian country, criminalised interracial marriage, and declared such children illegitimate. Blacks were forbidden to carry arms. Zinn writes:

> There was still another control which became handy as the colonies grew, and which had crucial consequences for the continued rule of the elite throughout American history. Along with the very rich and the very poor, there developed a white middle class of small planters, independent farmers, city artisans, who, given small rewards for joining forces with merchants and planters, would be a solid buffer against black slaves, frontier Indians, and very poor whites.
>
> Those upper classes, to rule, needed to make concessions to the middle class, without damage to their own wealth or power, at the expense of slaves, Indians, and poor whites. This bought loyalty. And to bind that loyalty with something more powerful even than material advantage, the ruling group found, in the 1760s and 1770s, a wonderful useful device. That device was the language of liberty and equality, which could unite just enough whites to fight a Revolution against England, without ending either slavery or inequality.[174]

To gain independence from the British crown, and take on its army and mercenary soldiers, American nationalists needed support, but

---

173 Zinn, 1999, p. 62.
174 Zinn, 1999, p. 57–8.

Chapter Three: Rebellion and Backlash

they lacked trained men, money, and weaponry. Zinn writes that "the reality behind the words of the *Declaration of Independence* was that a rising class of important people needed to enlist on their side enough Americans to defeat England, without disturbing too much the relations of wealth and power that had developed over 150 years of colonial history."[175] The liberal "language of liberty and equality" – taken not only from Locke, but also the Haudenosaunee Great Law of Peace – was "inspiring to all classes, specific enough in its listing of grievances to charge people with anger against the British, vague enough to avoid class conflict among the rebels, and stirring enough to build patriotic feeling for the resistance movement."[176]

While the 'committee of five' were drafting the *Declaration of Independence*, Abigail Adams (married to John) worried that English common law would remain the basis for family law following the revolution. As mentioned in Chapter Two, common law was derived from church law and codified by the English judge William Blackstone in 1770, in his four-volume *Commentaries*. It rendered women men's property, legalised wife beating, and criminalised divorce. Abigail wrote to her husband, saying:

> I long to hear you have declared an independency, and, by the way, in the new code of laws which I suppose it will be necessary for you to make, I desire you would remember the ladies, and be more generous and favourable to them than your ancestors. Do not put such unlimited power into the hands of husbands. Remember, all men would be tyrants if they could. If particular care and attention are not paid to the ladies, we are determined to foment a rebellion, and will not held ourselves bound to obey any laws in which we have no voice or representation.[177]

John responded: "I cannot but laugh. Depend upon it, we know better than to repeal our Masculine systems."[178]

---

175 Zinn, 1999, p. 74.
176 Dunbar-Ortiz, 2014, p. 26; Zinn, 1999, p. 68.
177 Buhle and Buhle, 1978, pp. 58–9.
178 Lerner, 1993, p. 9.

That liberal capitalism is a 'Masculine system', despite its claims to serve the freedom of individuals, is something feminists like economist Marilyn Waring, Cynthia Enloe and Susan Hawthorne have shown. Their work demonstrates that women's low economic status under capitalism does not derive from the undervaluing of particular forms of work, but the undervaluing, invisibilisation, and commodification of *women*. Waring says, "[t]he international economic system constructs reality in a way that excludes the great bulk of women's work – reproduction (in all its forms), raising children, domestic work, and subsistence production."[179] In Enloe's words, "Twin patriarchal values and beliefs underpin these low wages paid to employees in feminised jobs: anything done chiefly by women is not worth much; and, if it *were* a job worth much, it would be done by men."[180]

By 1776, Scottish economist Adam Smith 'got to tell the story' about why unbridled capitalism is the best possible economic system when he published the definitive text of capitalist theory, *The Wealth of Nations*. The book promotes free enterprise motivated by man's self-interest, and argued that wages should be determined by the 'invisible hand' of market demand, without government interference. Smith argued:

> Man ... has almost constant occasion for the help of his brethren and it is in vain for him to expect it from their benevolence only. He will be more likely to prevail if he can interest their self love in his favour, and show them that it is for their own advantage to do for him what he requires of them ... It is not from the benevolence of the butcher, the brewer, or the baker that we expect our dinner, but for their regard to their own interest.[181]

Marilyn Waring quips: "If Adam Smith was fed daily by Mrs Smith, he omitted to notice or to mention it."[182] Feminist analysis suggests

---

179 Waring, 1988, p. 25.
180 Enloe, 2017, pp. 138–9.
181 Smith in Waring, 1988, p. 23.
182 Waring, 1988, p. 23.

that the real 'invisible hands' of free market capitalism are those of the women who feed and clothe the world without any economic or political recognition. Susan Hawthorne puts her critique this way:

> Disconnection is structured into the system of neoclassical economics. Not only is it disconnected from the real biophysical world, it also pays little attention to the relationships between economic players, most of whom do not follow the model of 'rational economic man' pursuing 'his' own selfish interests. Many unacknowledged players are women, trying to maintain the lives of the people around them, including children and dependent men.[183]

Capitalism relies on a great deal of free labour that it needs to argue is *given*, and not *stolen*, without allowing an argument about human generosity to undermine the whole premise of economic rationality and human self-interest. Roxanne Dunbar-Ortiz, author of the *Indigenous People's History of the United States* (2014), argues that within a 'multicultural' framework that emphasises "the 'contributions' of individuals from oppressed groups to the country's assumed greatness," the idea of the "gift-giving Indian helping to establish and enrich the development of the United States is an insidious smoke screen meant to obscure the fact that the very existence of the country is a result of the looting of an entire continent and its resources."[184]

'Femininity' functions in exactly that way: as a 'smoke screen' meant to obscure the looting of an entire sex. When altruism is selectively affirmed within a capitalist economy explicitly premised on profit, accumulation, rationalism and the self-interest of man – and when it is conveniently associated both with the particular tasks required for free, and the particular people expected to do them – this indicates exploitation, not gift-giving.

As Silvia Federici argues, the witchcraze "paved the way to the confinement of women in Europe to unpaid domestic labour"

---

183 Hawthorne, 2002, p. 365.
184 Dunbar-Ortiz, 2014, p. 5.

after the simultaneous enclosure of the commons and claiming of church property by the Tudors.[185] It is not so much that the work is underpaid or marginalised, but that capitalism categorises women as commodities rather than contributors. The perception of women as wives and babymakers means that today, around the world, ten million girls are sold into marriage each year, and in 2006, according to Kajsa Ekis Ekman (2013) was the surrogacy industry in India was estimated to be worth $449 million USD.

Mass pauperisation of women also led to the rise, and industrialisation, of prostitution – a highly profitable industry. As human trafficking expert Siddharth Kara writes, "Drug trafficking generates greater dollar revenues, but trafficked women are more profitable. Unlike a drug, a human female can be used by the customer again and again."[186] By 1864, a law was passed in Britain called the Contagious Diseases Act (CDA), which dictated that women in or near military towns or navy ports where prostitution was rife could be examined for venereal disease, arrested, and imprisoned in 'lock' hospitals if they had syphilis. The CDA allowed soldiers to rape women, while ensuring that women took the blame and responsibility for the resulting spread of disease. This so-called 'harm reduction' approach to prostitution legislation – in which sexually transmitted diseases are considered 'harm', but rape is not – made women responsible for the sexual health of men who raped them. First implemented in Victorian England, it spread like a virus with European colonisation from the late nineteenth century and is still the legal model promoted by the international sex trade lobby today.[187]

The rise of capitalism also saw the industrialisation of subsistence tasks that women once did in the home, like housekeeping and

---

185 Federici, 2018, p. 48.
186 Kara, 2009, p. x.
187 The Act was opposed by Josephine Butler, a feminist who recognised that it gave men the right to violate women and then punish them for the harm done. Butler won her fight to repeal the CDA in 1886, and then took her fight to India, where the British army was selling women into prostitution in military towns using the same legal methods.

clothing production. Today, 80 per cent of domestic workers are women, as are the overwhelming majority of sweatshop workers, many of whom "earn so little that an entire month's wages would not buy a single item they produce."[188] At the beginning of the industrial revolution, when the textile industry was the largest and the commons were used to graze sheep for wool, "women comprised the undisputed majority of workers."[189] Some of the earliest strikes were carried out by women in the textile industry.

Just as women's poverty helps to secure a product supply for some of the world's major industries – like marriage, domestic work, surrogacy, and prostitution – employers benefit from the idea of femininity, the notion that domesticity and motherhood are women's true and 'natural' vocation. It helps them keep wages low, because it implies that women are ultimately supported by fathers and husbands and not 'serious' members of the labourforce, so they do not need to be paid as such. The low wages women are paid mean that many envisage marriage as "a way out of patriarchal factory toil" while low-paid jobs are an escape from "dependence on fathers and husbands."[190] This is the double bind discussed in Chapter Two, in economic action. Women's sexual subordination and 'femininity' makes for cheap labour, while poverty keeps us dependent, and sexually available.

Cynthia Enloe explains how industries and sectors that are not feminised are gendered from within (as we saw Naomi Wolf explain in Chapter Two, with examples from finance and the police). In tourism, for instance, we find that,

> the international business travellers are men, the service workers are women. Flight attendants in the United States began organising in the 1970s and won the right not to dress in uniforms that they believed turned them into airborne Playboy bunnies.[191]

---

188 Chamberlain, 2012.
189 Davis, 1983, p. 54.
190 Enloe, 1989, p. 165, p. 139.
191 Enloe, 1989, p. 33.

Agriculture provides another interesting example. While 'the farmer' generally conjures an image of a man, women produce over half of the world's food – in Africa, 60 to 80 per cent. Enloe explains that male agricultural workers are generally more visible because of the pride associated with men's work:

> Generally, crops that call for the use of machetes – tools that can also be used as weapons – are produced with large inputs of male labour: bananas, sugar, palm oil. Producers of crops that require a lot of weeding, tapping and picking hire large numbers of women, sometimes comprising a majority of workers: tea, coffee, rubber.[192]

On banana plantations, men could feel pride "for they were unquestionably performing men's work ... Whether a smallholder or a plantation employee, a banana man was a *man*."[193] By contrast, women hired by banana companies do low paid, often seasonal jobs that offer little chance at training or promotion and often include harmful chemical exposure, and "[s]exual harassment helps to control women working in the plantation factories."[194] The system of sexual oppression has never been consistently opposed either by liberals or by the Left.

The Left

Just as *ahamkāra* trumps intellect in the yogic philosophy of mind (as explained in Chapter Two), *identification* trumps values and rhetoric in politics and economics. This means that to understand any political tradition, you need to understand who it *serves*, not just what its proponents argue and *espouse*. The concept of 'liberty' can have a different meaning depending on who is asking for it, and where their bread is buttered. This is why principles like critical thinking and 'following the money' have always been cornerstones of leftist activism.

---

192 Enloe, 1989, p. 134.
193 Enloe, 1989, p. 135.
194 Enloe, 1989, p. 140.

As it turns out, women butter the bread, and most men do not want to draw attention to this fact – including those on the political left. Like liberals, the left have been reluctant to "repeal ... [their] Masculine systems" and have struggled to comprehend women's relationship to the power systems they despise.[195] After all, women are not by definition an economic class, but one of two sexes. Women's oppression is not based in economic relations, but sexual relations. We are not alienated primarily through wage slavery, but rape and relegation to the private sphere. Our relationship to the workforce involves the industrialisation of rape in prostitution, workplace sexual harassment, and the invisibilisation of life-sustaining work that does not lend itself to economic bargaining, like childcare, housekeeping, and food preparation. This work is invisibilised as "[w]omen's household and childcare work are seen as an extension of their physiology."[196]

Because the complex relationship women have with work, and the privilege men gain from ignoring it, the left prefers to endlessly delay dealing with 'the woman question'. Whether in unions or independence movements, women are told that our concerns will be heard 'Not now, later', after men's objectives are achieved. Countless books have been written by women critiquing this attitude within workers' struggles and independence movements all over the world. From Africa to Asia, the Pacific to Latin America, women who have participated in independence movements have echoed the words of Fawzia Fawzia, author of *Palestinian Women and the Revolution* (1984), who challenged male bias in the Palestine Liberation Organisation and wrote that:

> The main ideology which most Palestinians – including the so-called radicals – adopt with regard to 'the question of women' sets the priority as follows: 'to liberate the land, then the women'. The belief is that there is not enough time right now to develop ... the solution of the Palestinian 'women's question', although

---

195 Lerner, 1993, p. 9.
196 Waring, 1988, p. 23.

no one has developed any target date for when doing so would be feasible.[197]

In 1987, Grace Molisa (whose legacy aided my own politicisation) wrote these words in her poetry collection, *Colonised People*:

Vanuatu
Supports
Liberation
Movements
For
the Liberation
of Colonised People
Clear
Articulations
of support
For
freedom fighters
West Papua
French Polynesia
and Kanaky
Vanuatu
Womenfolk
Half
the population
Remain
Colonised
By
the Free Men
of Vanuatu[198]

In 1984, Ghanian novelist Ama Ata Aidoo wrote:

> If, as a woman, you try to flex your muscles as a revolutionary cadre where your comrades are predominantly male, you can hit the concrete wall with such force you might never recover your original self ... And don't be shocked if – when victory is won –

---

197 Fawzia in Morgan, 1984, p. 543.
198 Molisa, 1987.

they return you to the veil as part of the process of consolidating the revolution.[199]

In her essay 'Woman Worker', Valentina Dobrokhotova testifies to what the promises of socialism really meant for women in the Soviet Union. She writes that women's entry into the workforce effectively meant a promotion for men:

> It is becoming increasingly clear that the current equality means only giving women the right to perform heavy labor … On collective and state farms, women do the hardest and most exhausting work while men are employed as administrators, agronomists, accountants, warehouse managers, or high-paid tractor and combine drivers. In other words, men do the work that is more interesting and more profitable, and does not damage their health.[200]

Echoing the work of Enloe, Dobrokhotova writes:

> In the Soviet Union it is taken for granted that women will work on railroad beds, on road crews, on construction sites, and as janitors and cleaning ladies. Certainly men do not relish the prospect of sweeping out passenger cars, cleaning up after drunks, endlessly wiping tables, making up berths, and cleaning out toilets; as a result, conductors more often than not are women who have been instilled with the idea that this is 'women's work'. It should not be surprising that some women leave this 'women's work' for prostitution, which flourishes in our train stations, preferring even that humiliating 'profession' because it gives a woman at least some measure of freedom, some degree of choice.
>
> Of course, prostitution is ruinous for women. I do not want to justify it: I would like to point out the reasons behind it. Prostitution is a form of escape, and yet the woman really goes nowhere. She runs away from domestic exploitation and ends up in industrial exploitation; she runs away from both the first and the second, and ends up being sexually exploited.[201]

---

199 Aidoo in Morgan, 1989, p. 44.
200 Dobrokhotova in Mamonova, 1984, p. 8.
201 Dobrokhotova in Mamonova, 1984, p. 7.

The 'woman question' is not only tough for leftists to confront because it is complex and threatens men's position, but because understanding women's perspective requires a reassessment of how oppression is sustained on the most fundamental level. Is oppression primarily a matter of economic relations, or sexual relations? Does slavery begin in the workforce, or is it as Osho says – that "[s]ex repression, tabooing sex, is the very foundation of human slavery"?[202] If sexual relations *are* central to perpetuating oppression – do we want to know about that from *women's* perspective (aka feminism)? Do we want to hear about how sex repression means the silencing of women, about how rape silences women, about how prostitution industrialises rape and pornography normalises both, and how sexual liberation does not mean sexual licentiousness but *women's* liberation and a reunion of sex and love?

No.

Not now. Later.

As we shall see, the left's insistence on delaying these questions has left it with a fatal blind spot.

Neoliberalism

Spurred by the influence of thinkers like Marx, the nineteenth and twentieth centuries saw the emergence of a well-organised political left, including workers' unions that rebelled against industrial capitalism, Indigenous renaissance movements, successful independence struggles that ousted colonisers, and peace groups and conscientious objectors against military conscription, the Vietnam War, and the nuclear threat. Naomi Klein's book *The Shock Doctrine* explains that by the 1930s, this led to the rise of the welfare state: a compromise between the liberal establishment and leftist demands. Governments around the world started implementing socially progressive welfare and education policies, laws, regulations to protect workers, and free public healthcare.

---

202 Osho, 2002a, p. 110.

Free market capitalists following the tradition of Adam Smith were not happy, and in the 1950s, economist Milton Friedman was working on an economic model that would reverse the progress made by the left: the new liberalism, or neoliberalism. In the words of scientist and environmentalist Vandana Shiva, "neoliberalism is nothing more than the economic paradigm naturalising the violent imposition of corporate rule and the rule of the 1%." [203] By the 1980s, the World Bank and the International Monetary Fund had adopted Friedman's neoliberal policies, and began to hand out financial loans to governments on the condition that they undergo what is euphemistically called 'structural adjustment'.

Structural adjustment has three basic components. To receive loans, governments must 1) make natural resources, lands, and public infrastructure available for purchase by foreign corporations; 2) drastically cut back public spending on health, education, welfare, and social services, and 3) remove regulations and legal protections that restrict corporate profiteering, like minimum wage laws, price controls and/or environmental policies. One example of privatisation comes in the form of Export Processing Zones or EPZs: territories set aside by governments for overseas companies to establish factories on, with the offer of electricity, ports, runways, tax holidays, police protection and cheap labour.[204]

These structural adjustments amount to a contemporary enclosure movement, or privatisation of the commons. Just as the emergence of industrial capitalism was sugarcoated with rhetoric about liberty, the shock of structural adjustment is glossed over with storytelling about how a so-called 'free' market, in which private sector employers face minimal barriers to profiteering, fosters job and opportunity creation, and a 'trickle down' effect, that gradually enables the empowerment of the 'self-made' individual or employee, and 'choice' for consumers.

---

203 Shiva, 2018, p. 40.
204 Enloe, 1989, p. 159.

Naomi Klein points out that neoliberalism does not just induce, but follows, shock. People do not simply swallow the stories; disaster conditions have been crucial for imposing neoliberalism worldwide, which is why Klein calls neoliberalism "disaster capitalism." Before the IMF officially commenced its structural adjustment programs (SAPs) in 1983, neoliberalism was implemented in Chile under the military dictatorship of Augusto Pinochet after a military coup, and was imposed throughout much of South America similarly thereafter. SAPs were then imposed throughout Africa in the 1980s; in China and ex-Soviet countries after the fall of the Berlin Wall in 1989; in South Asia after the 1997-8 financial crisis, and in the Middle East after the United States invasion of Iraq and Afghanistan.

Whether it is a coup d'état, military invasion, financial crisis, natural disaster or epidemic,[205] shock creates the disorientation and debt that enables corporate hijacking, which must happen at a pace. In Chile, Friedman predicted that "the speed, suddenness and scope of the economic shifts would provoke psychological reactions in the public that 'facilitate the adjustment'."[206] In New Zealand, Roger Douglas, who was Minister of Finance in the Labour government that neoliberalised the country, wrote a paper on 'Successful Structural Reform' in 1989. He advised that "speed is essential – it is almost impossible to go too fast," and "once you start the momentum rolling, never let it stop."[207]

Klein explains that shock is used to disorient individual political dissidents as well as entire populations. She writes that "from Chile to China to Iraq, torture has been a silent partner in the global free-market crusade." It has involved,

> techniques designed to put prisoners into a state of deep disorientation and shock in order to force them to make concessions against their will ... The goal of this 'softening up' stage is to provoke a kind of hurricane in the mind: prisoners are

---

205 Klein, 2020.
206 Klein, 2007, p. 7.
207 Douglas, 1990, p. 3, p. 4.

so regressed and afraid that they can no longer think rationally or protect their own interests.[208]

Naomi Klein says one CIA manual that facilitated the adoption of neoliberal reforms was the 1963 *Kubark Counterintelligence Interrogation* manual, used in Chile. Its purpose was to "explain that the way to break 'resistant sources' is to create violent ruptures between prisoners and their ability to make sense of the world around them."[209] The *Kubark* manual drew heavily on experiments in so-called 'psychic driving', carried out by McGill University psychiatrist Ewen Cameron. CIA researchers became interested in Cameron's attempts to teach patients healthy psychological behaviours by creating a 'clean slate'. Cameron used both electroshock and extreme isolation on his subjects – but redefined these methods in his work as 'healing'.[210]

Just as the shock of rape causes a state of dissociation that creates the opportunity for 'hijacking' and courtroom gaslighting, and the 'pain laboratories' of the withcraze saw the emergence of modern femininity, under neoliberalism, shock creates the disorientation needed for structural adjustment to take place. Structural adjustment today is what enclosure was in the Tudor period: land is privatised and degraded, subsistence lifestyles are destroyed, wages drop, welfare and healthcare are harder to access. Under the Tudors, this simultaneous privatisation and pauperisation allowed for the rise of industrial capitalism and factories. Today, it means EPZs and multinational agribusiness and tourism profiteers. As Cynthia Enloe writes:

> These [neoliberal] policies have different implications for women and men in the indebted country, because women and men usually have dissimilar relationships to family maintenance, waged employment, public services and public policy-making. If a government does adopt the IMF package, feeding a family

---

208 Klein, 2007, pp. 15–16.
209 Klein, 2007, p. 16.
210 Klein, 2007, pp. 25–48.

and maintaining its members' health become more taxing. Food will cost more, while income coming into the household is likely to fall …

Thus the politics of international debt is not simply something that has an *impact* on women in indebted countries. The politics of international debt won't work in their current form *unless* mothers and wives are willing to behave in ways that enable nervous regimes to adopt cost-cutting measures without forfeiting their political legitimacy.[211]

Neoliberalism, like capitalism in general, depends on notions of feminine 'selflessness' because its measures require women to cope with anything from reduced quality of life to abject poverty while still keeping children fed and households running. Like ideas about liberty, consumer choice and trickle-down economics, ideas about feminine 'selflessness' sugarcoat the reality that "[j]ust like the environment, women are used up, turned over at a high rate, under conditions which threaten their future well-being."[212]

Environmentalist Wangari Maathai writes about how structural adjustment impacts women and families by forcing populations to export the food they producing as cash crops while importing what they need. After Kenya's neoliberalisation in 1986, Maathai observed:

> Children in the central region of Kenya were suffering from diseases associated with malnutrition. Many farmers had converted practically all of their land into growing coffee and tea to sell in the international market. These 'cash crops' were occupying land previously used for people to eat. Consequently, women were feeding their families processed foods like white bread, maize flour, and white rice, all of which are high in carbohydrates but relatively low in vitamins, proteins and minerals.[213]

---

211 Enloe, 1989, pp. 184–5.
212 Hawthorne, 2002, p. 118.
213 Maathai, 2008, pp. 122–3.

Chapter Three: Rebellion and Backlash

In Thailand, Sanitsudā 'Ēkkachai's *Behind the Smile* contains a collection of stories about the struggles Thai people have faced because of neoliberalism and its destruction of subsistence lifestyles through land privatisation and degradation. One of the stories comes from Moon, whose 15-year-old daughter In Wonglah left home two months before 'Ēkkachai visited. Moon lived on a hilltop in Chiang Rai province in Thailand, and her story is told under the heading, 'I didn't sell my daughter'. 'Ēkkachai writes:

> Moon looks like a frightened deer when asked about her daughter.
> 'No, I didn't sell my child. I didn't.' Her voice trembles. She looks at her mother-in-law sitting nearby, appealing for support
> ...
> 'I didn't sell her. I just borrowed money. She is working to pay off the debt. She'll come home soon,' she says, her voice breaking between sobs.

At the time her story was recorded, Moon was a single mother with four children in desperate poverty. A man came to her village and asked to take her daughter south for domestic work. Moon did not know he was a brothel owner, and wanted her daughter to come back quickly, so she decided to take as little money as possible from the man:

> 'That's why I only asked her boss for 2,000 baht. That's all I need to buy rice and food. They offered 10,000 baht for her. But I didn't want her to have to work long to pay off the debt. I want her to come back home'.[214]

In prostitution, debt is a trap: pimps simply keep adding expenses to the original amount 'owed' so that women can never pay their way out.

Marilyn Waring put it politely when she said that the "international economic system constructs reality in a way that excludes the great bulk of women's work." She could have said that the international economic system is a pimp that employs

---
214 Ēkkachai, 1990, pp. 175–9.

the same tactic of debt bondage that pimps use. As this tactic is passed like a baton from the IMF to governments to families to mothers and daughters, nobody believes that they have sold anyone, but increasing numbers of women are trafficked into the sex trade as the industry continues to grow. Many others are forced to travel overseas to find work and support their families from abroad, typically as nannies and domestic workers. Many national economies rely on the remittances sent home by women working abroad, away from home.[215] We can imagine the leaders of those countries telling us, 'I don't sell the women. I just borrowed money. They are working to pay off the debt. They'll come home soon'.

Cynthia Enloe offers another example of how the pimp analogy applies (as well as how the supposedly 'private' sexist behaviour of elites is politically indicative) in her book *Seriously!: Investigating Crashes and Crises As If Women Mattered* (1989). She discusses the 'DSK affair', named after former IMF managing director Dominique Strauss-Kahn. In 2011, six years before the #MeToo movement commenced, Strauss-Kahn violently raped a hotel maid named Nafissatou Diallo at the Manhattan Sofitel Hotel where she worked. Enloe explains that it is not coincidental that a leader of the IMF would behave this way, or that an organisation with an internal culture that fosters sexist abuse would also leave women carrying "the bulk of the burden for their government's debts."[216]

Siddharth Kara's book *Sex Trafficking* (2009) is crucial reading for those who wish to understand the link between IMF policies and the global expansion of prostitution. Echoing Klein's work on disaster capitalism, Kara writes, "[s]hrewd traffickers preyed on this desperation ... Because gender and minority disenfranchisement meant that women, children, and minorities were the hardest hit during times of socioeconomic crisis, these groups were the most heavily trafficked."[217] Kara also discusses how cultural notions of

---

215 Enloe, 1989, p. 185.
216 Enloe, 2013, p. 51.
217 Kara, 2009, p. 27.

femininity contribute to the problem, for instance in the example of Thailand, where Moon's daughter was taken. Kara writes about women's low status in the major religion of Buddhism, and says:

> Females cannot become monks and transfer religious merit to their parents, so the best they can do is to care for parents through financial contributions. Often uneducated and unable to find wage-paying jobs, poor Thai or hill tribe females turn to the country's prostitution industry as a primary vocation to fulfil parental obligations. 'Good' daughters work as prostitutes for many years and send home money to elevate the status of the family, whereas 'bad' daughters flee prostitution before their debts are repaid, or before they send enough money to provide for parents in old age.[218]

Kara tells the story of trying to help a Thai girl out of prostitution in the US, and how she refused to leave, fearing for her parent's welfare.[219]

The rapid expansion of the sex trade under neoliberalism explains the proliferation of sex industry marketing over the last several decades. The global sex trade lobby (Network of Sex Work Projects or NSWP) has become hugely influential and invested in rebranding the industry. We are now supposed to call prostitution 'sex work' to acknowledge its legitimacy. Women are 'sex workers' and we should think of pimps as job creators. The NSWP promotes a neoliberalised version of the so-called 'harm reduction' model of prostitution legislation first implemented in Victorian England through the Contagious Diseases Act.

In 1998, the International Labour Organisation (ILO), whose stated mission is "to advance social and economic justice," began briefing governments to fully decriminalise prostitution according to this model, which functions to legitimise the pimping and purchase of women for sexual use.[220] In 2003, New Zealand's Labour

---

218 Kara, 2009, pp. 175–6.
219 Kara, 2009, pp. 181–2.
220 Ekman, 2013, p. 3.

government followed the ILO's recommendations by passing the Prostitution Reform Act, and the Council of Trade Unions endorsed the move.

The political left has always been patriarchal, but endorsing prostitution has never been consistent with its ultimate concern for the poor and working class, or the position of its key thinkers, like Marx and Engels. Swallowing the notion that 'sex work is work' is perhaps the biggest compromise the labour movement could make, because it accepts rape not only as an inevitable aspect of human life – which would be bad enough – but as a basic working condition. I'm sorry, but don't unions exist to stop people from being fucked in the workplace? So, once unions *agree* to that, what exactly is there left to object to?

In 2016, Amnesty International followed suit by officially endorsing the legitimisation of prostitution as 'sex work'. Klein's *Shock Doctrine* offers some historic context for how this happened, context that speaks to the overall theme of liberalisation. Klein argues that in the Cold War period, the 1948 Universal Declaration of Human Rights became a "partisan battering ram, used by both sides ... to accuse the other of being the next Hitler."[221] In response to this, Amnesty International developed a doctrine of impartiality, including a decision to be financed exclusively by members, and to remain rigorously "independent of any government, political faction, ideology, economic interest or religious creed," in its own words.

In this spirit of impartiality, Amnesty International decided that "it was not necessary to determine *why* abuses were taking place but to document them as meticulously and credibly as possible." This explains why the organisation's 1976 report on Argentina, which was then undergoing neoliberalisation after a brutal military coup, "sheds no light on why the abuses were occurring." Klein believes that the cost of Amnesty's approach was "the intellectual honesty of the human rights movement." She adds that this 'impartiality'

---

221 Klein, 2007, pp. 118–121.

meant tacit endorsement of neoliberalism on the part of this movement.²²²

Nowadays, with neoliberalism comes prostitution, and vice versa: to endorse one is to accept the other. In fact, the phrase 'sex worker' echoes 'structural adjustment'. It is a euphemism that declares something real and alive – land, nature, values, culture, people, women – as being available for violation. In the market, the term 'sex worker' also has the same function that the term 'whore' does on the street and that the 'rough sex' defence has in the courtroom: it suggests that prostitution does not exist because of rape and men's exploitation of women's imposed economic dependence, but because women want and choose it for themselves as entrepreneurs.

As Kajsa Ekis Ekman explains in *Being and Being Bought: Prostitution, Surrogacy and the Split Self* (2013), this idea of the 'sex worker' requires us to imagine a prostituted woman both as an entrepreneur maximising her welfare by selling a product/service on the market, *and* the product/service being sold. The idea is based on a 'split self' concept that leverages the trauma response of shock and dissociation. In Ekman's book, she explores the way both prostitution and surrogacy are promoted by postmodern writers who buy into this split-self dualism. Many of these postmodernists call themselves feminists, like Kutte Jönsson and Torbjörn Tännsjö. Discussing surrogacy, Ekman comments:

> Jönsson writes that even if surrogacy implies both physical and psychological risks for women, prohibiting it is wrong because 'one restricts their opportunity to use their bodies in exchange for payment' (Jönsson, 2003, p. 220). Tännsjö, who is only in favour of altruistic surrogacy, observes that 'some of the criticism is well-founded' but that 'the risks both for the women and children are worth taking' (1991, p. 143). This is remarkable: by speaking of 'rights' and 'opportunities', these writers arrive at the view of surrogacy as a feminist right ('emancipation!' is [one] ... battle

---

222 Klein, 2007, pp. 118–121.

cry). Yet at the same time, they find it irrelevant whether women come to harm as a result.[223]

Discussing the work of philosopher H. M. Malm (1992, p. 297), Ekman writes:

> He experiments on both a literal level and a deeper, figurative level. On the literal plane, he uses concepts such as freedom, independence, individuals, free will and work. On this level, he claims that surrogacy is not exploitative, that it is not human trafficking, that it does not compromise women's integrity. On the figurative plane, he compares the woman with dead things. When he wants a metaphor, he uses a taxi driver who drives a car, a surgeon who performs an operation ... in other words, he creates a metaphor that *de facto* compares the woman's relationship to her body with a taxi driver's relationship to his car, even as he, on the superficial level, distances himself from these comparisons: 'To illustrate it, suppose you own a lawnmower. (I do not mean to suggest that women's bodies are on par with machines.)'.[224]

The postmodern art world also loves the idea of the 'split self' – the woman as both artist *and* canvas or 'site'. In *The Idea of Prostitution*, under the heading 'Prostitution performance art: public relations for the sex industrialists', Sheila Jeffreys explains how this postmodern tendency strengthened the relationship between the sex industry and the art world. "In the late 1980s a new phenomenon developed out of the pro-prostitution movement. This consisted of prostituted and ex-prostituted women, like Carol Leigh, Annie Sprinkle, Veronica Vera, who turned their life's experience of being abused by men in prostitution into careers as 'performance artists' and 'sex educators'."[225]

In *Public Cervix*, Sprinkle invites audiences to inspect her cervix with a speculum and flashlight. Sprinkle had a work called 'A Hundred Blow Jobs', in which she "gagged on this huge dildo" and "got in touch" with the pain she had suffered in prostitution.

---

223 Ekman, 2013, p. 140.
224 Ekman, 2013, quoting Malm, pp. 142–3.
225 Jeffreys, 1997, p. 84.

Chapter Three: Rebellion and Backlash

In Australia, Linda Sproule also made 'art' of pain – she would injure herself to the point of bruising for performances, before donning a negligee and high heels, and displaying her real wounds to audiences given torches to examine them. The artist Orlan has famously used her body as a 'canvas'.[226]

It is not hard to trace where these tendencies originate: combine the original shock of rape and the dualistic distortions of patriarchy with neoliberalism, prostitution and porn.

To bring us into the new millennium, add the internet, which is teeming with pornography bearing the stamp of its origins in the witch trials. In a world where rape, prostitution, online porn, and mainstream media objectification are rife, dissociation is a collective cultural issue, not just an individual trauma response. These factors combine and compound one another to create a climate of male sexual entitlement, body hatred, dissociation, dysphoria and anorexia – and *these are the disaster conditions that transgenderism exploits*.[227] They cause enough disorientation and split-self thinking to allow capitalism to advance into more intimate territory – from the commons and Indigenous lands to the unions, to sexuality, to sexual anatomy itself.

The mantra 'transwomen are women' announces womanhood itself as a frontier for commodification. Now, neoliberalism's 'structural adjustments' can be applied to human biology: "the penis is seen as a 'thing' to be gotten rid of. Female body parts, specifically the female genitalia, are 'things' to be acquired."[228] This is *the structural adjustment* (also known as 'shock therapy') of transgenderism: the silicone implants mimicking female breasts while parading them as sexual accessories rather than living tissue and part of the bond between mother and baby; surgical castration providing men with fake 'vaginas'; breast binders stunting growth so that teenage girls can pass for boys and avoid objectification; mastectomies

---

226 Jeffreys, 2005, p. 154, pp. 161–4.
227 Gerlich, 2019b. I have delivered a talk about this called 'Transgenderism, Neoliberalism and Rape Culture', on which this section draws heavily.
228 Raymond, 1979, pp. 30–31.

that remove any breast tissue that develops; testosterone lowering girls' voices irreversibly; forearm skin removed to fashion a 'penis' in phalloplasty; puberty blockers warding off normal adolescence and weakening bones. With the advance of transgenderism, the fact of biological sex is rhetorically ploughed over and substituted with the cash crop of 'gender identity'.

The story is that it is 'empowering' for the individual to reject biological sex and substitute it for a customised gender, one that is essentially constructed from pharmaceutical, 'beauty' and fashion industry consumables. Women who do *not* comply are labelled dissidents, nags, meddlers, terrorists, TERFs, conspiracy theorists – witches. Women who comply end up referring to *themselves* using an absurd new split-self vocabulary including terms like 'cis', 'incubator', 'menstruator', and 'vagina haver'.[229] This postmodern Newspeak echoes the way women are discussed in the surrogacy industry as 'gestational carriers', a term that "erases women," as Renate Klein argues.[230]

To unsuspecting members of leftist groups, becoming pro-'sex work' or pro-'trans' seems like a minor concession made to accommodate the special needs of small and neglected minorities. Indeed, many activist groups, women's organisations, student groups, and workplaces first absorb these ideas in the form of 'safer spaces' policies that claim to simply make the group more 'inclusive'. But the power of these concepts is such that once they are adopted, the re-prioritisation that they demand, and the policing of language that results, effectively liberalises any organisation that takes them on board. As Silvia Federici writes, "[t]here seems to be … a peculiar relationship between the dismantling of communitarian regimes and the demonisation of members of the affected communities that makes witch-hunting an effective instrument of economic and social privatisation."[231]

---

229 Cox, 2015; Murphy, 2016.
230 Klein, Renate, 2017, pp. 48–9.
231 Federici, 2018, p. 15.

Chapter Three: Rebellion and Backlash

The left has now largely swallowed the mantra 'transwomen are women'. The effect of this mantra is to consolidate the domestication of the whole political left – NGOs, peace groups, unions, socialist organisations – as they commit to, and prioritise, transgender mythology, purge feminists and independent critical thinkers from their ranks, and build stronger ties to the liberal political parties and big money also promoting gender identity, and funding the Pride Parades. The mantra is used like a threat against those who might question it, and the blackmail is allowing men to hijack women's organisations, rape crisis centres, safe houses and lesbian culture created during the Women's Liberation Movement of the 1970s and 80s.

Though both Naomi Klein and Silvia Federici support transgenderism, the ideology perfectly fits the patterns outlined in their important books. Transgender doctrine has proven an ingenious method for disorienting large groups of people, rendering them unable to "think rationally or protect their own interests," in Klein's words, and it lends a whole new, more intimate, meaning to the phrase 'enclosure' or 'structural reform'. Physically, the movement traps otherwise healthy people into life-long dependence on the medical establishment, and psychologically, it locks them into futile, defensive, and often aggressive battles for their perceived identities, against 'misgendering', so-called 'trans exclusionary radical feminists', and fictive 'anti-trans hate groups'.

Speaking of neoliberalism, Klein writes, "[t]his fundamentalist form of capitalism has consistently been midwifed by the most brutal forms of coercion, inflicted on the collective body politic as well as on countless individual bodies."[232] She could be speaking of transgenderism directly, just as Federici could when she says, "we have to think of the enclosures as a broader phenomenon than simply the fencing off of land. We must think of an enclosure of

---

232 Klein, Naomi, 2017, p. 18.

knowledge, of our bodies, and of our relationship to other people and nature."[233]

Transgenderism is no exception to the rules either of enclosure or neoliberalism. As the shock and disorientation spreads, the structural adjustment just becomes more intimate.

Postmodernism

Transgenderism – along with its contradictions and its disorienting effects – is supported in academia by postmodern theorists like Berkeley professor Judith Butler, author of *Gender Trouble* (1990), a sort of transactivists' Bible. In the *Guardian*, Butler recently mused:

> We generally think of sex assignment as happening once, but what if it is a complex and revisable process, reversible in time for those who have been wrongly assigned? To argue this way is not to take a position against science, but only to ask how science and law enter into the social regulation of identity.[234]

This is typical postmodern 'split self' obfuscation. When Butler refers to 'sex assignment', what is she talking about? Generally, transactivists use this phrase to refer to the moment that doctors identify the sex of a baby – the sex that is then recorded on a birth certificate, which some people wish they could change because they are not happy with it. This is dissociation, which is both painful and understandable, given the world we live in – but the idea that doctors routinely 'assign' sex is still as absurd as the idea that sex is 'reversible in time'.

The postmodern inclination to examine almost every concept as 'socially constructed' is not total baloney. Indeed, postmodernism shares the practice of radical questioning with Paulo Freire, feminism, and the *Tao*. In *Pedagogy of the Oppressed* (1970), Freire argued that no individual, and therefore no group, has the capacity to objectively know an entire concrete reality called 'the world'.

---

233 Federici, 2018, p. 21.
234 Butler, 2021.

Chapter Three: Rebellion and Backlash

As we live, each of us makes a 'world' through a creative process of observing, interpreting, and deciding. In Freire's words, "World and human beings do not exist apart from each other, they exist in constant interaction."[235] What Freire called 'the world', Andrea Dworkin called 'reality'. She wrote about,

> the distinction between truth and reality. For humans, reality is *social*; reality is whatever people at a given time believe it to be ... Reality is enforced by those whom it serves so that it appears to be self-evident. Reality is self-perpetuating, in that the cultural and social institutions built on its premises also embody and enforce those premises ...
>
> Truth, on the other hand, is not nearly so accessible as reality. In my view, truth is absolute in that it does exist and it can be found. Radium, for instance, always existed; it was always true that radium existed; but radium did not figure in the human notion of reality until Marie and Pierre Curie isolated it.[236]

All our communication is ultimately creative, our concepts constructed, and therefore so too is our 'world' and 'reality'. As Cynthia Enloe writes, "As one learns to look at this world through feminist eyes, one learns to ask whether anything that passes for inevitable, inherent, 'traditional' or biological has in fact been *made*."[237] With these statements, Freire, Dworkin, and Enloe echo the *Tao,* which famously states that:

> The Tao that can be told
> is not the eternal Tao.
> The name that can be named
> is not the eternal Name.
>
> The unnameable is the eternally real.
> Naming is the origin
> of all particular things.[238]

---

235 Freire, 1970, p. 32.
236 Dworkin, 1976, p. 109.
237 Enloe, 1989, p. 3.
238 Tzu/Mitchell, 2015, p. 1.

Truth is ultimately unnameable, and *life is a mystery* that, if it must be characterised, can only be characterised by change, by flux. What we call 'material reality' is a play of forms that arise, transform, pass away, and evolve. As we observe this play, we do not see absolute truths, only patterns of form. We speak and generalise about the patterns we see using signs, concepts, language, and metaphors that we agree upon and that ultimately become our 'world' or social 'reality'.

The problem with postmodernism is not its rejection of absolute truth, and we do not need to believe in absolute truths in order to perceive biological sex – we only need to have the capacity to observe patterns, a capacity that is crucial to the everyday functioning of human beings. Indeed to sense and respond to patterns is the reason why we have sense perception, cognition, memory, even muscle memory and reflexes. The pattern of sex is among the clearest and the first a human being identifies. The moment we are born, we instinctively look for our mother's breast. From the time we are toddlers, we start to actively identify who is a boy, girl, man, or woman. This is not because we have been persuaded about any 'truth', but because we have mammalian instincts and the ability to notice patterns. This is all it takes to recognise sex.

If you refuse to name this pattern, it must be because – as George Orwell famously wrote – "[t]he Party told you to reject the evidence of your eyes and ears."[239] Rejecting that evidence, on what basis can we accept anything that is even further removed from our own observable environment? The study and discussion of history, politics, foreign relations, wars taking place in countries we have never even visited – we must be unqualified to discuss any of this if we cannot discuss the patterns we can see for ourselves. In fact, language itself is constructed from generalisations based on patterns, each word being nothing but a social 'agreement'.[240] To relinquish the capacity to observe

---

239 Orwell, 1949/1989, p. 84.
240 Ruiz, 1997.

patterns, turn them into concepts using language ('that's a table,' 'that's a dog,' 'that's a man,' 'that's hot – don't touch!') is to exist in a bubble, untethered from social reality.

Clearly, postmodernists are selective about the kind of concepts they wish to deconstruct, and 'woman' is the top priority. Their rejection of truth and generalisation does not lead postmodern academics to leap from their office on the third floor in a gesture of defiance against the concept of gravity, or to walk into oncoming traffic on the way to work because they find Newtonian physics too ideologically restrictive. In fact, postmodern academics are so decadent about indulging in social artifice that they are literally incomprehensible to many people who are not as institutionalised as they are. There are ways of writing, publishing, teaching, speaking, and even dressing that form part of the academic 'world'. Is it not a little suspect for a group of people to accept facts, rules, patterns, and laws from the natural (like gravity and cause and effect) to the flagrant and institutional (like academic protocol, jargon, and attire) while becoming passionate about unravelling the concept of 'woman' – because suddenly it is immoral to observe, generalise and name?

This selectiveness is the mark of identification – *ahaṃkāra*. The difference between Freire, Dworkin, Enloe, and the *Tao* on one hand, and Butler and postmodernism on the other, is the difference between questioning concepts in the interest of 'humanisation' and solidarity with the oppressed, versus questioning concepts to consolidate external power in co-operation with the oppressor. Freire, Dworkin, and Enloe employ the idea of the world as discursively constructed not for the sake of it, but to help members of oppressed groups recognise the patterns of social conditioning, to 'eject' the oppressor from the mind, to 'see with our own eyes', and so change the world and restore it to love.[241] Freire said that "[t]he naming of the world, which is an act of creation and re-

---

241 Dworkin, 1976, p. 78.

creation, is not possible if it is not infused with love."[242] Without love as a motivation, endless questioning can only lead to a paradigm of meaninglessness, something the postmodern zeitgeist reflects.

Postmodernism is the theoretical framework that supports neoliberalism. Like Protestantism and liberalism, it ostensibly arose to challenge tyranny. Just as Luther's *Ninety-five Theses* opposed the Catholic Church and *The Declaration* opposed the rule of the British monarchy, postmodernism was a reaction to the rise of fascism and totalitarianism in the early twentieth century. That is why it claims to abhor imperialism and absolute truth. Yet, like John Adams writing the *Declaration*, it does not actually want to relinquish 'Masculine systems'. The solution, as Catharine MacKinnon writes in her magnificent essay 'Points Against Postmodernism', is to be vague: "Domination, postmodernists know exists, but they don't tell us how or where or why."[243]

Is this gaslighting? Literary theorist Terry Eagleton calls postmodernism a "cult of ambiguity and indeterminacy" that has bred "political illiteracy and historical oblivion."[244] As Somer Brodrib comments in *Nothing Mat(t)ters* (1992):

> The explosion of consciousness and responsibility, the death of meaning, is being proclaimed by postmodernism. All this is occurring as feminist critiques of the economy of patriarchal ideological and material control of women emerge from women's liberation movements.[245]

Postmodernism appropriated and distorted feminist approaches to theory and analysis, using almost all the tactics on the 'Power and Control Wheel'. MacKinnon, along with other feminists like Sheila Jeffreys, were involved with Women's Studies departments set up within universities by Women's Liberationists when postmodernism arrived on the scene. The anthology *The Sexual*

---

242 Freire, 1970, p. 68, p. 70.
243 MacKinnon, 2000, p. 702.
244 Eagleton, 1996, p. 5, p. 23.
245 Brodribb, 1992, p. 19.

Liberals and the Attack on Feminism (1990, to which both these authors contribute) analyses the coup that took place as Women's Studies departments were usurped and replaced with Gender Studies and queer theory.[246]

Feminist theory is distinct from fundamentalist ideologies precisely because it does not begin with a set of rigid, pre-constructed concepts, but with women's subjective experience and commitment to humanisation shared in consciousness raising. As MacKinnon writes, "Feminism's development as theory is impelled by the realities of women's situation."[247] It is constantly shaped and re-shaped as women pose questions about our lives and notice the patterns our experiences form. These patterns combine to form analysis, and this analysis is dynamic, changing as the times change. But the simple premise of women's humanity, from which women's experience arises and is spoken, does not change – because it is a premise based on love and observation, not dogma.

For postmodernists, who claim to abhor 'metanarratives', it does not matter that feminist analysis is developed from individual expression, observation and the desire for liberation. The fact that an incalculably vast accumulation of subjective experience and observation of social patterns led feminists like Andrea Dworkin to theorise about something called 'male supremacy' is still too much for postmodernists to stomach. So, the feminist discussion of patriarchy is dismissed as a simplistic generalisation that denies individual agency (even as the analysis is shaped by individuals), and is not nuanced enough, not whimsical enough, not malleable enough.

The irony of this is as follows: if subjective experiences form patterns, and if these patterns are not allowed to indicate anything about institutional power or 'Masculine systems', then those systems cannot be analysed and remain well protected. This is how postmodernism can *claim* to be fundamentally democratic and

---

246 Leidholdt and Raymond, ed., 1990.
247 MacKinnon, 2000, p. 688.

supportive of subjectivity and identity in theory, while supporting the misogynist monolith of neoliberalism in practice. It is also what prevents movements like #MeToo from posing a serious threat: such movements cannot evolve from testimony to analysis to collective action if they cannot theorise about sex-based oppression. That is why #MeToo is allowed so much media coverage: it offers women the illusion of progress.

The spokespeople for mass movements such as #MeToo are also under immense pressure to accept ideas developed in queer theory and Gender Studies departments by academics like Butler. In 2018, during a launch for Rose McGowan's book *Brave*, a man began to heckle McGowan about "transwomen," "genocide," and "white! Cis! Feminism!" from the audience. After initially responding calmly, McGowan became enraged and yelled,

> don't put your labels on me, don't you fucking do that ... I don't come from your planet, leave me alone. I do not subscribe to your rules. I do not subscribe to your language. You do not put labels on me or anybody. Step the fuck back.

She later issued an apology to *PinkNews*, saying:

> I would like to say I'm sorry. I didn't have the correct language. I am, you know, an older woman from Hollywood. It's not exactly the place for understanding new language, you know, had I said 'cis woman' – now I understand that that's what I should have said. And it's just been a learning process.[248]

These ideas constitute the 'backlash' to Women's Studies. In mind boggling displays of reversal and doublespeak, queer theory is now quite literally being sold to women as 'feminism' itself – a feminism in which the social reality of gender supposedly undermines the truth of biological sex; in which women ourselves are deemed unreal, an idea, and in which women must constantly apologise for not understanding the 'new language'.

---

248 McGowan in Braidwood, 2018.

Chapter Three: Rebellion and Backlash

Gender Studies is the academic discipline in which the stories that rationalise and justify the abuses of prostitution, pornography and transgenderism are produced. The capture and distortion of Women's Studies facilitated this process by allowing gender theorists to distort feminist arguments. Postmodernists take de Beauvoir's argument that "One is not born, but rather becomes, a woman" (something I realised intuitively when I watched Sandy's transformation in *Grease*) and turn it into an argument that sex is 'assigned' and that *men, not just girls, can become women!* Postmodernists take the feminist analysis of the patriarchal family as constructed and oppressive, and twist it into a defence of the surrogacy industry: if we can 'construct' one kind of family, what's wrong with 'constructing' another? The call to destigmatise female sexuality has become grounds to support the sex trade lobby's relabelling of prostitution as 'sex work', by calling it a form of individual female sexual emancipation.[249] And, as Enloe writes, "[f]eminists always pay attention to pronouns."[250] She means that feminists do not take for granted that when writers like Adam Smith refer to human behaviour in terms of 'mankind' and 'he', that these terms should be read as neutral and generic, rather than reflections of male identification. The currently fashionable so-called feminist concern with pronouns has become an absurd proposition that everyone must declare whether they are a he/him, she/her or they/them.

My first reaction to postmodernism was ambivalent. Today, young women are being forced to account for an abundance of even stranger, more counterintuitive and nonsensical, postmodern ideas around them, clearly coming from universities and media, and highly fixated on sex and identity. As they find other women with the same questions, they receive a masterclass in sexist obfuscation tactics. To come out of the fog, it will help these women to make

---

249 In 2017, I made a complaint to the Media Council about the promotion of prostitution as 'sex work' by student magazine *Salient* magazine over a period of five years (see Gerlich, 2017).
250 Enloe, 2013, p. 61.

a habit of asking the question: *who do these ideas really serve?* And are they really healing, humanising and loving – or do they promote fear, denial and desensitisation?

The liberal left

If postmodernism is defined by its identifications and not its stated values or objectives, then what exactly *are* its identifications? What are the basic loyalties of a paradigm that claims to abhor imperialism and absolute truth, while it promotes the split self as an unquestionable reality?

They are the loyalties of the new 'liberal left', a distinctly twenty-first century paradigm that resulted from the breaking of the left and the absorption of its leftovers into the liberal establishment. As Howard Zinn explained, assimilation has always been an important liberal tactic, and as Paulo Freire wrote:

> In a situation of manipulation, the Left is almost always tempted by a 'quick return to power', forgets the necessity of joining with the oppressed to forge an organisation, and strays into an impossible 'dialogue' with the dominant elites.[251]

Postmodernism allows for the reconfiguration of ideas required by this assimilation and 'dialogue' in academia.

This assimilation has given liberals a new arsenal to draw upon – the left's militant vocabulary of resistance, anti-capitalism, imperialism, neoliberalism, colonisation, heteronormativity and white supremacy. This vocabulary is hollowed of substance when absorbed into a postmodern paradigm of contradiction, but it is useful, because it appeals to deep human longings for freedom. Now, even mainstream politicians can claim to oppose capitalism and neoliberalism, as New Zealand prime minister Jacinda Ardern has done.[252]

---

251 Freire, 1970, p. 130.
252 Cooke, 2017.

Chapter Three: Rebellion and Backlash

The contradictions and vested interests of the liberal left reveal its identifications: a combination of the liberal identification with free marketeers wanting to escape the tyranny of the right, and the left's identification with the underdog. The result is that the liberal left identifies with any man who is not served by the conservative right, which still expects him to be a white, heterosexual breadwinner.

Liberal leftists will defend working men who struggle to put food on the table, gay men, black and Indigenous men, Muslim men, men who identify as women, men in gangs, incarcerated men, pimps, punters, pornographers, and men with mental health disorders. They will defend Islam, prostitution, marriage, homosexuality, and transgenderism ferociously, as varieties of freedom, for contradictory reasons.

There is nothing wrong with defending people who struggle, even if their interests disagree. The problem is that the liberal left does not oppose rape, and that is why it cannot understand, analyse, or address violence consistently, and that is why it runs into problems. It has no bottom lines about violence, what constitutes violence, when violence should be prevented at all costs, and when it should be excused as justified retaliation or emotional venting.

If a man's capacity to meet the heterosexual, paternalistic standards of 'protector' and 'provider' – even 'soldier' – are compromised, liberal-leftists will strive to accommodate his actions as 'reasonable' and rational, no matter how violent. His persecution or disadvantage, whether real, perceived or performed, is sufficient to render even his violence, and especially his violence against women, defensible. The lack of principle and the conflicts of interest are covered up with postmodern ideas of indeterminacy, and with 'virtue signalling' about the 'multiculturalism' critiqued by Roxanne Dunbar-Ortiz, and 'inclusivity', 'love' and 'kindness'.

Meanwhile, a woman cannot name her own sex without fear of losing her job, livelihood, social network, sense of safety, and reputation – because acknowledging sex makes a woman 'violent'.

Robin Morgan's *Demon Lover* (1989) is the classic text on the violence of the left.[253] Morgan shows how in order to defend men who conduct acts of terrorism in reaction to United States imperialism, as well as men in gangs or in prison for violent crime, leftists tend to view terrorism and violence as stemming from violation, desperation and poverty. It is a sort of last resort or lashing out. This begs the question of why women, who are more routinely violated, and more economically disadvantaged as a group than men are, do not lash out violently at anywhere near the same rate.

As Kathleen Barry explains, oppression renders men incapable of carrying out the duty of protection that men everywhere – husbands, fathers, soldiers – are told is their duty as men. "Violated self-determination of a people brings about resistance," says Barry. Of course. She adds: "When men are made inferior, their condition is reduced to that of women. That is intolerable to most men. Those men in turn force women's status to lower levels."[254]

And what happens when these men 'lash out' at each other? If a gay man beats a Muslim man, or vice versa, what does a liberal leftist do? Ignore it? Defend it? Excuse it? As Zinn writes, "inspirational language to create a secure consensus is still used, in our time, to cover up serious conflicts of interest in that consensus, and to cover up, also, the omission of large parts of the human race" (namely women).[255]

While terrorism, gang and other criminal violence can be defended and explained away by leftists as a result of poverty and abuse inflicted by the state, they will drop their militant opposition to the state and even US imperialism if an emasculated man requires it of them. In 2017, Donald Trump, then-US president (POTUS), announced plans to ban men who identify as women from the US military, saying they cost too much to employ. After Trump's announcement, I watched Peace Action Wellington (PAW), the

---

253 Morgan, 1989.
254 Barry, 2011, p. 107.
255 Zinn, 1999, p. 73.

Chapter Three: Rebellion and Backlash

group with whom I protested the arms conference, argue against the ban. This meant that they had to take a position that voluntary enlistment in the US military could possibly be seen as a 'human right'. As Enloe argues, "an equal opportunity preoccupation ... implies that the military is 'just one more employer', an employer that happens to measure success in terms of kill ratios rather than miles-per-gallon or rates of profit."[256]

Enloe calls the military the 'epitome of patriarchy'.[257] A man who voluntarily enlists is a male conforming to masculine norms, *and* participating in imperialism. The credibility of his claim to any sort of female or feminine psychology or interior are questionable on every level. What can they be based on? In the thrill of occasionally trading in guns and camouflage for lipstick and women's underwear – how is that not sexism?

The sexism of the left is the door through which liberals have managed to stride in with their state, corporate and university sanctioned ideas that 'sex work is work' and 'transwomen are women', and as Marilyn French wrote, "The assertion of female inferiority prepares the ground for men's subjection, because the principle of superiority ramifies endlessly."[258]

So, three things broke the left. The most significant is its common ground with external power systems: male bias. In seeking to unite men who share a condition of oppression, and to build an analysis of class that takes male dominance for granted, revolutionary leaders left in place the seed of the left's own demise. The second factor is backlash from the state by force, torture and infiltration, carried out during the era of McCarthyism and by agencies like the CIA, the FBI's counterintelligence programs or COINTELPRO (Counter Intelligence Program, 1956–1971). The third is absorption into the liberal establishment. In a 1982 issue of *Broadsheet*, Māori rights activist Donna Awatere wrote

---

256 Enloe, 1983, p. 150.
257 Enloe, 1983, p. 132.
258 French, 2002, p. 179.

that the trade union movement, built on the premise of 'collective bargaining', is "inherently reformist in nature." She argued that,

> the Trade Union Movement is not committed to replacing the economic set up but merely to reducing the amount of their labour power which is taken off on profit by the owner class ... It is *part of the structure* of Capitalism and is one of the key ways Capitalism's stability is ensured ... The Union function, then, is to represent workers commercially in dealings with the Capitalist class ... The Trade Union Movement plays by Capitalism's rules in too many ways for it to be a threat (italics and capitals in original).[259]

Over the last decade, the political left has revealed more about its underlying identifications. With the emergence of Pride Parades, many activists shifted their concerns away from the 99 per cent, or the 'immense majority' (in Marx's words) whose solidarity could topple the ruling class, to very specific minorities like 'black trans sex workers' who would appear to win in a contest of 'oppression Olympics'.[260] At the same time, the left has begun turning a blind eye to the state and corporate investment in social movements, at a time that wealth is being concentrated in the hands of an ever-smaller *minority* of billionaires.

Protest itself is starting to look more and more franchised, with a constant procession of social movements emerging with slick brands, logos, merchandise, spokespeople, party political affiliations, corporate sponsors and large marketing budgets. In my region of Wellington, it has become rare to see marches or protests without party political spokespeople. Banks fund the Pride Parades, politicians promote the Green New Deal at climate change marches, and "[w]e are reaching the point where there is no distinction between our 'movements' and the coalitions created to further our oppression and servitude."[261]

---

259 Awatere, 1982, p. 27.
260 Fischer, 1970, p. 78.
261 Morningstar, 2019.

Chapter Three: Rebellion and Backlash

Yet as Freire writes, "It would be a contradiction in terms if the oppressors not only defended but actually implemented a liberating education."[262] Influencers and people in positions of authority might bring glamour to public events, but they cannot *liberate*. In fact, if people could be liberated by the elites, that would only reinforce the power dynamic, since, as Sonja Johnson put it: "anybody that can *let* you, *owns* you."[263]

In short, we cannot hope to be saved by celebrity spokespeople, progressive politicians, and franchised movements. Everyone who wants freedom must dispel the fog for themselves, whether through solitary reflection, consciousness-raising groups, or a combination. As Freire said, "the great and humanistic and historical task of the oppressed [is] ... to liberate themselves and their oppressors as well."[264] It cannot happen the other way around.

---

262 Freire, 1970, p. 26.
263 Johnson, 1989, p. 26.
264 Freire, 1970, p. 26.

CHAPTER FOUR

Fatal Contradictions

> *I have never really understood exactly what a liberal is, though, since i have heard 'liberals' express every conceivable opinion on every conceivable subject. As far as i can tell, you have the extreme right, who are fascist, racist capitalist dogs like Ronald Reagan, who come right out and let you know where they're coming from. And on the opposite end, you have the left, who are supposed to be committed to justice, equality, and human rights. And somewhere between those two points is the liberal. As far as i'm concerned, 'liberal' is the most meaningless word in the dictionary. History has shown me that as long as some white middle-class people can live high on the hog, take vacations to Europe, send their children to private schools, and reap the benefits of their white skin privileges, then they are 'liberals'. But when times get hard and money gets tight, they pull off that liberal mask and you think you're talking to Adolf Hitler. They feel sorry for the so-called underprivileged just as long as they can maintain their own privileges.*
> —Assata Shakur, *Assata: An Autobiography*[265]

Today, many of us live with a simultaneous sense of urgency and paralysis as our personal and social challenges compete for priority while they are seeming impossible to reconcile. We are constantly implored to 'act':

> White silence is violence.
> Fight for your lives before it's someone else's job.
> Pussy grabs back.
> Be kind.
> Act as if the house was on fire.
> Stay home, save lives.

---

265 Shakur, 2014, p. 188.

These imperatives always seem righteous, but on close inspection, they contradict. If we want to make a positive impact in the world, we need to take a closer look at the stories we are being told about what needs defending and against what imminent threat. In this chapter I provide an opportunity to do that by offering a broad overview of political events between 2014 and 2020, focussing on Pride and the promotion of transgenderism; Black Lives Matter and prison abolition; mainstream feminism; climate change activism, and the 2019 Christchurch massacre.

Prisons

Around 2014, two campaigns kicked off that shaped progressive politics in the years to follow: the annual Pride Parades, and Black Lives Matter (BLM). Both position themselves as radical, but they each have a different set of objectives, tone, aesthetic, and attitude toward the state. BLM was established to challenge racialised state violence and incarceration by holding demonstrations in response to the shooting of black men by white police officers in the US. They have rallied on behalf of Dontre Hamilton, Eric Garner, John Crawford III, Michael Brown, Ezell Ford, Laquan McDonald, Akai Gurley, Tamir Rice, Antonio Martin, Jerame Reid, George Floyd and others. As I said in the Introduction, BLM representatives promote prison abolition as part of its opposition to state violence and racism.

The Pride Parades share many of the same supporters as BLM demonstrations, but Pride is state sanctioned and corporate funded. In New Zealand, the police started marching in the Auckland parade in 2014, and the following year, ANZ Bank launched its 'GAYTMs', which are ATMs decorated in rainbow-coloured rhinestones to honour Pride. The parades are famed for extravagance and exhibitionism. In 2018, the Auckland Pride programme included KIWIFIST, marketed on the event website as "New Zealand's biggest arse-play event ... A full-on, five-hour-plus, gathering of gay and bi men into fisting and arse-play big-time!" Organisers offered slings,

Chapter Four: Fatal Contradictions

toys, lubricants, "touch-up douche facilities" and a clothes check-in for $30 at the door.

These are not just expensive, fetishistic street parties though, we are told. They are anti-establishment marches that celebrate the decriminalisation of homosexuality, and demand visibility for vulnerable and marginalised 'trans people'.

In New Zealand, one group has been vocal about wanting to re-radicalise the festival from the outset: People Against Prisons Aotearoa (PAPA), formerly No Pride in Prisons (NPP). PAPA is New Zealand's most vocal prison abolitionist group, much like other anti-fascist or 'antifa' organisations, and is led by Emmy Rākete, a young man who identifies as lesbian. PAPA sought to ban police from marching in Pride as soon as they joined, and in 2015, three members confronted police and security at the event. Rākete was hospitalised with a broken arm and later said, "I wish I'd heard that Corrections were marching sooner." PAPA were better prepared in later years.

PAPA shares a prison abolitionist position with BLM, except that their priorities are more specific and niche. Their stated reason for wanting to ban police from Pride was the Department of Corrections' treatment of 'trans prisoners'.[266] PAPA has 50 'abolitionist demands' which include requesting that Corrections "allow for the immediate placement of all trans prisoners in a prison of their choosing," "end the practice of incarcerating trans people," "enable consistent, high-quality access to gender affirmation surgery and hormone replacement therapy" and "allow all prisoners access to the underwear, other clothing, and makeup of their choice." The group does not want the police marching at Pride so long as they do not honour these demands.[267]

Promoting transgenderism is a high priority for PAPA. It is likely that in New Zealand, all prisoners who identify as the opposite sex are male. This can be deduced from the fact that most trans-

---

266 Furley, 2017.
267 No Pride in Prisons, 2016.

identified people in the general population are male, and there are approximately 10,000 incarcerated men in New Zealand's prisons, compared with 800 women.

These numbers point to the gendered nature of violent crime: 95 per cent of all violent crime inflicted on both men and women is committed by men. Even though only one in ten sexual assault cases results in a conviction in New Zealand, sexual assault is still one of the most common offences for which men are sentenced.

Yet Indigenous women are the fastest growing incarcerated group, and this is true for Canada, the US, Australia, and New Zealand, where women are being incarcerated for crimes associated with poverty, like theft and welfare fraud (in some US states, women can also be charged for miscarriage and abortion). Māori women, who comprised one per cent of the female prison population in the 1980s, made up 64 per cent in 2018.[268] In New Zealand, the South Auckland and Arohata women's prisons are so full that women at Arohata have been placed in self-contained units at a nearby men's prisons.

Since violent crime and the rapid imprisonment of Indigenous women for crimes of poverty and self-defence would seem to be the single clearest illustration of the capitalist, racist and criminal injustice of the prison system, it is significant that, in contrast with its support for a small number of male 'trans prisoners', PAPA's demands make no mention of ending the incarceration of women.

What's more, analysis of violent crime in New Zealand reveals gendered patterns in which a "significant proportion" of men who murder women employ "overkill – where the violence used was far beyond what was necessary to cause death," while women who kill overwhelmingly act in self-defence.[269] This data, reported by the New Zealand Family Violence Death Review Committee, makes the question of why Indigenous women are the fastest growing prison population even more pertinent, and suggests we place urgent

---

268 Mau, 2018.
269 New Zealand Family Violence Death Review Committee, 2017, p. 10.

Chapter Four: Fatal Contradictions

priority on their release.[270] Instead, PAPA's second demand is to "prevent the implementation of any public sex offender register," something that *increases* the onus on women to act in self-defence.[271]

A feminist position would suggest that violent men can take their pick from any and all available prison cells – whether in men or 'women's' facilities, and however the men identify – *once all women are released from prison*. When the men are arranged comfortably, we can start transforming the prison system into a rehabilitative one that serves the purpose of creating a world without rape.

In contrast, PAPA's prioritisation of sex offenders and transgenderism not only ignores women, it puts them at risk. In 2015, PAPA lobbied to have Jade Follett, who had been sentenced to 21 months for stabbing a man four times, rehoused into a women's prison. It took just hours for Corrections to comply.[272] In the UK, Karen White (born Stephen Wood) raped four women within days of being moved into a women's prison on the same pretence. In New Zealand, Corrections have admitted that between January 2017 and August 2018, at least six assaults were committed against women by trans-identified prisoners, most likely all males, ostensibly rehoused to honour their gender identities.

The continued campaigning for the rights of men to be placed in facilities according to their gender identities and regardless of their crimes, makes prison abolition look like something other than a 'leftist' and 'antifascist' social justice movement. Indeed, in a podcast made by Rākete and friends as the Sh*t Hot People's Politburo, Rākete described the Pride Parade he wants to see: "I wanna see people fucking on a float … If there is not wall to wall

---

270 According to the New Zealand Family Violence Death Review Committee report, in the seven years from 2009 to 2015, there were 92 deaths caused by intimate partner violence. Seventy offenders were male compared to 22 female; 63 women and 29 men were killed. The report showed that when women kill, it is for different reasons than men: 83 of these deaths followed a recorded history of abuse, and in 82 of those cases, women were the primary victim. In 67 cases those women were killed, and in 16 cases they killed in self-defence.
271 No Pride in Prisons, 2016.
272 Maxwell, 2015.

sex down Queen Street, I don't want to have any of it."²⁷³ Where do these fantasies come from, and how do they affect what such activists do in the name of human rights? Do they indicate anything about why antifa activists do not like prisons and police, other than because of their supposed anarchist beliefs and passion for justice?

It does often seem that the fundamental concerns of today's liberal left boil down to male sexual licence and impunity rather than justice. This is illustrated in the way they view feminists, as well as female inmates and victims of violence.

A narrative that victims-are-offenders-are victims is central to prison abolitionism. From BLM founder Patrisse Cullors, Angela Davis and Gabor Maté to Rākete, abolitionists often cite poverty, colonisation and trauma as major factors that drive criminal offending and increase the likelihood of incarceration. Men like Follett and Wood become viewed as 'victims of circumstance' within this framework. They may well be – but this framing neglects to consider that poverty, colonisation and trauma are not leading women to commit rape routinely or employ overkill while murdering their partners.

'Restorative justice' is the system many abolitionists suggest should replace incarceration. It involves dealing with violent crime through 'honest dialogue' in victim-offender mediation sessions, family group conferences, and 'peacemaking circles'. Restorative justice advocacy has become popular, and in August 2018, New Zealand's Labour government held a $1.6 million Justice Summit with restorative justice high on the agenda.²⁷⁴ When ActionStation's Laura O'Connell Rapira was interviewed regarding the summit, she explained that "the truth is 77 per cent of people who are in prisons currently have once been victims of family or sexual violence, and so victims and offenders are often the same people."²⁷⁵

Jayne Crothall's experience of the Justice Summit is illuminating. Crothall is the mother of a girl who was murdered at the age of

---

273 Rākete in Rahera, 2019.
274 1News, 2018.
275 Radio New Zealand, 2018

Chapter Four: Fatal Contradictions

three by a man who broke into their family home in 1997. So when Crothall attended the summit, she had some questions about the idea that victims and offenders are the same people. In response, she was told that she does not know what it means to be a victim, because she is white and privileged.[276] "This is a horrendous summit for victims," she told an audience of around 500. "We've been re-victimised."[277] Such is the tension between restorative justice advocacy and feminism at present.[278]

Prison abolitionists neglect to consider the gendered nature of violence. When feminists raise the issue, nowadays we are labelled 'TERFs', for revealing that we know that biological sex is real. Compare the liberal left's reluctance to discuss men's violence with its willingness to punish so-called 'TERFs' for talking, and you can see the identifications of this movement. All concerns for compassion, historic trauma, and honest dialogue go out the window when a supposed 'TERF' stands accused. Labour Party MP Louisa Wall demonstrated this at a Pride Board meeting in November 2018. Defending police participation at Pride, she argued:

> The police are doing an amazing job at diversifying. Some of you may not even know, they won a diversity award this year ... The police aren't bad ... The police are exemplifying, at the moment, diversity and inclusion. And that's the irony of this decision, okay ... My whole thing is I don't want any fucking TERFs at the Pride Parade![279]

Wall's final exclamation seems out of place, but it was followed by loud applause that must have relieved her of some of the tension she felt while having to liaise between the police, and the anarchist factions within Pride.

---

276 Here I would like to recommend Catharine MacKinnon's 1991 essay 'What is a White Woman Anyway?'
277 Stewart, 2018.
278 To explore this further, I recommend the essay collection *Restorative Justice and Violence Against Women*, edited by James Ptacek (2010), and Andrea Dworkin's 1979 essay, 'For Men, Freedom of Speech; For Women, Silence Please' (in Dworkin, 1988).
279 For the full recording of Wall's speech, see Speak Up For Women, 2018.

When the Pride board did announce that police uniforms would no longer be welcome, the police responded by withdrawing from the event altogether. The Defence Force followed, and PAPA were initially thrilled, until there was a corporate exodus. The 2019 parade was officially cancelled, and the board was left with an ambitious crowdfunding project. When ANZ Bank withdrew its sponsorship, PAPA tweeted that this amounted to "holding the Auckland Pride Board to ransom." The comment was interesting considering that when ANZ launched its GAYTMs, prison abolitionists vandalised them as corporate 'pinkwashing'.[280] It seems that PAPA objected to ANZ's dirty money until it was gone.

This whole palaver was a great illustration of the chaos of the liberal left. You can see how misogyny and the will to ignore rape leads to contradictions and inconsistent positions on violence, justice, trauma, compassion, the state, and big money. It leads figures like Wall to promote 'inclusion' while working to exclude women from public events, and 'anarchists' to promote top-down state and corporate funded ideologies when those ideologies appear sufficiently sexually transgressive. That such contradictions are a feature of patriarchal society is something that transgenderism makes abundantly clear.

Feminism

It is hard to tell how nominal anarchists dreaming of "wall to wall sex down Queen Street," might have really felt about a president of the United States who was once on the cover of *Playboy* and bragged that "I grab women by the pussy." The left tended to disagree with the surge of 'heartbeat bills' that followed Trump's inauguration – laws banning abortion from around six weeks of pregnancy, which is before many women even know they are pregnant – yet in *Right Wing Women* (1983), Dworkin questioned whether the left's 'pro-choice' stance is really grounded in solidarity with women. She says:

---

280 The Wireless, 2015.

Chapter Four: Fatal Contradictions

It was the brake that pregnancy put on fucking that made abortion a high-priority political issue for men in the 1960s – not only for young men, but also for the older leftist men who were skimming sex off the top of the counterculture and even for more traditional men who dipped into the pool of hippie girls now and then.[281]

The left certainly does not match its pro-choice stance on abortion with consistent solidarity with women. Following Trump's inauguration in 2017, 370 Women's Marches took place across the United States in one day – the largest single-day protest in US history. Activist Krista Suh designed pink knitted 'pussy hats' with cat-like 'ears' for protesters to wear, and these quickly became iconic. But given the rise of transgenderism from 2014, writer Marie Solis claimed that:

Suh's pussy hats set the tone for a march that would focus acutely on genitalia at the expense of the transgender community. Signs like 'Pussy power,' 'Viva la Vulva' and 'Pussy grabs back' all sent a clear and oppressive message to trans women, especially: having a vagina is essential to womanhood.[282]

These sorts of criticisms and disclaimers are commonplace in what passes for feminism today. Even Chanel Miller's book, *Know My Name*, contains a disclaimer that when she talks about victims of rape, "I say *her*, but whether you are a man, transgender, gender nonconforming, however you choose to identify … I seek to protect you."[283] This whole sentence, if taken seriously, quietly undermines the whole premise of challenging women's oppression. This is now standard, Rose McGowan's book launch, as previously discussed, providing another example.

In December 2018, I attended an abortion rights rally at New Zealand parliament that followed these lines. Abortion Law Reform Association New Zealand (ALRANZ) teamed up with Organise Aotearoa to plan the rally. Organise Aotearoa is run by Rākete and

---

281 Dworkin, 1983, p. 94.
282 Solis, 2017.
283 Miller, 2019, p. viii.

has been heralded as the "return of socialism" to New Zealand on liberal website *The Spinoff*.[284] They used Twitter to threaten that "If any known transphobic people attend, especially if they're carrying transphobic signs or banners, people can point them out to our ushers and they will be asked to leave."

Since ALRANZ now claims that "not all women can get pregnant, and not all people who might need an abortion are women," a 'transphobic' sign can be anything relating to specifically female rights or anatomy.[285]

At the rally, Green Party politician Jan Logie reminded protesters that "women and pregnant people have a right to make choices that are the best for them." One activist led a chorus of, "solidarity forever, for the union makes us strong," the relevance of which was unclear. The national coordinator from New Zealand Prostitutes' Collective, Catherine Healy, had also been invited to speak. She used the occasion to plug a recently published book about 'sex workers' called *My Body, My Business* (Wilton, 2018).

We live in a time when feminism looks to be in the ascendent, but its most public iterations are distinctly neoliberal. The concepts of 'sex workers', 'cis women', and 'TERFs' prevent Women's Marches and the #MeToo movement from posing a real challenge to the status quo. This is what Freire refers to as "cultural invasion" by the oppressor – as well as "divide and rule," since it leads to so much splintering and antagonism.

The prioritising of so-called 'transwomen' and even more specific groups like 'black trans sex workers' within today's pseudo-feminism is frequently justified with the concept of *intersectionality*. But the word has been distorted, like other concepts that emerged from second wave feminist consciousness raising and Women's Studies departments. In the 1970s and 80s, women learned to see and name the misogyny they normally lived with unconsciously. The term 'intersectional' was intended:

---

284 Braae, 2018.
285 Abortion Law Reform Association New Zealand, 2018.

> To describe how interlocking systems of power combine, overlap and intersect with each other to affect women's experiences and opportunities. The term reminded feminism [sic] that women are not *one* homogenous category since our experiences are affected by different axes of oppression ...[286]

bell hooks' *Feminist Theory from Margin to Centre* (1984) was key to the creation of this concept within the women's movement. Specifically, hooks showed how feminist analysis is affected when the compounding of race, class and sex oppression are accounted for. So, an important primary feminist practice, while keeping in mind the overall objective of women's humanisation, is to ask critical questions about how social norms, propaganda or proposals for change might affect *working class women of colour*: women affected by all three major types of global oppression. When these questions are asked and investigated honestly, they always help people see beyond the blinkers of privilege and bring important information to the table.

But the liberal left has decided that *intersectionality* means consistently prioritising men who claim a female identity, and this idea now permeates every feminist initiative, ultimately disconnecting feminism from women's real lives and feelings, as in McGowan's example.

This leaves women who do seek genuine change to battle in small movements with very limited capacity. Throughout 2018, midwives, nurses and teachers – all overworked, female-dominated professions – protested New Zealand's Labour government under prime minister Jacinda Ardern. In May, midwives marched to parliament, with the chair of the Wellington Region of the College of Midwives, Siobhan Connor, saying that the average take-home hourly income for urban midwives is $12.80 – and for rural midwives, $7.23. She said, "Midwives are leaving the profession because of this – and then women lose access to maternity care."[287]

---

286 Brunskell-Evans, 2020, p. 18.
287 *New Zealand Herald*, 2018.

In July 2018, nurses also went on strike: 92 per cent of all nursing staff in New Zealand are women, according to the Nursing Council. Registered nurse Danni Wilkinson explained, "We're not asking to be millionaires. We're asking to be able to afford to live where we can take care of the patient population."[288]

Teachers, unable to make the Ardern government listen to their demands, marched in August 2018 and again in May 2019. Of teaching staff in New Zealand, 72 per cent are women. In an article outlining teachers' demands and why she voted to strike, primary school teacher Lisa Geraghty wrote:

> I want my students to have the education they deserve. I want them to have teachers who have time to teach them. I want them to have teachers who aren't exhausted, burnt-out, and feeling undervalued.[289]

I know from experience that women are groomed to accept the burn-out culture Geraghty refers to right from teacher training.

In 2019, the current events site *Newsroom* reported that on average, Child Youth and Services (CYFS – which recently rebranded to Oranga Tamariki) confiscates three Māori babies from mothers staying in maternity hospitals each week.[290] A young mother told journalist Melanie Reid that "If I had three wishes it would be to keep my baby, have a house, and to have Oranga Tamariki leave me alone." Reid reported that this young woman had been left alone in a hospital room overnight as police and CYFS staff tried to take her baby. Two midwives – Ripeka Ormsby and Jean Te Huia from Māori Midwives Aotearoa – were locked out of the hospital for trying to intervene.

Te Huia had appeared in the media in April that same year, in a *Sunday* documentary called *The Black Hole,* which drew attention to the fact that approximately one in four mothers are affected

---

288 Lewis, 2018.
289 Geraghty, 2019.
290 Reid, 2019.

Chapter Four: Fatal Contradictions

by perinatal depression and anxiety in New Zealand. Te Huia said, "[t]he problems that we are seeing are more social than clinical. There's partnership issues, there's poverty, lack of housing … There's a sense of shame and blame when you can't cope." She asked an important question: "Does this government really care about Māori women? Do they care about the workforce, that's overworked? Do they care about us, as women, in this country?"[291]

That is the question.

These protests would be made immeasurably more effective if they recognised the common problem of women's oppression and joined together. Transgenderism, one-step sex self-identification, and proposed hate speech laws protecting 'gender identity', prevent this, by rendering the word 'woman' meaningless, and threatening to make the recognition of sex, and therefore sex-based oppression, *criminal*. How can we measure the implications of this, in a context where rape is commonplace, and women need to speak about sex and oppression?

It seems that many women have become numb to the frustration because we are so used to seeing our own lives and occupations as foggy and solitary endurance tests that we barely realise when our opportunity for collective action is taken away. Ongoing campaigns against the 'pay gap' cannot help – and are in fact disingenuous and pacifying – wherever they do not address the promotion of prostitution and redefinition of sex. As Cynthia Enloe writes, "women's labour is made cheap by preventing women from organising."[292] When feminism is domesticated, it also prevents us from recognising the link between 'private' and 'public', between our feelings, lives, and cultural contexts – and the significance of, for instance, electing a sex abuser as president.

---

291 Television New Zealand, 2019.
292 Enloe, 1989, p. 166.

Violence and the climate

In January 2018, Trump was goading North Korean leader Kim Jong Un on social media. He tweeted:

> North Korean Leader Kim Jong Un just stated that the 'Nuclear Button is on his desk at all times'. Will someone from his depleted and food starved regime please inform him that I too have a Nuclear Button, but it is a much bigger & more powerful one than his, and my Button works!

Meanwhile, by 2021, over 200,000 civilians had died in Iraq due to conflicts following the 2003 US invasion. A US-backed Saudi Arabian assault on Yemen, begun in 2016, left almost half the population starving while the death toll climbed to 70,000 by 2020.[293]

By 2017, the city of Aleppo in Syria had been bombed to rubble; Damascus was struck in August 2013, by rockets containing the chemical agent sarin. Up to 1,729 people were killed. When the Assad government violently put down protests following the Arab Spring, it marked the beginning of a civil war, and a refugee crisis. In September 2015, a photograph of Aylan Kurdi – a three-year-old Syrian boy of Kurdish ethnic background – circulated in western media. The boy was lying face down on a Turkish beach, after drowning in the Mediterranean Sea, fleeing Syria.

Amidst the devastation, the fundamentalist organisation Islamic State of Iraq and the Levant, emerged and spread. Islamic State carried out bombings in Paris in 2015, and Brussels in 2016.

Trump came to power in part because of a reactionary rise of white supremacy in Europe and America. In 2016, Unite the Right marchers in Charlottesville, Virginia, carried tiki torches, chanted "You will not replace us," and clashed with BLM supporters. As reported by Nellie Bowles in *The New York Times*, their slogan is shared with the neo-Nazi group Identity Evropa, and both reference 'replacement theory', popularised by French philosopher Renaud

---

293 Laursen, 2021, p. 12.

Chapter Four: Fatal Contradictions

Camus. Replacement theory is a contemporary expression of the colonialist idea that if white women do not bear enough children, white people will be 'replaced' by the 'other'. The ideology influences far-right political parties across Europe, as well as the right-wing web, where white men who fear 'replacement' congregate on sites like 4chan and 8chan. Brenton Tarrant, a white supremacist who murdered 50 people in a mosque and Islamic Centre in New Zealand in 2019, used such websites.[294]

Mass shootings are a norm in the US. Two months after Trump tweeted about his Nuclear Button, a gunman shot and killed 17 students at Marjory Stoneman Douglas High School in Parkland, Florida. Students from over 3,000 schools across the US participated in a School Walkout to demand gun control. Ten days later, in the face of backlash from the National Rifle Association, then-high school senior Emma Gonzalez stood before an audience in Washington DC at an event called March For Our Lives. "Six minutes and about 20 seconds," she opened:

> Six minutes, in a little over six minutes, 17 of our friends were taken from us, 15 more were injured, and everyone, absolutely everyone in the Douglas community was forever altered. Everyone who was there understands. Everyone who has been touched by the cold grip of gun violence understands.

Gonzalez listed the names of the students who were killed by Nikolas Cruz, who had entered her school with an AR-15 rifle. She took a lengthy pause:

> Since the time that I came out here, it has been six minutes and 20 seconds. The shooter has ceased shooting, and will soon abandon his rifle, blend in with the students as they escape, and walk free for an hour before arrest.
>
> Fight for your lives before it's someone else's job.[295]

By 18 May that year, 17-year-old Dimitrios Pagourtzis had killed ten people at Santa Fe High School using his father's revolver

---

294 Bowles, 2019.
295 Gonzalez, 2018.

and shotgun, and in November, Ian David Long, an ex-Marine, used a semi-automatic pistol to kill 13 people at a student bar in California. Parkland, Sutherland Springs church, Pittsburgh synagogue, Orlando, Las Vegas – American place names have become references to mass shootings and gun violence, attacks that occur too regularly to be blamed on 'lone wolves' taking advantage of lenient legislation.

Despite all of this abject violence, there is much consensus that climate change – specifically the prospect of a two degree rise in global temperatures – is the definitive issue of our time. Our age has been marked by natural disasters throughout the world – tsunamis in Japan and the Philippines, hurricanes and cyclones in Haiti, Vanuatu, Fiji and Puerto Rico, and fires in Indonesia, Brazil, California, Canada and Australia. The mainstream solution to the problem of climate change is informed by the Paris Agreement, a set of 'solutions' formulated by world leaders at a 2015 United Nations conference. The Agreement focuses on reducing carbon emissions to keep global warming under two degrees. Mainstream environmentalism is geared around achieving this by substituting fossil fuels for 'biofuels' and 'renewables' and encouraging investment in 'green' energy.

In his book, *The Green Zone: The Environmental Costs of Militarism* (2009), Barry Sanders explains why we cannot so easily divorce the issue of violence from climate change. He says that "the greatest single assault on the environment, on all of us around the globe, comes from one agency ... the Armed Forces of the United States."[296] Sanders points out that US military aircraft consume close to two million reported gallons of oil every day, and that,

> the Pentagon is the largest single consumer of petroleum in the world, using enough oil in one year to run all of the transit systems in the United States for the next 14 to 22 years ... The military also consumes one-quarter of the world's jet fuel ... The world's militaries combined are responsible for an astonishing two-thirds

---

296 Sanders, 2009, p. 78.

Chapter Four: Fatal Contradictions

of the ozone-depleting, greenhouse gas, chlorofluorocarbon, or CFC-113, released into the atmosphere.[297]

He writes that,

> even if every person, every automobile, and every factory suddenly emitted zero emissions, the Earth would still be headed first and at full speed toward total disaster for one major reason. The military – that voracious vampire – produces enough greenhouse gases, by itself, to place the entire globe, with all its inhabitants large and small, in the most imminent danger of extinction.[298]

Of course, it is not only jet fuel behind the environmental impacts of the military. It is the shooting, firing, exploding and incinerating; the chemical attacks, cluster bombs, cannon rounds, napalm and depleted uranium. Sanders points out that "targeted bombing involves blowing up highly volatile and extremely strategic sites like fuel and weapons depots, power plants, fertilizer plants, and chemical plants, releasing much more toxic waste into the atmosphere." All this causes air pollution, poisoned water, and contaminated produce, not to mention cancer, increased child mortality rates, and mass murder. Looking at the environmental impacts of militarism makes it impossible to sustain the false distinction between environmental destruction and violence. Sanders writes:

> How bizarre to think about installing "an environmentally sensitive culture" inside the military. We might then boast to the Iraqis: Notice how little fuel we consumed to destroy your homeland. The reasoning is absurd.[299]

Reflecting on this, I think of my university friend feeling so much responsibility for human destructiveness that she struggled to buy groceries. I think of Swedish climate change activist Greta Thunberg speaking with US television presenter Trevor Noah about the 'Greta

---

297 Sanders, 2009, p. 50.
298 Sanders, 2009, p. 22.
299 Sanders, 2009, p. 57.

Effect', the name for behaviour changes motivated by the desire to stop climate change. Noah asked Thunberg about how the Greta Effect changed her mother's life:

> Noah: Your mom is an opera singer, and she stopped flying, which means she couldn't perform the way she used to. Do you sometimes feel bad that she can't perform, or are you more excited that she's not part of, I guess, polluting the planet?
>
> Thunberg: I don't care, honestly, about how she performs. She's doing musicals now. So, I mean, she had to change career, but it wasn't that big.
>
> Noah: And the planet is the most important thing for you?
>
> Thunberg: Yeah, I mean – for all of us, I think, it should be.[300]

Thunberg is not wrong to suggest we should prioritise the planet, and I think the basic principle of not using what you don't need is excellent. However, a world where women feel shame and guilt about their diets, creative career ambitions, and need to make short car trips to buy groceries and collect children from school – because of a climate change issue largely driven by military and industrial behaviour – does *not* make sense to me. In fact, patriarchy and neoliberalism *rely* upon the model of guilt, shame, pressure, restricted movement, creative shrinking, and *general austerity for women* – and as Audre Lorde famously warned, "the master's tools will never dismantle the master's house."[301]

The link between climate change, violence and gender is also expressed through the issue of 'man camps'. Sanders points out that the Pentagon is the world's largest landlord, since the US military occupies approximately thirty million acres of land worldwide.[302] Feminists call military bases, as well as resource extraction sites like mines, 'man camps' for the obvious reason that

---

300 Noah, 2019.
301 Lorde, 1984, p. 110. Consider too that in the television adaptation of Margaret Atwood's dystopian novel *The Handmaid's Tale*, the rulers of Gilead boasted of their carbon neutral status.
302 Sanders, 2009, p. 36.

Chapter Four: Fatal Contradictions

they are overwhelmingly populated by men. In 2019, a Canadian National Inquiry on Missing and Murdered Indigenous Women was published and found,

> 'substantial evidence' that natural resource projects increase violence against Indigenous women and children, and that 'work camps', or 'man camps', associated with the resource extraction industry are implicated in higher rates of violence against Indigenous women at the camps and in the neighbouring communities.[303]

In Canada, Wet'suwet'en activists – who oppose a plan to clear forests and build a pipeline through their community in northern British Columbia – object not only to the environmental destruction but to the installation of 'man camps' in their community.

Protests against further environmental destruction continue. In 2016, Sioux protestors resisted the installation of the Dakota pipeline near Standing Rock Indian Reservation. By August 2019, Indigenous women were marching to protest Brazilian president, Jair Bolsonaro's, systematic burning of the Amazon, as reports of a record number of forest fires hit the mainstream media.

In the Netherlands, activist Raki Ap asks why, in a time of BLM protests and climate change strikes, people are not making clearer links between the two. Specifically, he wants to know how the simultaneous environmental destruction and genocide in his native West Papua can be ignored at a time where people around the world are apparently concerned about racism *and* climate change. He says, "If we had cared about the lives of the people of the Global South, and the lives of Indigenous peoples, we would not have had this climate crisis. It's that simple."[304] To me, the point Ap is making is not about guilt, but independent thinking. If today's anti-racist and climate change movements were truly sincere and *grassroots,* wouldn't they be more localised, diverse, and proactive about identifying and addressing urgent matters?

---

303 Office of the Wet'suwet'en, 2019.
304 Ap, 2021.

Out of the Fog: On politics, feminism and coming alive

Neither Ap, nor Vandana Shiva, are convinced that climate change can be reversed through technological solutions. In her 2007 book, *Soil Not Oil*, Shiva wrote about how demand for so-called 'green' energy is destroying rainforests, which are "being bulldozed to plant soy and palm."[305] At the time the book was published, 22.2 million hectares had been converted to soy plantations in Brazil, and 21 per cent of Brazil's cultivated area was soy. Between January 2003 and 2007, nearly 70,000 kilometres of the Amazon rainforest had been cleared for biofuel production.

The 2021 book *Bright Green Lies* is another text that questions the assumptions and primary objectives of 'bright greens', the new breed of environmentalists who hope that "green technology and design, along with ethical consumerism, will allow a modern, high-energy lifestyle to continue indefinitely."[306] The book fundamentally challenges the idea of 'green cities', and the 'false solutions' of solar and hydropower, wind farms, electric cars, industrial recycling, biofuels and 'green energy'.

The authors of *Bright Green Lies* note a transition away from the nature-focused environmentalism of figures like Rachel Carson, whose 1962 book *Silent Spring* informed readers about the harms of pesticides while celebrating the beauty and life-giving complexity of soil and water. Carson's writing is so clearly and beautifully driven by love of the living world. Nowadays, as outlined in *Bright Green Lies*, figures like Naomi Klein say that, "The polar bears? They still don't do it for me ... stopping climate change isn't really about them, it's about us."[307] Bill McKibben, founder of 350.org, writes about the "peril that civilisation is in" under headings such as 'Civilisation's Last Chance' as though civilisation, and not nature, is in danger.

In 2018, Thunberg became the face of the global climate movement. The tech company We Don't Have Time (partnered with Al Gore's Climate Reality Project) tweeted a photo of the then 15-year-old activist conducting a solitary protest outside the Swedish

---

305 Shiva, 2009, p. 82.
306 Jensen, Keith and Wilbert, 2021, p. xxi.
307 Jensen, Keith and Wilbert, 2021, p. 24.

parliament in August.[308] The photo was captioned with the words, 'Imagine how lonely she must feel'. Within a fortnight, Thunberg made the front page of a Swedish paper and the cover of *The Guardian* and, by January 2019, she addressed the World Economic Forum in Davos. There Thunberg famously declared that "solving the climate crisis is the greatest and most complex challenge that homo sapiens have ever faced." She added:

> Adults keep saying, "We owe it to the young people to give them hope." But I don't want your hope. I don't want you to be hopeful. I want you to panic. I want you to feel the fear I feel every day. And then I want you to act – I want you to act as you would in a crisis. I want you to act as if the house was on fire. Because it is.[309]

One year after the March for Our Lives – on 15 March, 2019 – young people from 2,000 cities worldwide joined another school walkout, this time inspired by Thunberg: the School Strike 4 Climate. This was a global campaign pitched as a way for children to hold adults to account by demanding they take action on climate change, specifically by calling for governments, businesses and political leaders to honour the Paris Agreement.

That is a day no New Zealander will forget. By lunchtime, students were gathered in town and city centres with coloured placards, drums, horns and whistles. Politicians from across the political spectrum addressed them. By the time they dispersed, the country's terrorist threat level had been raised to 'high' for the first time in history.

The Christchurch massacre

At 1.40 p.m., a 28-year-old Australian white supremacist named Brenton Tarrant emailed his 174-page manifesto 'The Great Replacement' to Parliamentary Services. He was standing outside Al Noor mosque in Christchurch, dressed in military garb and armed

---

308 Here I draw on the work of Morningstar, 2019.
309 Thunberg, 2019.

with an AR15 rifle. It was the hour of Friday prayer. After sending the email, Tarrant went inside the mosque and shot and killed 42 people, uploading a livestream to Facebook. When the Armed Offenders Squad arrived at 1.46 p.m., Tarrant had already left for the Linwood Islamic Centre. Police finally spotted and apprehended him 13 minutes later, after he had killed another seven people. One man died later, in hospital.

The people Tarrant murdered came from India, Egypt and the Middle East. Nine came from Pakistan, six from Palestine, and several were refugees – from Somalia, Syria and Afghanistan.

The day after the massacre, Prime Minister Ardern travelled to Christchurch to meet with Muslim leaders at a refugee resettlement centre. She offered financial assistance to the families, reassuring them that "this is not New Zealand," and that the country was "united in grief." She later tweeted:

> What has happened in Christchurch is an extraordinary act of unprecedented violence. It has no place in New Zealand. Many of those affected will be members of our migrant communities – New Zealand is their home – they are us.

The last three words became a catchphrase in the weeks and months to follow, a slogan to match widely shared images of Ardern in hijab.

Police patrolled mosques with semi-automatic rifles while New Zealand's terrorist threat level remained on 'high', and Ardern announced in parliament that she would refuse to say Tarrant's name. She said:

> He sought many things from his act of terror but one was notoriety, that is why you will never hear me mention his name. He is a terrorist. He is a criminal. He is an extremist. But he will, when I speak, be nameless.[310]

---

310 I have no problem with this tactic, but I think it can be followed to the point of superstition (especially in the context of a culture committed to sexual obfuscation and that refuses to discuss male violence plainly), where people get 'spooked' at the mention of a name, thereby paradoxically infusing the name with an almost supernatural 'power', as in the 1988 film *Beetlejuice*. Journalists and writers who wish to relay the facts of an event plainly are then accused

Chapter Four: Fatal Contradictions

Ardern received wide praise for this move, which created a taboo around any mention or report of Tarrant's name.

On 23 March 2019, before a panel discussion on NewsTalk ZB, Morgan Godfery tweeted "i'm on the panel tomorrow afternoon. who should I call out … give me names people." Screeds of names and lists of public figures who could be considered white supremacists were sent back.

Tarrant's livestream was taken offline, and by June, Philip Arps – a well-known Christchurch-based white supremacist – was sentenced to 21 months in prison for distributing the livestream to 31 people, and asking a friend for a 'kill count' to be added. Chief censor David Shanks also deemed Tarrant's manifesto objectionable, making it illegal to possess or share. Still, by November, journalist Annabel Hennessy reported in *The West Australian* that right-wing extremists were using video games like Minecraft and Grand Theft Auto to 'recreate' the Holocaust and the Christchurch massacre, and to offer mass shooting 'tips'.[311]

Ardern had donned the hijab not only to visit with Muslim leaders on 16 March but in public appearances in the week following the massacre. Several female broadcasters and television presenters followed her lead, and Auckland doctor Thaya Ashman declared a 'Headscarves for Harmony' day with approval from New Zealand's Islamic Women's Council and Muslim Association. An image of police officer Constable Michelle Evans stationed on patrol outside Christchurch Memorial Park Cemetery with a rose pinned to her uniform, wearing a hijab and armed with a rifle, also went viral online, receiving wide praise.

Ardern became a global icon. An image of her in hijab was projected onto the Burj Khalifa in Dubai, the world's tallest building,

---

of evoking this 'power' if they simply name the perpetrator, as if doing so is somehow tantamount to endorsing mass murder. There are also, of course, times when name suppression is considered in the opposite way: as a way of granting perpetrators unwarranted *protection*, as in the case of Grace Millane's killer Jesse Kempson. In any case, these questions seem to me to be a distraction from the more important task of examining the root causes of violence.

311 Hennessy, 2019.

accompanied by the word, 'peace'. Each day, many Saudi Arabian women walk past that building, their faces, bodies and identities censored by full burka. Ardern was praised in *The Washington Post* and ranked second in a *Fortune* magazine list of great world leaders, while Oprah Winfrey called on women to "channel our inner Jacindas."[312] Several articles echoed a message about Ardern's legitimisation of 'feminine' leadership.[313]

At the beginning of the COVID-19 crisis in April 2020, Ardern provided another example of such leadership: she announced that she would take a 20 per cent pay cut for six months "in solidarity" with frontline workers and those who lost their incomes because of COVID-19 and lockdowns. The pay cut was symbolic, of course. It did not represent a redistribution of wealth or directly improve anyone else's life. But many teachers, nurses, and hospitality workers are women, and Ardern's move functioned as a signal about the need to work harder and expect less, willingly.

It is important to note that widespread praise for 'feminine leadership' is not necessarily good news for women. Whether it involves promoting hijabs or pay cuts, it is not an automatic indicator that women are gaining status or respect in leadership or otherwise.

Here it is worth recalling the work of Cynthia Enloe, quoted in Chapter Three: "The politics of international debt won't work in their current form *unless* mothers and wives are willing to behave in ways that enable nervous regimes to adopt cost-cutting measures without forfeiting their political legitimacy."[314] Enloe's work shows how messages about femininity from political leaders are always designed to communicate expectations to women, especially in times of austerity.

---

312 *New Zealand Herald*, 2019.
313 Karlis, 2019, 'New Zealand Prime Minister Jacinda Ardern and the power of "feminine" leadership'; Karim and Krewel, 2019, 'Is there a "feminine" response to terrorism?' Rizvi, 2019, 'Jacinda Ardern just proved typically "feminine" behaviour is powerful'.
314 Enloe, 1989, pp. 184–5.

Following the Christchurch massacre, Ardern also took swift action on gun laws, bringing them under immediate review. This resulted in a ban on most semi-automatic firearms, and a buyback scheme for these guns was announced, while people began voluntarily turning in legal guns to police.

The owner of Gun City, David Tipple, admitted that his store sold four guns and ammunition to Tarrant, and that he resented the firearms debate. He said, "I don't see firearms as the villain. I see psychology as the villain."[315] Clearly, Tipple wanted to stay in business while he was in the spotlight following the massacre and revelations that Tarrant had ordered ammunition from his store. Yet there is truth to this assertion that *psychology* is the ultimate distinguishing feature of a killer, and this argument was also made by feminist Sophie Walker in *The Metro*. Walker wrote that "attacks like the Christchurch shooting won't stop until links between toxic masculinity and terror are recognised." She continued:

> The Manchester bomber punched a female classmate in the head because he disapproved of what she was wearing; the Charlottesville attacker had previously repeatedly beaten his mother and had threatened her with a knife; the London Bridge attacker had emotionally and physically abused his wife; the man behind the 2016 Orlando nightclub mass shooting had physically abused his wife on a regular basis.[316]

Three days after the Christchurch massacre, 37-year-old Gokmen Tanis shot eight people on a tram in the Dutch city of Utrecht, killing three of them. Tanis had been detained in 2017 on rape charges.

Commentators are generally more inclined to compare men like Tarrant with other racially and politically motivated mass murderers like Anders Breivik, who killed 69 participants of a Workers' Youth League (AUF) summer camp in Norway, in 2011. They do not tend to make the link to the likes of Elliot Rodger,

---

315 Duff, 2019.
316 Walker, 2019.

who killed seven people in Isla Vista in 2014 after making a video about how he wanted to punish women for rejecting him; or to Marc Lépine, who killed 14 women in the 1989 Montreal Massacre while yelling, "You're all a bunch of fucking feminists." Yet, as journalist Nellie Bowles and feminist author Robin Morgan noted in their responses to the massacre, the title of Tarrant's manifesto was a reference to replacement theory, as were the opening lines: "It's the birthrates, it's the birthrates, it's the birthrates." Morgan said:

> Sex is the first political point of agreement that a white supremacist recruiter online uses. Remember that they are approaching teenage and early twenties males who are preoccupied with sex anyway … Once a group of young men in an online forum agrees that declining white birthrates are an existential threat, then the conversation turns to policies.[317]

Consider that on the day of *his* attacks, Breivik electronically distributed a manifesto in which he called for the deportation of all Muslims from Europe, and blamed feminism for a European 'cultural suicide'. Do we have to guess at how this man got away with treating women, before his massacre in 2011?

After New Zealand's gun laws were changed, police commissioner Mike Bush announced that Armed Offenders Squad patrols will be trialled in the Canterbury district as well as Manukau and Waikato. On 18 October 2019, Bush explained:

> The Police's mission is that New Zealand is the safest country. Following the events of March 15 in Christchurch, our operating environment has changed … The introduction of ARTs [Armed Response Teams] improves our ability to respond to rapidly evolving events and incidents with highly-trained specialist skills and expertise, minimising risks to our people and the public.[318]

Ardern urged New Zealanders to do their bit in stopping the spread of "extremism" and "the viruses of hate, of fear" emphasising the

---

317 Morgan, 2019.
318 New Zealand Police, 2019.

role of social media. At a remembrance service in Christchurch on 29 March, she promised that "We will remember the tears of our nation," and read aloud words from the national anthem:

> From dissension, envy, hate
> And corruption, guard our state
> Make our country good and great
> God defend New Zealand

The same month, author Morgan Godfery, who is a prison abolitionist and BLM supporter, tweeted his request that Ardern "promises the full weight of the New Zealand state and society will come down upon every single white supremacist." Since 2014, BLM had been asking us to consider that the state and state institutions are fundamentally racist. Now, it seemed that one of the New Zealand Left's respected intellectuals was calling on the Prime Minister to act as a leader in the effort to dismantle white supremacy. This either meant that he, along with other progressives, had changed his mind on the role of the state in perpetuating racism – or that he was calling for her to initiate mutiny.

Another year later, and COVID-19 trumped all other considerations, from climate change to state and racial violence. In January 2020, the World Health Organisation declared the virus a "public health emergency of international concern," after it began spreading from its possible origin at a food market – or a lab? – in Wuhan, China. The coronavirus and the associated lockdowns ground everything to a halt.

By Thursday 26 March 2020, New Zealand had closed its borders, shops, and schools. Services deemed 'essential' were still operating, but the public was asked to stay home and remain two metres away from each other when "undertaking essential shops." Ardern clarified that there would be "no tolerance" for breach of orders, and that "the police and the military will be working together."

By 29 March, a journalist reported being stopped by a police officer while making a delivery. The officer did not accept his letter of permission. "All of a sudden my life and what I'm allowed to do, comes down to which officer happens to talk to me at that time," he wrote.[319]

Whistleblower Edward Snowden, whose work "triggered an international eruption of loathing toward the surveillance capitalists" in 2013, warned that governments are responding to COVID-19 by building the "architecture of oppression."[320] So much has changed in the political landscape since 2013, that this opinion now positions Snowden as a 'conspiracy theorist' among many of those who once defended him.

Speech

After the Christchuch massacre, the regulation of speech became just as contested as guns. By May 2019, an Auckland man began distributing anti-Muslim pamphlets to letterboxes. The pamphlets were brought to police for investigation. The bookshop franchise Whitcoulls temporarily banned the book *12 Rules for Life*, by clinical psychologist Jordan Peterson, famous for his status on the 'intellectual dark web'. Green Party politician Golriz Ghahraman spearheaded a call to fast track a review of New Zealand's hate speech laws.

This legislation already criminalises the incitement of racial disharmony, something that did nothing to stop Tarrant's clearly racially motivated social media activities and his planning of a terrorist attack two years in advance, with three months focused on the specific Christchurch location. Nevertheless, the Greens wanted not only to review, but to extend hate speech laws to protect religion, gender identity, and sexual orientation. This would have effectively criminalised feminism, by deeming the acknowledgement of biological sex 'hate' under law.

---

319 Manch and Devlin, 2020.
320 Zuboff, 2019, p. 511; Dowd, 2020.

Chapter Four: Fatal Contradictions

The Green Party's stance on what constitutes hate reflects the loyalties of the liberal left. They have historically spoken out to support the speech of whistleblowers like Snowden as well as WikiLeaks founder Julian Assange and former US army soldier Bradley 'Chelsea' Manning, all three of whom belong to a tradition of men opposing the conservative impulse to promote 'national security' at the expense of civil liberties and media freedom. In 2018, Ghahraman advocated for Manning to be allowed to enter New Zealand despite his criminal record. "What is it about her that would pose a risk to us?" asked Ghahraman. "She's done her time – do we say that she should be silenced forever?"[321]

It would be nice if the Green Party would ask the same questions about the feminists it seeks to silence indefinitely with hate speech laws that protect gender at women's expense. But liberals like the Greens are just as keen as anyone in politics to silence women, as well as their opponents.

In the UK in 2018, a man going by the name of Aimee Challenor ran to become Green Party deputy leader. He has referred to a critic of transgenderism as a 'cunt', and prides himself on having developed a mass-blocking tool on Twitter, with the handle @Blockterfs. In 2017, Challenor claimed the tool had rendered 50,000 people invisible on the timelines of those who wish not to witness critiques of transgenderism.[322]

Challenor withdrew his bid to become deputy leader following revelations that his father David, also a well-known Green Party figure, had served as his election agent.[323] The problem was not nepotism, but that David Challenor had been sentenced to 22 years in prison for raping, torturing, and electrocuting a ten-year-old girl. During the criminal trial, the girl testified that David dressed as a little girl or a baby in a nappy during the torment, which took place in 2015 at a house used as an official Green Party address.

---

321 1news, 2018a.
322 Campbell, 2018.
323 In the UK, an election agent is legally responsible for the conduct of a candidate's political campaign.

Aimee knew about this and was not suspended. Journalist Julie Bindel writes:

> The Green Party did, however, take swift action when it suspended Olivia Palmer earlier this year, who stood as a candidate in the 2015 and 2017 General Elections, because she "misgendered" transwoman Munroe Bergdorf during a TV debate, Genderquake. Bergdorf has previously referred to a woman as "hairy barren lesbians" and insulted another as a "butch lezza."[324]

Neither the concept of 'free speech', nor hate speech laws, are designed to protect women. If we were to define the basic concepts of the free speech versus hate speech debate on feminist terms, it would look like this: *freedom* is a world without rape. *Hate* is the promotion of rape. In Andrea Dworkin's words, "Rape is widespread. One characteristic of rape is that it silences women."[325] *Silencing* is the fear, intimidation and exclusion from the public sphere that women experience in a rape culture. As Susan Hawthorne writes in her book *Bibliodiversity: A Manifesto for Independent Publishing*:

> Censorship is not only the straightforward culling and banning of the words of writers and artists, and the imprisonment, torture or killing of those who utter rebellious words. It also ventures into the realm of social conditioning. In *Pornography and Silence* (1982), Susan Griffin makes the connection between the violence of pornography and women's silence. She argues that the silence is as much internal as external. This is also the case for colonised peoples in general.[326]

What's more, "Free speech, when resorted to by Rupert Murdoch or a pornographer, silences those who do not have media empires behind them."[327] Looking at the world from women's perspective requires that we rethink the meaning of freedom, hate, speech, and silence.

---

324 Bindel, 2018.
325 Dworkin, 1988, p. 223.
326 Hawthorne, 2014, p. 47.
327 Hawthorne, 2014, p. 47.

Chapter Four: Fatal Contradictions

Traditionally, the phrase 'free speech' is a reference to the First Amendment of the US Constitution, which prevents the government from making laws restricting speech. Dworkin pointed out that both the Constitution and First Amendment were – like the *Declaration of Independence* – written by white male landowners who owned black slaves and women as chattel. The First Amendment was never intended to grant people the right to a public voice, but to protect those who already have one. There are two problems with this for feminists: one is that feminism *does* seek to move the voices of women out of the private sphere and into the public, so it does require that women *gain* the capacity to speak where it is not granted. In this effort, the First Amendment is of little use. As Dworkin said:

> The First Amendment is now being used in an almost metaphoric way for freedom of speech as though ... [it] protects everybody's right to speech and it doesn't. It's not a grant to individuals of a right to speak. If it were, you would be able to go to the government and you would be able to say, "I need four minutes on NBC ..."[328]

What's more, when women face backlash for supposedly speaking out of turn in private and public (as I have done), Dworkin says:

> It doesn't stop a man from punching you out for what you said ... It doesn't stop anybody from using economic recriminations against you for what you say. It doesn't stop anybody from deciding you're an uppity bitch because of what you say and they're going to hurt you because you said something that they didn't like.[329]

In fact, 'free speech' can be used to defend this behaviour, which leads us to the second problem with the First Amendment: it supports men's impunity, and encourages activists to redirect support towards some of the most vile political actors. As a result, Dworkin comments:

---

328 Dworkin, 1990/1997, p. 205.
329 Dworkin, 1990/1997, p. 204.

> They have convinced many of us that the standard for speech is what I would call a Repulsion Standard. That is to say, we find the most repulsive person in the society and we defend them. I say we find the most powerless people in the society – and we defend *them*.[330]

For those who promote free speech in the 'metaphoric' sense, not taking the limitations of the First Amendment for granted, the phrase becomes even more ambiguous. Not just the government, but even private companies and the public are expected to protect freedom of speech. Many free speech advocates are unclear about their views on the status of protest itself: sometimes they consider protests, like rallies and picket lines, a form of speech that should be protected. Other times, protest represents *objection* to speech that the government should intervene in. Sometimes *harassment* is framed as protest and then defended in the name of 'free speech'. It seems to depend on which side they are on.

David Seymour, New Zealand's libertarian ACT party leader, is a free speech advocate. He defends feminists who challenge transgenderism in the name of free speech, but he has also defended campaigners harassing women at an abortion clinic using the same catchcry. Because, as Hawthorne writes, "the word 'free' is ambiguous" and "the term 'free speech' sounds innocuous" it can be used to justify almost *anything* in politics.[331] It becomes a vehicle for anyone's agenda, anyone who wants to promote their own interests while building support from other political actors.

Think of the contradiction with Seymour: if conservatives have a right to harass women at abortion clinics, don't women have a right to tell them to fuck off and leave us alone? Would Seymour defend that response on the grounds of free speech too (if so, why defend both sides of a neverending argument)? Or would he consider it an action *against* free speech? Free speechers simply draw these lines as they see fit.

---

330 Dworkin, transcribed from a video recording now removed from YouTube.
331 Hawthorne, 2014, p. 39.

Chapter Four: Fatal Contradictions

Many people who promote free speech sincerely – including feminists – are really making a plea for tolerance and civil discourse. These people are asking us, culturally, to develop our capability to deal with disagreement or difference through debate and conversation, rather than hostility and mudslinging. They underestimate the problem: an inability to disagree civilly is not what divides us. Rape is what divides us. Rape, the fetishisation of violence, objectification, brutality, fear, identification, denial, projection, blame. Promoting 'tolerance' understates the madness we live with. And when this leads people to promote 'free speech', and thus buy into an associated 'Repulsion Standard', it not only constitutes a significant departure from the project of ending rape, it can lead feminists to the bizarre position of defending both the whistleblower and the perpetrator at once.

This happened when Canadian feminist and founder of website *Feminist Current*, Meghan Murphy, filed a lawsuit against Twitter after having her account removed in 2019. When Trump also had his account deleted, Murphy argued that "It's not a good thing that Trump was banned from Twitter" because "free speech isn't just for one side … it's for all sides."[332] So is freedom itself, of course: it is for everyone. The feminist argument is that freedom for everyone requires the end of rape, and we can only arrive there by purposefully amplifying the voices of women, even if that means men get less airtime. As Hawthorne says,

> 'free speech'… indeed is frequently made to sound important to a state of social freedom, but when one looks a little closer, 'whose' freedom counts, becomes the determining factor of whether it really represents the idea of 'freedom'.[333]

This is what both Freire and Dworkin taught. Environmentalist poet Will Falk makes this point beautifully too, in a poem he wrote while living at Thacker Pass in Nevada as part of an occupation to stop lithium mining there. The poem is called 'First, There's the World',

---

332 Murphy, 2021.
333 Hawthorne, 2014, p. 39.

and echoes Dworkin's point that freedom of speech begins with integrity of the body. It asks:

> For what is poetry without the voice?
> and what is the voice
> if not for the world that makes the voice possible?[334]

I'm sure Falk, whose work currently revolves around protecting the wildlife at Thacker Pass from being bulldozed for profit, would agree that to arrive at the world in which speech is truly free – that is, a world without rape or coercion – male elites will have to withstand losing more than their Twitter accounts.

Feminism as Reform

Many of the feminists who promote 'free speech' in the face of misogynist accusations of 'transphobia' are part of the new 'gender critical' trend, represented by reformist lobbies like A Woman's Place UK. These campaigns call for governments to protect the interests of all women (or 'female people', as we are now sometimes called), and the work involves strategic public advocacy, branding, slogans, flyers and merchandise. As British radical feminist Julia Long writes in an article titled 'A Meaningful Transition?', these groups are premised more on negotiation and bargaining with external power than Freire's call for 'humanisation'. Long writes,

> … the British gender critical movement has shown very little willingness to reject wholesale the pernicious language of transgenderism. High-profile groups such as A Woman's Place UK (WPUK) and Fair Play for Women insist that they are in favour of the rights of 'trans people', habitually use the terms 'trans woman' or 'transwoman', and use 'she' pronouns for men who demand it. Paradoxically then, much of what is written and spoken in the name of British gender critical feminism in fact does the

---

334 Falk, 2021.

ideological work of transgenderists for them, promulgating their fictions as legitimate and valid through speaking their language.[335]

Long notes that in 2018, two male cross-dressers – Kristina Jayne Harrison and Debbie Hayton – spoke at a third of all WPUK events between them. The reason is not a mystery: one of Harrison's talks is the second most popular of all the talks on the WPUK YouTube channel. WPUK justifies these men's participation as a matter of 'kindness', since they have undergone a 'meaningful transition'. This leaves women like Long – who do not accept the idea that some transgenderism is 'meaningful' – lumped with the stigma of being 'unkind'. This replicates patriarchal dynamics of 'niceness', repression and avoidance of guilt-by-association discussed in Chapter Two. Freire also warned that when campaigners silence those among the oppressed to keep up appearances:

> Each time they say their word without hearing the word of those they have forbidden to speak, they grow more accustomed to power and acquire a taste for guiding, ordering and commanding.[336]

In Freire's work, the urge to make liberation into a 'campaign' is a pitfall. To him, revolutionary 'praxis' involves revolutionary leaders and members of an oppressed class learning to decipher the 'limit situation' they face, through critical reflection and dialogue that leads to transformative action infused with the goal of *humanisation*. This action changes a situation, which is the goal – for people to transform reality together, not to try to influence one another with slogans.

For Freire, this work is necessarily grassroots and collaborative. It is not premised on any quest for external power, whether through negotiation with authority figures or popularity. Someone becomes a 'revolutionary leader' because they are committed to the task of humanisation, not because of title or formal appointment. He writes:

---

335 Long, 2020.
336 Freire, 1970, p. 115.

After all, the task of the humanists is surely not that of pitting their slogans against the slogans of the oppressors, with the oppressed as the testing ground, 'housing' the slogans of first one group and then the other. On the contrary, the task of the humanists is to see that the oppressed become aware of the fact that as dual beings, 'housing' the oppressors within themselves, they cannot be truly human.[337]

I experienced the same dynamic that Julia Long identifies. On Christmas Day in 2016, I set up an online group for people who shared my concerns about transgenderism and prostitution in New Zealand. By mid-year 2018, the group included about 50 people, most of whom I knew offline. I left the group at that time, because I wanted to reduce my time on social media and have smaller and more focused conversations. After this, members of the group formed a public lobby called Speak Up For Women (SUFW), which campaigns to challenge (though not definitively oppose) sex self-identification laws.

SUFW would not associate with me. At their first public event, the spokeswoman gave a talk in which she included a generous acknowledgement: "Thanks to Renée, for bringing us all together and sending us on our way."[338] After this, the lobby's decision to act as if I do not exist became more decisive, while they have happily worked alongside Seymour and Labour Party MP Louisa Wall, who had publicly exclaimed that she does not want "fucking TERFs at the Pride Parade" in 2018. SUFW's website claims that the group started after they "met each other online," as if by accident. Reading such lines felt like my years of organising were dumped into one of the 'memory holes' used to incinerate records in George Orwell's *Nineteen Eighty Four*.

To me, the real threat gender poses is in the way it isolates. As transgender ideology spreads, it alienates and dehumanises women while shoring up old and fundamental patriarchal positions

---

337 Freire, 1970, p. 76.
338 O'Brien, 2020.

Chapter Four: Fatal Contradictions

in the culture at large. For years, I felt that this tactic of gaslighting, shaming and alienating women who dissent was the most crucial thing for feminists to resist. I felt that building grassroots solidarity that broke down women's isolation was much more important than seeking popular appeal or high-powered allies, and that is what I worked towards.[339]

This approach comes down to recognising transgenderism as a backlash, a 'countermove'. As Harriet Lerner writes, "Our job is to keep clear about our own position in the face of a countermove – not to prevent it from happening or to tell the other person that he or she should not be reacting that way." She says:

> It *is* our job to state our thoughts and feelings clearly and to make responsible decisions that are congruent with our values and beliefs. It is *not* our job to make another person think and feel the way we do or the way we want them to. If we try, we can end up in a relationship in which a lot of personal pain and emotional intensity are being expended and nothing is changing.[340]

What Lerner calls keeping "clear about our own position," is what Freire calls "adhesion to freedom," and it is the basis of liberation movements. The power of second wave feminism lay in a commitment to freedom and longing for sisterhood so deep that its visionaries could not be seduced by external power. The great works of that moment, like *Sister Outsider* and *Gyn/Ecology;* poems like *The Dream of a Common Language* and *Monster*, demonstrate this. For Women's Liberationists, as for Freire, authentic power, individual freedom, and collective liberation were not separable, neither did they require approval from husbands, fathers, politicians or journalists.

In *The Creation of Feminist Consciousness* (1993), Gerda Lerner also laments the tragedy that the urge to negotiate, being so ingrained in

---

339 Gerlich, 2019a.
340 Lerner, 1989, p. 39. In his poem 'Half is Never Enough', Khalil Gibran wrote, "If you refuse then be clear about it / for an ambiguous refusal / is but a weak acceptance."

women, means that we have been doing precisely that for the 5,000 years that patriarchy has existed. She writes:

> This ultimate consequence of men's power to define – the power to define what is a political issue and what is not – has had a profound effect on women's struggle for their own emancipation. Essentially, it has forced thinking women to waste much time and energy on defensive arguments; it has channelled their thinking into narrow fields; it has retarded their coming into consciousness as a collective entity and has literally aborted and distorted the intellectual talents of women for thousands of years.[341]

The implication here is that it is *precisely the habit of negotiation that feminism – allegiance to freedom for women – challenges us to break.* In Freire's words:

> The oppressed have been destroyed precisely because their situation has reduced them to things. In order to regain their humanity they must cease to be things and fight as men and women. This is a radical requirement. They cannot enter the struggle as objects in order *later* to become human beings.[342]

By September 2019, SUFW announced that it would be holding an event at Massey University called 'Feminism 2020', marketed as a chance to "hear the feminists they don't want you to hear, uncensored." The event took place in the very city I had been trying to speak for four years. While it was organised by people I knew, I found out about it along with the public – when it was advertised. One speaker was flown in especially from Canada at great expense, and she and three other speakers were shown in the promotional posters with taped mouths to represent silencing. I have never felt as invisible in my life as I did that month. I felt ghost-like; not real.

While as a child I had always found Athena and her owl compelling when I turned to myths and stories to make sense of the world; in 2019, I became drawn to exiled women like Circe,

---

341 Lerner, 1993, p. 10.
342 Freire, 1970, p. 50.

Chapter Four: Fatal Contradictions

Medusa and Cassandra, looking for what they could teach me about ostracism.

In the myth of Cassandra, she was a princess from the city of Troy with many suitors, including the gods Zeus and Apollo. Apollo gives Cassandra the gift of prophecy to try and seduce her, and is outraged when she continues to reject him. He spits in her mouth (probably a euphemism) and puts a curse on her: *Cassandra, you will remain clairvoyant, but now, no one will believe you.* As time goes by in the story, Cassandra foresees many things including the sacking of Troy and the death of her brothers, but the curse holds. Nobody believes her, and the experience of being met with doubt every time she speaks the truth eventually drives her mad.

To me, this myth speaks to the female experience of growing up and trying to maintain a semblance of self-determination while confronting the realities of sexual harassment and male entitlement. These realities form patterns, and based on those patterns, women can make predictions. These predictions are normally unconscious, made by our nervous systems as they sound the alarm when we encounter something we recognise as a stressor based on earlier experience. What makes a woman a feminist is simply that she becomes conscious of these patterns. She gains the ability to watch and name patterns of male entitlement in her personal life and in society, and this allows her to make predictions … that most people would not believe. As Hawthorne writes, Cassandra "was an ancient feminist with the same problem of being disbelieved that many feminists face."[343]

In the original myth, Cassandra's predicament drove her mad. In 2019, it was easy for me to see why. I was a woman trying to speak and being censored and disbelieved at every turn. I could find no organisation or legal mechanism – and very few individuals – that could relate to my position. Bringing people together who *did* understand felt a bit like building a life raft, and after being thrown off the raft, I carried a sinking feeling around for many weeks.

---

343 Hawthorne, 2020, p. 9.

It scared me to think that this state of rejection and invisibility would be my life for the foreseeable future, and that I had reached a point where there was little I could do about it.

Massey University cancelled SUFW's 'Feminism 2020' event, citing "health, safety and wellbeing obligations" and its "duty of care to its community."[344] By 2021, SUFW were organising public events around the country, some of which were also cancelled, including two public library events. An event at Wellington's Michael Fowler Centre went ahead despite being protested by hundreds of people – one source claiming that more than a thousand protestors rallied.[345] In a city of only 200,000, that number is extraordinary, and I commend the bravery of a small group of women standing up to such a crowd. At the same time, the protests seemed to show that the strategy of discarding me had not helped this group to become palatable and well-treated after all. I sometimes wondered if they still felt that trading in solidarity for likeability had been worth it.

My own priority became learning how to face the world as an individual with little chance of finding the sort of community I once thought I could. After I stopped trying to argue my case, or redeem the situation, I had to confront being on my own. I found inspiration in many places, including a passage in feminist author Vicki Noble's book *Shakti Woman* (1991). Noble describes a breakthrough she had in her marriage to her psychologist husband Jonathan, with whom she spent the first three years of married life frequently arguing – incidentally, about the concept of 'the feminine'. Jonathan held a sort of 'yin' concept of the feminine as being watery and receptive, whereas for Noble, 'the feminine' was more like the Indian goddess Kali, fierce and arresting. Noble felt betrayed at the idea that her husband held this belief that she felt minimised her very existence. Then, one night, she dreamt the title and structure of *Shakti Woman*:

> This healing dream freed me from the futile arguments …
> It redirected me in a clear and unmistakable way onto my own

---

344 Long, 2019.
345 Crossland, 2021.

path of choosing to honour my own authority and to encourage other women to do the same. My need for Jonathan's approval lessened in the face of the compelling suggestion from my own unconscious that I communicate the truth of my experience to the world rather than argue with him about it in our tiny arena of the couple.[346]

Isn't feminism this very breakthrough, writ large?

---

346 Noble, 1991, p. 2.

CONCLUSION

Cassandra's Power

Care about people's approval and you will be their prisoner.
—Lao Tzu, Tao Te Ching[347]

With what shall we replace this figment, this dream of 'equality'? I suggest that it was part of a long and ancient nightmare and that we just let it go. It needs no replacement. Feminist anarchy is simple: self-love resulting in love of others out of which springs behaviour in the best interests of everyone. To some that sounds impossible. But it is not nearly so complicated, not nearly so difficult to maintain, as patriarchy, and it is home to the human heart, where it longs to go, where it knows it is possible to go, where, guided by the rising of women out of self-hatred and out of our consequent facilitation of men's destructiveness, it is heading at the speed of light.
—Sonia Johnson, Wildfire[348]

Liberation is thus a childbirth, and a painful one. The man or woman who emerges is a new person, viable only as the oppressor-oppressed contradiction is superseded by the humanisation of all people.
—Paulo Freire, Pedagogy of the Oppressed[349]

I want a wild politics.
—Susan Hawthorne, Wild Politics[350]

In her book *Soil Not Oil*, Vandana Shiva conceives of external versus authentic power in the language of a 'mechanistic paradigm' opposed to the 'living energies' of nature personified by the

---

347 Tzu/Mitchell, 2015, p. 8.
348 Johnson, 1989, p. 109.
349 Freire, 1970, p.31.
350 Hawthorne, 2002/2022, p. 375.

goddess Shakti. In a chapter titled 'Unleashing Shakti: Our Power to Transform', she writes that, "In the dominant paradigm, 'energy' refers to oil and coal, which are mined from the earth," whereas,

> energy is Shakti – the primordial power of creation, the self-organising, self-generative, self-renewing creative force of the universe ... Shakti comes from the root 'sak', meaning 'the capacity to do', 'to have power'. Shakti is power. Shakti is force. Shakti is the personification of primordial energy ... and potentialities of nature. The universe is an expression of Shakti and an infinite reservoir of power.[351]

When feminist anarchist Sonia Johnson reflects on the same contrast between external and authentic power, she concludes that the existence of both means that women are not marginalised under patriarchy purely by virtue of involuntary exclusion and exploitation. We are indeed excluded by nature:

> Power is the generative, positive stuff of life ... Since genuine power stems from integrity and can exist only in the presence of integrity, women cannot possibly have power in men's misogynist system (and of course men, being misogynist, cannot have power either) ...
>
> To me this means in reality I am excluded from patriarchy not by the fact of men's control but by my own women's values, my own perspectives, my own female way of being human in the world. These values, these perspectives, these ways make patriarchy alien to me and to all women, put us physically, emotionally, and spiritually outside their system. Outside their system, then, is where we genuinely live and have our being; any other notion is pure illusion.[352]

This might all seem abstract or esoteric if Vicki Noble had not provided us with a perfect example of what a leap from external to authentic power looks like. She switched from trying to improve her own life by changing her husband's mind by arguing with him

---

351 Shiva, p. 134, p. 136.
352 Johnson, 1989, p. 87.

repeatedly about a 'supposedly intellectual' issue, to channelling her views and her impulse to speak into the effort of writing a book on the topic for the world to read.

This, too, is the essence of Harriet Lerner's teaching in *The Dance of Anger* – that even, perhaps especially, when we are the victim in a situation, we must claim creative *response-ability* if we want change. 'Response-ability' is yet another expression of 'authentic power'. Wherever we do not have the capacity to change another person or situation, we still have the capacity to act on our own feelings, our own vision, and *respond*.

Feminists often resist the idea of talking about the responsibility of women, or of victims, for good reason. The reason is that there is no shortage of narratives about 'responsibility' in the public realm. The 'bootstraps' narratives we are so used to don't help, only exacerbate feelings of guilt, shame, and inadequacy. So to clarify what I mean by the term, let's imagine that Noble's husband was not gentle (as she reassured readers), but aggressive and condescending in his opinions about femininity. The fact that Noble has *response-ability* for her own needs and views would not imply that she is to be blamed for his arguments, aggression, or the situation itself. It simply means that a shift from external to authentic power is not only *possible* for her regardless of her husband's behaviour – it is key to her own liberation regardless of his behaviour.

Cassandra

I learned this lesson for myself when I was 'abandoned', for lack of a better term, by the feminist community that I helped bring together. Losing this group was a personal nightmare, because I had no more ideas about how to find or build a support network. I felt quarantined, like Circe on the island of Aeaea, or Cassandra finding no one to believe her. I felt I could not reach people, and it gave me a surreal sense of not really existing in any way that was corroborated by others – only *I* knew who I was, and that nothing about me warranted banishment to obscurity. That nobody else could or would confirm it made me feel like a ghost, my real self completely invisible to the outside world.

It was grief that taught me the difference between external and authentic power. I became angry and frustrated with the feminists who left me behind because they felt it would help them cultivate relationships with politicians, broadcasters, and journalists. Of course, every feminist wants to live in a world in which feminism is popular: but to me, making it so required solidarity, grassroots consciousness raising, and breaking down the walls of the 'private sphere' that segregate women from each other. It did not mean leaving 'undesirable' women – in this case, me – behind, to cultivate a more appealing public image.

At first, I tried to explain this in political terms, but when I was ignored, I grieved, and like all emotions do, grief brought me images. It showed me pictures of women I knew, gathering together without me, in the name of feminism, but it also brought me images of myself. I saw myself sitting alone, on top of my bed, asking questions, looking for answers, reading, taking notes, writing, writing, writing – I saw my innocence and dedication. My point here is not to argue for that innocence, or to appear pitiful in the in the face of 'villainous' women or suggest that nobody offered me friendship. It's that my grief seemed to have a purpose: to focus my attention on parts of me that no one else would ever see or protect on my behalf, and show me the pain of allowing these parts to go neglected.

When I became conscious of all of this, it changed me. For years, I had seen myself as a sort of generic 'woman', one among many, trying to act on behalf of us all. My intention was always to act in solidarity with women worst affected by patriarchal oppression. I believed that once there was a group around me, this kind of solidarity would extend to me. I thought that was the idea: feminism exists to end rape by undermining women's alienation and relegation to the 'private sphere'. To this end, we act in solidarity, amplify each other's voices, and make sure that even if that innocent and dedicated woman inside us all is ignored and trashed by the whole world, she will not be ignored and trashed by *us*. This was my understanding.

Grief showed me that however hard I may have tried to turn myself into an embodiment of the feminist cause, a representative of the interests of an entire 'sex class', I *do*, in fact, care about myself and my own, individual life. It also showed me that no one else was going to care about my life *for* me. If I felt that the dedicated woman I am was not being done justice, I was going to have to be the first one to remedy the situation. So I took all my attention away from short-term, reactive projects and social media, and focused it on slower burning, creative ones that I felt would honour not only a cause, but my own time and energy, even if the work was never recognised by others.

Another helpful image I saw in my mind's eye, as I worked through grief and anger, was the image of a staircase. In the picture, the wealthiest people with the most influence in the world were at the top of the staircase. They were conservatives, clutching to their position. A step below were the liberals, arguing for why they should be on top. Another step below were individual politicians I could recognise, like Seymour, Wall, and the Greens. A step below them was the left, and government-funded women's organisations, and below them, Speak Up For Women, trying to get the attention of those on the steps above. On the bottom stair was me, trying to be heard by Speak Up For Women.

This image showed me how ridiculous my position was, and the irony of being angry with a group of people for seeking external power instead of solidarity. I saw that in needing the group so badly, I was seeking external power too, just from an even more helpless and demoralised position. I was seeking attention from them, while they were seeking the attention of political representatives who were seeking the attention of the public in order to gain votes, influence, notoriety, and move up the staircase. I saw that the only reason I could be stuck in this position was if I was seeking the same thing everyone else was: external power. The horrifying indignity of this image broke the spell the second I saw it. I knew that if I had any character or integrity, I would get off the staircase.

I also asked myself, what had compelled the group to abandon feminist principles for the sake of popularity? Only one answer made sense to me: feminine socialisation. The need for approval and validation that lodges itself in the psyche and manifests continuously as intense social pressure. At first it seemed counterintuitive to me that this would explain things, because this feminist group had all the intellectual and moral resources needed to *resist* such impulses, which was indeed what they purported to do. But it was at this time that I learned the lesson conveyed in Chapter Two, that *identification trumps intellect*. Neither education nor politicisation automatically change our conditioned habits. Needless to say, this is true for me also.

At first, this realisation scared me, because it implied that I could not trust anyone, even people with whom I seemed to share understanding. One implication of all this was that I had to get real about my capacity at the scale of one. I had to untangle my feelings of moral duty and obligation from my actual response-ability, and to learn the true meaning of *acceptance*. For instance, as an individual, I of course cannot 'end rape'. I cannot 'smash the patriarchy'. If rape is society's core problem, I cannot do much about it. I cannot even stop *one man* from doing it, if he has the intent. I cannot ensure that he is held to account. I cannot stop anyone from promoting rape through objectification, or ignoring it when it should be addressed. Nothing I say or do can change anyone else's behaviour. Being unable to 'get' a group of feminists to hear my plea for solidarity taught me that definitively, through experience. The filmmaker Nina Paley puts it this way: "It all comes down to this. Can people change? Yes. Can you change them? No."[353]

This turned out to be a healthy and valuable lesson. If I had become a dedicated hiker rather than a feminist, I would have at some stage had to learn the same lesson: if I go on a bush expedition

---

353 From a public Facebook post made on 16 November, 2019.

with a group, just because there are people around me does not mean I should unconsciously rely on them for my safety. This is not cynicism, and it does not amount to a belief that if I fall into a ditch, no one will come to my aid. It just means that I need to be the one to watch my step, carry a First Aid Kit, and know how to dress a wound. However much we crave solidarity and belonging, we must contend with our own lives like they are just that: ours. There is nothing new about this revelation, I just came to it in an unconventional way, and a bit late.

I finally saw the truth that I must accept what I cannot change. I had to let go of my inflated sense of moral duty and focus instead on response-ability. And not only on my responses to the most awful aspects of human existence, but to life as a whole – my *real, felt* life, that which I love. As Hawthorne writes, "[r]ape works to increase and substantiate women's feelings of powerlessness."[354] I may not be able to do anything about rape, but I *can* dream of a world without it. And I *can* use that vision to act, and address my own sense of powerlessness. In other words: I may not be responsible, but I *can* respond.

In short, grief helped me begin to shift from fruitlessly trying to change what is outside me, to acting on what is inside me. For me, this was the value of the Cassandra experience, which author Carol Christ calls "the experience of nothingness." In being cut off from access to external power of any kind, I had no choice but to discover the alternative. I was invited to discover authentic power – that which cannot be taken or denied. In her book *Diving Deep and Surfacing*, Christ explores the way that this shift takes place in women's fiction writing. She discusses how violation, self-negation, and social and cultural invisibilisation compound to "the experience of nothingness" among women, and says that among many female protagonists of feminist fiction,

> the experience of nothingness often precedes an awakening, similar to a conversion experience, in which the powers of being

---

354 Hawthorne, 2019, p. 60.

are revealed. A woman's awakening to great powers grounds her in a new sense of self and a new orientation in the world. Through awakening to new powers, women overcome self-negation and self-hatred and refuse to be victims.[355]

The Shift

I call this 'awakening' The Shift. In *Know My Name* (2019), Chanel Miller writes about her experience of awakening, of how her attitude to court processes transformed from rule abiding negotiation with representatives of external power, to something much more anarchic:

> Throughout the legal process, I felt like I was always trying to keep up, to not mess up, learn court jargon, pay attention, follow the rules. I wanted to fit in and prove I could do what was expected of me. It had never occurred to me that the system itself could be wrong, could be changed or improved.[356]

In other words, "I wanted to fix everything, straighten it out one by one. Explain explain explain. But this defensiveness would carry over into my regular life."[357] After a merciless cross examination in which Miller's answers are constantly interrupted and struck from the record, she writes:

> I lost it, throwing open my arms, pleading, *I didn't know where my sister was. I didn't know where I was* ... I let go, emptying my lungs into the grape-sized microphone. Guttural sounds crawled out of my throat, long and loud. I didn't collect myself, didn't take my little sip of water, didn't daintily dab at the tips of my eyes, didn't say, *I'm okay*, just decided, you will wait for as long as it takes. This is it, everybody. Here it is, you did it.
>
> Not a single person in the room knew what to do with this unhinged wailing. But I had finally come to the end of an answer without interruption. I felt manic, it was intoxicating, everyone

---

355 Christ, 1980, p. 13.
356 Miller, 2019, p. 139.
357 Miller, 2019, p. 49.

forced to swallow my siren sounds. *Calm, collected, centred, strong, bullshit,* I abandoned all of it, had no intention of stopping, had lost the little voice that told me to reel it in, could only think release, release, release.[358]

Reflecting on the shift she underwent, Miller says, "[k]icking and screaming is not a sign you have lost your mind. It's a sign you have stepped onto your own side. You are learning, finally, how to fight back. Rage had arrived to burn the timidness away."[359]

In her book *Untamed*, author Glennon Doyle offers another illustration of The Shift, and the role of rage in reclaiming power. She tells the story of leaving her husband Craig, after trying to redeem their marriage when he was repeatedly unfaithful. As her anger waxed and waned, she began to observe it carefully. She saw that it flared when she was physically or emotionally intimate with Craig, and eased when she watched him with the children. At first, this made her feel confused and inconsistent, and she assumed that forgiveness would eventually come to her if she was patient. Then, one evening, Doyle was sitting on her living room couch with Craig, and she was silently fuming. Meanwhile, he was oblivious, enjoying the TV show. She recalls:

> All the fire was in me. None in him. I thought, 'How can this anger be about him? He can't even feel it … If this anger is in me, I am going to assume it is *for* me.' I decided to stop being ashamed and afraid of my anger, to stop being ashamed and afraid of myself.
>
> From that moment on, whenever anger arose, I practised staying open and curious … I noticed that anger flooded my body whenever I opened myself up to Craig emotionally or physically. My anger lifted completely when I watched him with the children. Before I started paying close attention, I thought this meant that I was flip-flopping. But over time, I began to understand that my anger wasn't arbitrary. It was incredibly specific. My anger was repeating, 'Glennon, for you, familial intimacy with Craig is safe. Physical and emotional intimacy are not.' I knew this. My body

---

358 Miller, 2019, p. 166.
359 Miller, 2019, p. 222.

knew this. And I had been ignoring what I knew. *That* is why I was so angry. I was angry at myself ...

... Eventually, I decided to stop abandoning myself, which meant honouring my anger. I didn't need to prove to anyone else whether leaving was right or wrong. I didn't need to justify my anger anymore. What I needed to do was forgive the father of my children. I was able to do that as soon as I divorced him.[360]

Feminism of all varieties is full of such anarchic shifts. Indeed, the third chapter of Gerda Lerner's book *The Creation of Feminist Consciousness* (which is the first chapter on the history of feminism) is called 'Self-authorisation'. The chapter essentially asserts that western feminism began when individual mediaeval feminist mystics began to simply *claim* authentic power, despite mediaeval European notions that "women are born inferior, have a weaker mind and intellect, are more subject to emotions and sexual temptations than men and that they need to be ruled by men."[361]

In the anthology *Societies of Peace: Matriarchies Past, Present and Future* (2009), Zapotecan shaman Dona Enriqueta Contreras advocates for self-authorisation when she writes, "Women must take back their authority," referring to the authority women possessed within matriarchal cultures.[362] This statement echoes Vajra Ma's assertion, in *From a Hidden Stream: The Natural Spiritual Authority of Women* (2016), that matriarchal cultures recognised women's 'natural spiritual authority'. Ma clarifies that this authority is not about external power, superiority or dominance – rather, *to author* means *to create*. "A life-giving source authors life, naturally," she writes. "Authority thus is an inherent part of life-giving, of authorship ... Authority is where life comes from."[363] True, undistorted authority is synonymous with creativity, with response-ability.

---

360 Doyle, 2020, pp. 261–2.
361 Lerner, 1993, pp. 46–7.
362 Contreras, in Göttner-Abendroth, 2009, p. 78.
363 Ma, 2016, p. 17.

Conclusion: Cassandra's Power

In *Sisters in Spirit: Haudenosaunee (Iroquois) Influence on Early American Feminists* (2001), Sally Roesh Wagner argues that the suffragists – and women like Matilda Joslyn Gage (mentioned in Chapter Two) – learned what liberation could look and feel like from Indigenous women who exercised this authority. She asks the question, "How did the radical suffragists come to their vision, a vision not of Band-Aid reform but of a reconstituted world completely transformed?" and concludes, "They believed women's liberation was possible because they knew liberated women, women who possessed rights beyond their wildest imagination: Haudenosaunee women."[364] Haudenosaunee women (commonly known as Iroquois) were not bought and sold in marriage, not ashamed of their bodies, not subordinate, not afraid of the men of their own clans or of the 'dark'.

If matriarchal cultures are where we all originate – cultures in which women experienced a 'natural spiritual authority' – it follows that The Shift arises from an ancient impulse. That is why Doyle says that, "If we want to taste freedom instead of control / Then we must relearn the soul's native tongue."[365] While the feelings and experiences associated with reclaiming personal authority are deeply personal and individual, The Shift is also *natural*, and forms patterns and discernible movements, like many streams finding their way back to the sea. Among these are the movements for natural birth, reproductive autonomy, lesbian feminism, and women's lands. In *Wisdom Rising* (2018), Tsultrim Allione illustrates The Shift when she recalls giving birth to her daughter at home:

> By evening, I had been in hard labor for eight hours when the doctor arrived from Seattle. My labor wasn't progressing, and he thought the baby's head was in the wrong position. Suddenly I thought: I have to get this baby out! It's up to me, no one else can do this. What do I need to do?

---

364 Wagner, 2001, p. 41.
365 Doyle, 2020, p. 67.

I tuned in to my body, got off the bed and onto the floor on my hands and knees, and told the doctor to leave me. I began weaving and shaking back and forth, up and down. My husband tried to approach me to tell me to be calm and breathe quietly, but I told everyone to get out of the way. I wasn't nice and calm; I was fierce and clear ... And before long, I held my newborn daughter in my arms.[366]

My understanding of the politics of birth comes from US midwife Mary Lou Singleton, and Joyous Birth founder Janet Fraser in Australia, both of whom are personal friends. I met Mary Lou at San Francisco airport, on the way to a women's festival. On the long journey and throughout the weekend, she blew my mind. At one point, I shared a lunch table with her and several others as she discussed midwifery. Mary Lou explained the prevalence of obstetric violence in hospital childbirth, and when someone asked for her views on birthing centres where women can give birth in pools and not on their backs on hospital beds, she said something like this: "When women give birth in those centres, they tend to go home saying, *'I had such an amazing midwife'*. When they give birth at home, they say, *'I CAN DO ANYTHING!'*"

As she almost roared those last words, goosebumps rippled over my skin as an aliveness awakened inside me. Intuitively I sensed that Mary Lou was not only advocating for women's autonomy in childbirth, but promoting a restoration of agency more profound than I had ever considered myself capable of. I knew she believed this power was natural and could apply to any woman in any area of life. It was not that I *thought* that's what she meant. My *body* responded to her as if something within me was trying to reach out to grasp hold of her words and pull them inside, where they would stay and gestate and change me for good.

There is an important and overlooked correspondence between the restoration of authentic power that Singleton and Fraser promote in birthing, and the restoration of agency required to

---

366 Allione, 2018, p. 14.

become a political activist. Fraser speaks of this when she writes about the way that feminists tend to dilute our desire for authentic power to placate and negotiate with representatives of external power and for the sake of public palatability. She says:

> I saw the mainstream birth advocacy groups around me, frightened to promote the only real model of one-to-one midwifery that existed, for fear of being seen as crazies. I did ask members of these groups why they didn't promote birthing outside of hospitals to women when they expressed concern about the way the system processes and treats women. The answer was usually something like: 'We work for all women and we don't want to be seen to be pushing our own barrow'.[367]

This is the same pattern that I witness among 'gender critical' feminists who dilute their opposition to transgenderism with claims to be non-partisan and in favour of 'trans rights', negotiating for whatever women's rights can still be held onto once that oppressive pseudoscience has been swallowed. While this looks like 'pragmatic' political manoeuvring and concession making, the foregoing of authentic power in favour of bargaining with the external power is just like Noble arguing with her husband endlessly and fruitlessly. To understand the cost of this approach, listen to Mary Lou explain why she does midwifery:

> I love midwifery. It brings together all the parts of my self: my feminism, my spirituality, my love of life, my love of babies, my love of women, my desire to live in a world full of women who are *crackling* with their own power – it was, and remains, who I am, and birth activism to me is … the most primary activism for humanity. Birth is the rite of passage *into* humanity.[368]

This is just the undiluted, unapologetic, goosebump-inducing, juicy passion that women tend to stop speaking with when we are looking for external validation. When *we* decide to moderate our own voices, we ultimately opt out of reclaiming the very freedom

---
367 Fraser, 2020, p. 11.
368 Singleton in Fraser, 2021.

we put all our energy into convincing others we need and want. As Janet Fraser says:

> What women really lack is autonomy in our lives … We have rights on paper, which may well form the easier part of social change. What we don't have is *respect* in reality, just lip service about it. When we engage in the kinds of harm minimisation and impact amelioration that traditionally serves as [feminist and] birth advocacy, we cement the existing status quo. We can hold the best intentions possible, but without women's autonomy and personhood front and centre, none of it matters.[369]

Another movement that Mary Lou introduced me to is the movement for reproductive autonomy. Before meeting her, I did not know that the Women's Liberationists of the 1970s and 80s had taught themselves about safe, self-induced abortion practices and menstrual extraction, processes outlined in texts such as *A Woman's Book of Choices* (1992) by Carol Downer and Rebecca Chalker.[370] Essentially, second wave feminists worked to reclaim the wisdom that was taken away from women during the witchcraze, before gynaecology was established as a male-dominated profession. Sonia Johnson writes how the Women's Liberationists realised that,

> it didn't take a man's eye to see a woman's cervix, it didn't take an American-Medical-Association, male-trained mind to diagnose the health of our reproductive organs or to treat them …
>
> So in learning to examine our own sexual organs, to diagnose and treat our own cervical and vaginal ailments, to do simple abortions, to deliver babies, and in beginning to think seriously about developing our own safe, effective, natural contraceptives and getting the word out, women were moving out of colonisation, out of slavery.[371]

Johnson compares this movement for reproductive autonomy with the legalisation of abortion in the US in 1973. While Roe versus

---

369 Fraser, 2020, pp. 13–14.
370 Singleton in Murphy, 2017.
371 Johnson, 1989, pp. 23–4.

Wade may have been a victory for women, men had their own reasons for supporting it (as Andrea Dworkin noted, see Chapter Four), and the law reform also helped women forget about the goal of re-establishing the terrain of women's sexual health as women's own. "We forgot that anybody that can *let* you, *owns* you," Johnson wrote.[372]

During the same Women's Liberation Movement, lesbian feminists argued that the best contraception was a 'misterectomy'. At a time that women were supposed to be celebrating the birth control pill, many were asking why women should alter their body chemistry so significantly for little or no benefit. Shere Hite's 1977 *Hite Report* on female sexuality exposed the previously private reality of women's profound dissatisfaction with heterosexual practices, noting that orgasm through penis-in-vagina sex alone was rare for women.[373] So, feminists asked – why all this fuss about heterosexual sex? Why does it appear to be *mandatory* if women rarely enjoy it? Why *must* it happen even in the face of risking unwanted pregnancy, sexually transmitted disease, and the heartbreak that occurs when we feel used for someone else's gratification? "Women's sexuality has been largely ignored independent of men's sexuality," Susan Hawthorne wrote in 1976.[374]

By 1980, Adrienne Rich published her landmark essay, *Compulsory Heterosexuality and Lesbian Existence*.[375] The piece outlines the various ways that patriarchy shapes, controls and monitors women and female sexuality, and argues that this "pervasive cluster of forces, ranging from physical brutality to control of consciousness ... suggests that an enormous potential counterforce is having to be restrained."[376] Rich called this counterforce *woman identification*, or *lesbian existence*, and wrote:

---

372 Johnson, 1989, p. 26.
373 Jeffreys, 1997, pp. 237–8.
374 Hawthorne, 1976/2019, p. 31.
375 Rich, 1980/1996.
376 Rich, 1980/1996, p. 132.

> Woman-identification is a source of energy, a potential springhead of female power, violently curtailed and wasted under the institution of heterosexuality. The denial of reality and visibility to women's passion for women, women's choice of women as allies, life companions, and community; the forcing of such relationships into dissimulation and their disintegration under intense pressure have meant an incalculable loss to the power of all women to change the social relations of the sexes, to liberate ourselves and each other.[377]

Janice Raymond also wrote about The Shift away from male-defined femininity to lesbian feminism:

> Men, of course, invented the feminine, and in this sense it could be said that all women who conform to this invention are transsexuals, fashioned according to man's image. Lesbian-feminists exist apart from man's inventiveness, and the political and personal ideals of lesbian-feminism have constituted a complete rebellion against the man-made invention of woman, and a context in which women begin to create ourselves in our own image.[378]

Another second wave movement to promote female kinship, autonomy, and response-ability was the establishment of women's lands. In Australia, Chris Sitka helped to establish such lands and says – in an essay beautifully titled 'Sheltering Out in the Open' – that as a result, she is committed to the cause of Women's Liberation, "[n]ot because I intellectually prefer it, but because I have emotionally experienced it."[379] Sitka's writing captures the way that freedom is real for her – not just a political concept. She explains:

> The land Herself embraced me and nurtured me. She gave me confidence and strength. Both my body and mind muscles grew. I walked and ran and swam and rode on horses and loved my own body deeply and unconditionally. Not least because no one,

---

377 Rich, 1980/1996, p. 139.
378 Raymond, 1979, p. 106.
379 Sitka, 2019, p. 172.

including the women I lived amongst, ever judged me for how I dressed, or didn't dress at all; or how wild and unkempt my hair was as I tangled with vines and got dirty churning up clay.[380]

She recalls:

> We sang day and night. We sang our joy and our hope for women. We sang to the land and to each other. It was a primal kind of love. An expanding love that circled the Earth and boomeranged back to us.[381]

As Chris Sitka expresses so well, the call to authentic power, or humanisation, comes to us, as individuals, in the form of *feeling* – something Audre Lorde beautifully argues too, in her essay 'Poetry is Not a Luxury'. Paulo Freire refers to the feeling of longing as the fuel of 'humanisation', and Glennon Doyle refers to this longing as 'electric restlessness':

> But while I made school lunches, wrote memoirs, rushed through airports, made small talk with neighbours, carried on with my outer life, I felt an electric restlessness buzzing inside me. It was like constant thunder rolling right there beneath my skin – a thunder made of joy and pain and rage and longing and love too deep, scalding and tender for this world ... Maybe we are all fire wrapped in skin, trying to look cool.[382]

Wild Politics

As legendary anarchist Emma Goldman (1869–1940) wrote, "the individual instinct is the thing of value in the world. It is the true soul that sees and creates the truth alive, out of which is to come a still greater truth, the re-born social soul."[383] The constant tug within the individual soul also has political implications for contemporary anarchist writer Darren Allen, author of *33 Myths of the System*.

---

380 Sitka, 2019, p. 173.
381 Sitka, 2019, p. 170.
382 Doyle, 2020, p. 45.
383 Goldman, 1979, p. 51.

It is "why anarchism, in its profound and primal sense, is the instinct that won't go away."[384]

The term anarchism, like much of the English language, seems to have been claimed by transgressive men. Anarchism has such a bad name these days that it led the environmentalist Derrick Jensen to write an unpublished book titled, 'Anarchism and the Politics of Violation'.[385] He talks about those activists (like those in the opening passages of Chapter Four) who consider that "all constraints on their behaviour are oppressive, and so for whom the point of anarchism is to remove all constraints."[386] Yet to my mind, these activists have as much right to define the word 'anarchism' as transactivists have to define 'feminism' or postmodernists to redefine 'woman'. Their attempts are distortion in action, as Allen suggests when he writes:

> A certain kind of idiot is drawn to anarchism, just as a certain kind of idiot is drawn to classical music, team sports or Hello Kitty ... Violent young atheists wearing anarcho-acceptable (ideological) attire, reading Palahniuk, playing hardcore music in violent demos, living in filthy squats,[387] and sharing dank memes fantasising about exterminating pigs, are not hard to come by, but they no more represent anarchism than Cliff Richard represents Christianity or Margaret Thatcher represents women.[388]

The key problem with nominal anarchism is much like the problem with postmodernism: it is well and good to question everything, or to reject all claims to power, but without love as a motivation, conditioned identifications remain intact and the practice of subversion and challenge descends into nonsense. It is inescapable that the rejection of external power *requires* a shift to authentic power. Without it, we cannot reach a state of 'no ruler', the etymological meaning of anarchism.

---

384 Allen, 2021, p. 301.
385 Jensen, 2018.
386 Jensen, 2018.
387 "Not that there is anything wrong with squats," Allen footnotes.
388 Allen, 2021, p. 286.

Conclusion: Cassandra's Power

Historically, Emma Goldman is perhaps the most well-known feminist anarchist, and she defined anarchism as follows:

> ANARCHISM: The philosophy of a new social order based on liberty unrestricted by man-made law; the theory that all forms of government rest on violence, and are therefore wrong and harmful, as well as unnecessary.[389]

A dream of liberty unrestricted by man-made law is not a dream of everyone out for themselves, but of all our streams undammed. When Goldman refers to 'man-made law', she means external power; when she talks about 'liberty', she means authentic power. This is clear from Goldman's critique of the women's suffrage movement. She felt it was ill-advised for women to frame the *vote* as a *right*, when the *state* is an *imposition*. "Alas," she wrote, "for the ignorance of the human mind, which can see a right in an imposition."[390] Goldman felt that women should give up the quest for 'equality' with men under patriarchy. Instead, she argued:

> Her development, her freedom, her independence, must come from and through herself. First, by asserting herself as a personality, and not as a sex commodity. Second, by refusing the right to anyone over her body; by refusing to bear children, unless she wants them; by refusing to be a servant to God, the State, society, the husband, the family, etc., by making her life simpler, but deeper and richer. That is, by trying to learn the meaning and substance of life in all its complexities, by freeing herself from the fear of public opinion and public condemnation. Only that, and not the ballot, will set woman free, will make her a force hitherto unknown in the world, a force for real love, for peace, for harmony; a force of divine fire, of life-giving; a creator of free men and women.[391]

Goldman's belief in the 'individual instinct' as a basis for anarchist action meant that she did not have a predetermined view of what

---

389 Goldman, 1910/1979, p. 50.
390 Goldman, 1911.
391 Goldman, 1911.

the outcome of such action should be, since "Anarchism is not, as some may suppose, a theory of a future to be realised through divine inspiration." [392] Another way of putting this is to say that anarchism is necessarily a politics of collective response-ability. Anarchism is to politics what The Shift is to individual life.

Yet, we live in an age of countermoves and appropriation, one where the naked emperor reigns. Distortion is his rule, and it follows this formula:

eros + male identification = distortion

Male identification, or masculinity (as defined in Chapter Two), distorts all political values and spiritual principles. It turns *power* from *authentic* to *external*. It turns *sex* into *gender* and female erasure. True selflessness is the same as authentic power – it is an individual's deep understanding that they are a piece of universe, not separable from the life as a whole: the Buddhist monk and activist Thich Nhat Hanh called this *interbeing*. This form of Buddhist 'selflessness' is antithetical to the codependency that is at the heart of female socialisation. Feminine socialisation requires that women dam up our own life energies to be seen as 'giving' and 'good.' Interbeing is the dismantling of those dams and restoration of our place in the sea of life, an experience that unleashes *bodhicitta*.

Distortion also turns loving kindness, the Buddhist *maitri*, into that aforementioned domesticated, feminine 'kindness' that Gabor Maté warns us is associated with autoimmune disease, that politicians increasingly implore us to live by, and that Buddhist teacher Pema Chödrön calls 'idiot compassion'. Chödrön says that "there are three near enemies of compassion: pity, overwhelm, and idiot compassion."[393] This 'kindness' is based on damming and denying, not listening to, our deepest longings.

Distortion also turns *infinite growth* into capital accumulation, rather than the growth John Dewey referred to when he said, "growth is the characteristic of life." It turns *responsibility* into *blame*,

---

392 Goldman, 1911/1979, p. 60.
393 Chödrön, 2018, pp. 77–8.

which is why the phrase *response-ability* is more useful: it helps us reclaim the idea of *responsibility* from the political conservativism and 'bootstraps' thinking that distorts it. While liberalism turns *freedom* into *privilege* or *licentiousness*, the annual Pride Parades turn *pride* – which in its authentic form, is a deep gratitude for one's own life – into *exhibitionism*.

Distortion leads us to keep all sorts of ideas at bay, because of their connotations. Look at the word *surrender*: under patriarchy, it comes to denote *capitulation*, because the factor of male identification makes us assume that the surrender is *to an oppressor*, rather than to *nature*, the intelligence of life. True surrender is Vicki Noble giving up arguing with her husband to write a book; Chanel Miller 'emptying her lungs' into the grape-sized courtroom microphone; Tsultrim Allione tuning into her body while giving birth, telling the doctor to "leave me". It is Glennon Doyle listening to and acting on her anger at her husband. To *truly* surrender is to listen to our instincts and deeper wisdom – rather than "always trying to keep up, to not mess up ... [to] follow the rules," in Miller's words. To surrender authentically does not mean to capitulate – it means to give up on trying to change what is outside us in favour of honouring what lives within. We may still *want* external reality to change – but we accept it may not. Changing external reality is no longer a *condition* for action.

Not only distorted concepts, but distorted political movements dominate the landscape. Nominal environmentalism claims to want to stop climate change without making the necessary shift in loyalty from civilisation to nature. Instead, it promotes greenwashing: lithium mining is 'green' because it produces electric cars; deforestation is environmentally friendly because today's cash crops are 'biofuels'. Nominal feminism claims to 'smash the patriarchy' without making the necessary shift in loyalty to women, instead promoting the idea that 'transwomen are women.' However well populated these movements are, greenwashing is not environmentalism, just as transgenderism is not feminism, and men are not women.

As Susan Hawthorne writes, "[r]esistance to appropriation is important in developing a wild politics."[394]

What's more, anarchism is necessarily self-defined. In *33 Myths*, Darren Allen addresses the awkwardness of redefining an entire political tradition according to one's own understanding. He anticipates being asked, "who are you to say what anarchism really is? And to exclude those [nominal anarchists] who don't fit your narrow definition?" Allen's says his answer to this challenge is his 'entire book'. My own answer to the same question is to assert that true anarchism is not about intellectual adherence to a political tradition – that would be a paradox. It is, primarily, a Shift that is *felt and experienced* (and can have many names, just like the *Tao*).

What Allen calls 'primal anarchism', Shiva calls 'unleashing Shakti', and Hawthorne calls 'wild politics'.[395] While Allen names the 'intelligence of life', as his inspiration, Shiva and Hawthorne's language denotes a politics inspired and informed by biodiversity.

In whatever way we speak about it, The Shift from reactivity to response-ability, from arguing and negotiation to creativity, from external and mechanistic to living and authentic power, must necessarily be invented, discovered, defined (and even named) by each person who undertakes it for themselves. It does not really matter whether we call this transformation 'primal', 'wild', or 'anarchic', as part of a process of 'humanisation', 'liberation', or becoming 'untamed', through the aid of 'Shakti', 'eros', 'God', undistorted 'authority' or 'the intelligence of life'. What matters is that it is *felt* and *authentic* and not *appropriated*. Accordingly, I agree with Allen that Krishnamurti is one of the best examples of an anarchist thinker: he constantly implored the people in his audiences not to believe him, but to "Go and find out for yourself."

---

394 Hawthorne, 2002/22, p. 370.
395 I cannot resist mentioning Chellis Glendinning here, who uses the phrase 'primal matrix' to refer to the same phenomenon in her book *My Name is Chellis and I'm in Recovery from Western Civilisation* (1994).

The Individual

Many feminists and leftists who are concerned with changing the material conditions affecting the lives of oppressed people through collective action, are allergic to individualism and popular ideas of individual 'empowerment'. As you might anticipate by now, I think we would be well advised not to accept the monopoly that liberals appear to have on the individual – because, like any other value we are fed in a patriarchal society, liberal individualism is a distortion. This means the very idea of 'the individual' deserves another look.

In 1892, suffragist Elizabeth Cady Stanton did this when she made a speech called 'The Solitude of Self' that her closest comrade, Susan B. Anthony, advised her not to deliver. Stanton insisted the speech was the best thing she had written, and gave it anyway.[396] She said:

> The strongest reason for giving woman all the opportunities for higher education, for the full development of her faculties, her forces of mind and body; for giving her the most enlarged freedom of thought and action; a complete emancipation from all forms of bondage, of custom, dependence, superstition; from all the crippling influences of fear – is the solitude and personal responsibility of her own individual life. The strongest reason why we ask for woman a voice in the government under which she lives … is because of her birthright to self-sovereignty; because, as an individual, she must rely on herself. No matter how much women prefer to lean, to be protected and supported, nor how much men desire to have them do so, they must make the voyage of life alone, and for safety in an emergency, they must know something of the laws of navigation. To guide our own craft, we must be captain, pilot, engineer; with chart and compass to stand at the wheel; to watch the winds and waves, and know when to take in the sail, and to read the signs in the firmament over all.

---

396 Morgan, 1982/1994, p. 241.

Later in the speech, she writes that,

> there is a solitude which each and every one of us has always carried with him, more inaccessible than the ice-cold mountains, more profound than the midnight sea; the solitude of self. Our inner being which we call ourself, no eye nor touch of man or angel has ever pierced. It is more hidden than the caves of the gnome; the sacred adytum of the oracle; the hidden chamber of Eleusinian mystery, for to it only omniscience is permitted to enter.
>
> Such is individual life. Who, I ask you, can take, dare take on himself the rights, the duties, the responsibilities of another human soul?[397]

Stanton and Anthony realised that The Shift requires a reassessment of the significance of the individual to social and political change. The prospect is threatening to many radical feminists, Marxist, or communist thinkers who not only value collective action above all, but also *material analysis*. Neither *self*, not *authentic power*, are ultimately material. They cannot be seen, pointed to, placed on a table, evidenced, dissected, and analysed. What's more, many people who become interested in the indefinable self and conclude that 'everything is energy', say that this means that they can magnetically attract social change using the law of attraction, the power of manifestation and high vibes. They make claims about how 'I contain multitudes', and "quantum physics helped me understand my queer identity."[398]

To many radicals, it is liberals and libertarians who cultivate this insufferable fixation on their indefinable selves. Not people with their eyes open, not feminists who know all too well what a woman is and what the effects of systemic oppression are. For those who are aware that women around the world share a condition of oppression that is evidenced by the facts of our living conditions and the events of our lives, *like rape*, it is very uncomfortable to

---

397 Stanton in Buhle and Buhle, 1978, pp. 325–7.
398 Arora, 2018; Al-Kadhi, 2018.

venture into the territory of the ephemeral and indefinable. What a distraction from the task of addressing what we *do* know and *can* see!

Yet, affirming the power of individuals does not have to mean delusion, just like responsibility does not have to mean blame, surrender does not have to mean giving in, and anarchism doesn't mean compulsive transgression. In fact, to spiritual teachers, our ability to be alone, to confront our shadows, to embrace the solitary aspects of existence – these are all prerequisites to true freedom. And only the solitude of deep meditation leads to the question *who am I?* that can allow us to go beyond that "illusion of … a separate self" that results from social conditioning and is so inextricable from all our social problems.[399] Through meditation we can independently realise *interbeing*: that we are not separate from life itself, from universal existence. That our bodies are impermanent, organic processes, made of earth and water, displaying the likeness of ancestors we have never met, constantly in dialogue with the rest of life: fed by energy from the sun converted by plants and soil into sugars – plants that also form part of our own breathing apparatus. To truly understand that we *are* life is the only authentic power we can have, and not only the wellspring of mysticism but the lifeblood of social change.

Following the private longing to know ourselves *as* life itself is the only authentic way to gladly embrace response-ability *for* life itself, without this being an overwhelming, guilt-ridden, or performative gesture. In today's world, we are so often motivated by terror, or the desire to 'fix' or 'save' the world. This is perfectly natural, given the scale, severity and proliferation of atrocities and threats that we face. But no matter how bad things become, the facts remain: we cannot 'fix' external reality (or it would have been done already by activists past); the only power we have is our response-ability; and the only sincere and sustainable way to activate it is not through fear or heroism, but the understanding

---

399 Osho, 2001, p. 36.

that, as Krishnamurti put it, "you are the world."[400] When people reconnected with this wisdom contemplate what course of action would be in their own, individual best interests, they are really asking themselves, *what is in the interest of life?* They automatically prioritise natural law, 'Gaia's laws', over societal rules.

This – not random, reckless antisocial behaviour – is the basis of anarchism.[401] As Allen writes:

> The word 'anarchy' means, in the dictionaries of the system, disorder; despite the fact that actual anarchists, with a few insane exceptions, have never been opposed to order. The question which anarchists seek to ask is what order, or whose. Anarchists believe that the only society worth living in is based on some kind of *natural order,* that which naturally or intuitively regulates individual and collective life. For authoritarians this does not exist. They see no evidence of it. What they see in 'intuition' is erratic emotionality ... Nature might be finely ordered, formally beautiful and good eating; but it cannot be trusted. To organise a society therefore must entail suppression and control of our natural instincts. Result; people become resentful, bored, stupid and violent ... which is to say *disordered*.[402]

Knowing ourselves *as life* is necessarily the basis of a truly anarchic, wild politics. It is something we all long to do, can only do alone, following our feeling, our 'electric restlessness'. This orientation, this commitment to knowing ourselves as life, provides the only true and lasting source of energy and wisdom to make The Shift and face the inevitable resistance, countermoves, and backlash.

For Emma Goldman and Paulo Freire alike, liberation was a creative process, neither a matter of negotiation, nor insisting on certain predetermined outcomes. Authentic power is not *control*, and the truth is that we cannot change external reality so that it matches our vision. We can act on this vision, and it can be as large as our hearts dictate – but we cannot know how the story ends.

---

400 Krishnamurti, 1972.
401 Shiva, 2008, p. 137.
402 Allen, 2021, p. 281.

Conclusion: Cassandra's Power

Real anarchism does not try, nor attempt to delineate how human beings 'should' organise their lives without external power dominating. In Hawthorne's conception, 'wild politics' is as indescribable as biodiversity – it is emergent and creative; there is no blueprint. As Goldman wrote:

> 'What I believe' is a process rather than a finality. Finalities are for gods and governments, not for the human intellect … In the battle for freedom … it is the *struggle* for, not so much the attainment of, liberty, that develops all that is strongest, sturdiest and finest in human character.[403]

Allen writes that "we don't know how innumerable people in innumerable situations are going to set about organising their lives. And thank God we don't."[404] This means, "What kind of world *can* emerge from anarchist principles is … an open question."[405]

I love this open question. It allows each of us to act according to our own capacity, our authentic power – and to collaborate on that basis, without clinging to the 'group' for dear life. That is what freedom is, and what distinguishes it from oppression and rule following. This is also what makes freedom scary, because a lack of rules or template implies total responsibility. It also implies that freedom is a way of life, a series of decisions, a process, a creative commitment – not a destination we arrive at. If many of us began to embrace this response-ability, make this commitment, we would not then have to agree on some predetermined template of social organisation – we would get to *discover* what sort of movement is made out of our cumulative, cross-pollinating creativity. As Allen writes:

> In an anarchist group whoever has more ability or sensitivity than the others naturally 'takes the lead'. Nobody with any intelligence, anarchist or otherwise, would refuse to *unthinkingly obey* an experienced sailor in a storm. Indeed, the hallmark of

---

403 Goldman, 1979, p. 35.
404 Allen, 2021, p. 292.
405 Allen, 2021, p. 287.

ability and sensitivity is that neither compel … Thus a primal anarchist society is, actually, *full* of leaders.[406]

To many people this political vision may appear simultaneously idealistic (full of leaders?) daunting (full response-ability?) and morally insufficient (People are dying! We *must* fix the world! In *this* way! Now!). I don't deny these concerns, but I am simply interested in what is real, true, possible, and mobilising, rather than what is futile. As Sonja Johnson asks:

> Every day patriarchy comes for *you* again, to get your mind and heart again, to destroy you, body and soul. If you cannot extricate yourself from its grasp, if you are imprisoned, how can you expect yourself to free anyone else?[407]

Liberation is not about achieving something prescribed and predetermined. It is revealed as we 'eject the oppressor' from our minds and rediscover our own power and response-ability. This is humanisation; this is our contribution to human evolution, the one we long to make. This is *coming alive*. It is what we are here for. As Chanel Miller writes, "Society thinks we live to come after him. When in fact, we live to live. That's it."[408]

---

406 Allen, 2021, pp. 283–4.
407 Johnson, 1989, p. 56.
408 Miller, 2019, pp. 290–1.

Bibliography

1news. 2018. '"Trans women are women" – Minister for Women Julie Anne Genter responds to some feminists' concerns transgender rights will compromise their own'. 1 news. 9 July. <https://www.1news.co.nz/2018/07/09/trans-women-are-women-minister-for-women-julie-anne-genter-responds-to-some-feminists-concerns-transgender-rights-will-compromise-their-own/>.

1news. 2018a. 'Green MP slams effort to bar US whistle-blower Chelsea Manning from NZ – "She's done her time."' 1news. 29 August. <https://www.1news.co.nz/2018/08/28/green-mp-slams-effort-to-bar-us-whistle-blower-chelsea-manning-from-nz-shes-done-her-time/>.

1news. 2018b. 'Final breakdown of $1.6 million bill for Government's Justice Summit labelled "talkfest" by National, is released'. 1news. 27 September. <https://www.1news.co.nz/2018/09/27/final-breakdown-of-16-million-bill-for-governments-justice-summit-labelled-talkfest-by-national-is-released/>.

Abortion Law Reform Association New Zealand. 2018. 'ALRANZ and the Transgender Community'. ALRANZ website. 4 December. <http://alranz.org/alranz-and-the-transgender-community/>.

Achterberg, Jeanne. 1990. *Woman as Healer*. Boston: Shambhala.

Al-Kadhi, Amrou. 2019. 'Gender identity: "What quantum physics taught me about my queer identity"'. BBC Ideas. 19 March. Accessed via YouTube.

Allen, Darren. 2018. 'Anarchism at the End of the World', expressiveegg.org. 10 December. <https://expressiveegg.org/2018/12/10/anarchism-at-the-end-of-the-world/>.

Ap, Raki. 2021. 'Free West Papua Campaign Spokesperson Raki Ap On Racism and Climate Change'. Free West Papua Campaign Nederland. 28 February. Accessed via YouTube.

Arora, Priya. 2018. 'Poet Alok Vaid-Menon: "I Am Part of Something Greater than Myself."' *Huffpost.com*. 14 October. <https://www.huffpost.com/entry/alok-vaid-menon_n_5b27dae4e4b0783ae12bd140#:~:text=What%20have%20you%20learned%20about,is%20thrilling%2C%20beautiful%20and%20wonderful>.

Awatere, Donna. 1982. 'Alliances with Pacific Island People, White Women, the Trade Union Movement, and the Left'. *Broadsheet*. October. Vol. 103, pp. 24–9.

Barry, Kathleen. 2010. *Unmaking War, Remaking Men*. Melbourne: Spinifex Press.

Benazzo, Maurizio and Zaya Benazzo. 2021. *The Wisdom of Trauma*. California: Science and Nonduality.

Bieringa, Luit and Jan Bieringa. 2016. *The HeART of the Matter*. Wellington: BWX Productions.

Bilek, Jennifer and Mary Ceallaigh. 2016. 'In the Absence of the Sacred: The Marketing of Medical Transgenderism and the Survival of the Natural Child'. In Ruth Barrett (ed). *Female Erasure*. Lebec, California: Tidal Time Publishing, pp. 138–170.

Bindel, Julie. 2018. 'Why are so many LGBT organizations caving to trans activists and losing lesbians?' *Feminist Current*. 29 August. <https://www.feministcurrent.com/2018/08/29/many-lgbt-organizations-caving-trans-activists-losing-lesbians/>.

Bowles, Nellie. 2019. '"Replacement Theory," a Racist, Sexist Doctrine, Spreads in Far-Right Circles'. *New York Times*. 18 March. <https://www.nytimes.com/2019/03/18/technology/replacement-theory.html>.

Braae, Alex. 2018. 'Socialism is back, baby, and it doesn't want your vote'. *The Spinoff*. 4 October. <https://thespinoff.co.nz/politics/04-10-2018/socialism-is-back-baby-and-it-doesnt-want-your-vote>.

Braidwood, Ella. 2018. 'Rose McGowan to the transgender community: I'm "profoundly sorry."' *PinkNews*. 18 January. <https://www.pinknews.co.uk/2019/01/18/rose-mcgowan-transgender-apology/>.

Brodribb, Somer. 1992. *Nothing Mat(t)ers: A Feminist Critique of Postmodernism*. North Melbourne: Spinifex Press.

Brown, Brené. 2015. *Daring Greatly*. London: Penguin Random House.

Brunskell-Evans, Heather. 2020. *Transgender Body Politics*. Mission Beach: Spinifex Press.

Buhle, Mari Jo and Paul Buhle. (eds). 1978. *The Concise History of Woman Suffrage*. Chicago: University of Illinois Press.

Buhner, Stephen. 2004. *The Secret Teachings of Plants: On the Intelligence of the Heart in the Direct Perception of Nature*. Rochester: Bear and Company.

Butler, Judith. 2021. 'Why is the idea of "gender" provoking backlash the world over?' *The Guardian*. 23 October. <https://www.theguardian.com/us-news/commentisfree/2021/oct/23/judith-butler-gender-ideology-backlash>.

Campbell, Beatrix. 2018. 'Somewhere in England's Green and Pleasant Land …' beatrixcampbell.co.uk. September. <http://www.beatrixcampbell.co.uk/author/bc/>.

Carson, Rachel. 1951/2014. *The Sea Around Us*. London: Unicorn.

Chamberlain, Gethin. 2012. 'India's clothing workers: "They slap us and call us dogs and donkeys."' *The Guardian*. 25 November. <https://www.theguardian.com/world/2012/nov/25/india-clothing-workers-slave-wages>.

Chen, Ellen. 1974. 'Tao as the Great Mother and the Influence of Motherly Love in the Shaping of Chinese Philosophy'. *History of Religions*, 1 August, pp. 51–64.

Cheyne, Brenda. 2003. *Getting to Peace: A Guide to Healing after Rape and Abuse.* Wellington: Dove.

Chödrön, Pema. 2018. *The Places That Scare You.* Boulder Colorado: Shambhala.

Christ, Carol. 1980. *Diving Deep and Surfacing: Women Writers on Spiritual Quest.* Boston: Beacon Press.

Cline, Sally and Dale Spender. 1987. *Reflecting Men at Twice Their Natural Size.* London: André Deutsch.

Cooke, Henry. 2017. 'Jacinda Ardern says neoliberalism has failed'. *Stuff. co.nz.* 12 September. <https://www.stuff.co.nz/national/politics/96739673/jacinda-ardern-says-neoliberalism-has-failed>.

Cox, Susan. 2015. 'Are we women or are we incubators? An interview with Mary Lou Singleton'. *Feminist Current.* 13 October. <https://www.feministcurrent.com/2015/10/13/are-we-women-or-are-we-incubators-an-interview-with-marylou-singleton/>.

Crossland, Jack. 2021. 'More than 1000 gather at Wellington's transgender rights rally'. *New Zealand Herald.* 15 July. <https://www.nzherald.co.nz/nz/more-than-1000-gather-at-wellingtons-transgender-rights-rally/AVOBAGIKQJ2P6QYTD2TWG7FDP4/>.

Cukor, George. (Director). 1944. *Gaslight* [movie]. California: Metro-Goldwyn-Mayer.

Daly, Mary. 1978. *Gyn/Ecology: The Metaethics of Radical Feminism.* Boston: Beacon Press.

Daly, Mary. 2021. 'Mary Daly – Gyn/Ecology – The Fire of Female Fury'. Feminist vhs archive 1 March. Accessed via YouTube.

Dashu, Max. 1998. 'Reign of the Demonologists'. *Suppressed Histories Archives.* <https://www.suppressedhistories.net/secrethistory/ReignD.pdf>.

Davis, Angela. 1983. *Women, Race and Class.* New York: Vintage.

Davis, Angela. 2003. *Are Prisons Obsolete?* New York: Seven Stories Press.

Dewey, John. 1916/2004. *Democracy and Education.* New York: Dover Publications.

Dines, Gail. 2010. *Pornland: How Porn Has Hijacked Our Sexuality.* North Melbourne: Spinifex Press.

Dispenza, Joe. 2017. *Becoming Supernatural: How Common People are Doing the Uncommon.* California: Hayhouse.

Domestic Abuse Intervention Project. <https://www.theduluthmodel.org/wheels/faqs-about-the-wheels/>.

Douglas, Roger 1990. 'The Politics of Successful Structural Reform'. *Policy,* Autumn, pp. 2–6.

Dowd, Trone. 2020. 'Snowden Warns Governments Are Using Coronavirus to Build "the Architecture of Oppression."' *vice.com.* 10 April. <https://www.

vice.com/en/article/bvge5q/snowden-warns-governments-are-using-coronavirus-to-build-the-architecture-of-oppression>.

Downer, Carol and Rebecca Chalker (eds). 1992. *A Woman's Book of Choices*. New York: Seven Stories Press.

Doyle, Glennon. 2020. *Untamed: Stop Pleasing, Start Living*. London: Penguin.

Duff, Michelle. 2019. 'Gun City's David Tipple: Firearms aren't the villain'. *stuff.co.nz*. 19 March. <https://www.stuff.co.nz/national/christchurch-shooting/111376049/gun-citys-david-tipple-firearms-arent-the-villain>.

Dunbar-Ortiz, Roxanne. 2014. *An Indigenous People's History of the United States*. Boston: Beacon Press.

Dworkin, Andrea. 1974. *Woman Hating*. New York: E.P. Dutton.

Dworkin, Andrea. 1976. *Our Blood: Prophecies and Discourses on Sexual Politics*. New York: Harper and Row.

Dworkin, Andrea. 1983. *Right Wing Women: The Politics of Domesticated Females*. New York: Perigree.

Dworkin, Andrea. 1988. *Letters From a War Zone: Writings 1976–1987*. London: Secker and Warburg.

Dworkin, Andrea. 1990/1996. 'Dworkin on Dworkin'. In Diane Bell and Renate Klein (eds). 1996. *Radically Speaking*. Melbourne: Spinifex Press, pp. 203–217.

Dworkin, Andrea. 2002. 'Heartbreak'. Radcliffe Institute Schlesinger Library talk. c-span.org. <https://www.c-span.org/video/?169293-1/heartbreak>.

Eagleton, Terry. 1996. *The Illusions of Postmodernism*. Cambridge: Blackwell Publishers.

'Ēkkachai, Sanitsudā. 1990. *Behind the Smile: Voices of Thailand*. Bangkok: Thai Development Support Committee.

Ekman, Kajsa Ekis. 2013. *Being and Being Bought: Prostitution, Surrogacy and the Split Self*. North Melbourne: Spinifex Press.

El Saadawi, Nawal. 1980/2015. *The Hidden Face of Eve*. London: Zed Books.

Enloe, Cynthia. 1983. *Does Khaki Become You?: The Militarisation of Women's Lives*. Boston: South End Press.

Enloe, Cynthia. 1989. *Bananas, Beaches and Bases: Making Feminist Sense of International Politics*. London: Pandora Press.

Enloe, Cynthia. 2013. *Seriously! Investigating Crashes and Crises as if Women Mattered*. Berkeley: University of California Press.

Enloe, Cynthia. 2017. *The Big Push: Exposing and Challenging the Persistence of Patriarchy*. Oxford: Myriad Editions.

Falk, Will. 2021. 'When I Set the Sweetgrass Down'. Unpublished poetry collection.

Federici, Silvia. 2018. *Witches, Witch-Hunting and Women*. Oakland: PM Press.

Fischer, Ernst. 1970. *Marx in His Own Words*. Middlesex: Penguin.

Foster, Judy. 2013. *Invisible Women of Prehistory: Three Million Years of Peace, Six Thousand Years of War*. North Melbourne: Spinifex Press

Fraser, Janet. 2020. *Born Still: A Memoir of Grief*. Mission Beach: Spinifex Press.
Fraser, Janet. 2021. 'Hear Me Raw: Episode 3'. *Despatches from the Matriarchy*, via patreon.com. 24 December. <https://www.patreon.com/posts/60271032?fbclid=IwAR2iLHrhz2WDAiUnd0cxajVrUYrPmCer0_i55_wYeJsd1N4JXuu3-X8h4LU>.
Freire, Paulo. 1970/1993. *Pedagogy of the Oppressed*. London: Penguin Books.
French, Marilyn. 2008. *From Eve to Dawn: A History of Women in the World: Volume I: Origins: From Prehistory to the First Millennium*. New York: The Feminist Press.
Friedan, Betty. 1963. *The Feminine Mystique*. London: Penguin.
Furley, Tom. 2017. 'Corrections not welcome at Auckland Pride Parade'. Radio New Zealand. 2 February. <https://www.rnz.co.nz/news/national/323603/corrections-not-welcome-at-auckland-pride-parade>.
Gage, Matilda Joslyn. 1893/1980. *Woman, Church and State: The Original Exposé of Male Collaboration Against the Female Sex*. Massachusetts: Persephone Press.
Geraghty, Lisa. 2019. 'I'm a teacher. Here's why I voted to strike'. *The Spinoff*. 13 May. <https://thespinoff.co.nz/society/13-05-2019/im-a-teacher-heres-why-i-voted-to-strike/>.
Gerlich, Renée. 2013. 'Homeopathy'. *Dominion Post*. 'Your Weekend' Summer Fiction series, pp. 12–13.
Gerlich, Renée. 2017. 'Sex trafficking by deceit and complicity: An exchange with Salient magazine and the Press Council'. <https://reneejg.net/2017/10/sex-trafficking-salient-press-council/>.
Gerlich, Renée. 2018. 'Suffragists Fought for the Female Sex'. *Quillette*. 24 September. <https://quillette.com/2018/09/24/suffragists-fought-for-the-female-sex/>.
Gerlich, Renée. 2019a. 'Feminists Must Think Radically to Reject Sex Self-Identification Laws'. reneejg.net. March. <https://reneejg.net/2019/03/think-radically/>.
Gerlich, Renée. 2019b. 'Transgenderism, Neoliberalism and Rape Culture'. IWD Brisbane. 16 October. Accessed via YouTube.
Gerlich, Renée. 2020. 'Cassandra Lives: From politics to the courtroom, women are disbelieved'. *Feminist Current*. 23 December. <https://www.feministcurrent.com/2020/12/23/cassandra-lives-from-politics-to-the-court-room-women-are-disbelieved/>.
Giles, Mary E. 1982. *The Feminist Mystic and Other Essays on Women and Spirituality*. New York: Crossroad.
Gimbutas, Marija. 2001. *The Living Goddesses*. Berkeley: University of California Press.
Glendinning, Chellis. 1994. *My Name Is Chellis and I'm in Recovery from Western Civilisation*. Boston: Shambhala.
Göttner-Abendroth, Heide. (ed.) 2009. *Societies of Peace: Matriarchies Past, Present, and Future*. Toronto: Inanna Publications and Education Inc.

Goldman, Emma. 1911. *Anarchism and Other Essays*. Second Revised Edition. New York and London: Mother Earth Publishing Association.

Goldman, Emma. 1979. *Red Emma Speaks: The selected speeches and writings of the anarchist and feminist Emma Goldman*. London: Wildwood House.

Gonzalez, Emma. 2018. 'Emma Gonzalez's powerful March for Our Lives speech in full'. *Guardian News*. 25 March. Accessed via YouTube.

Gay'wu Group of Women. 2019. *Songspirals: Sharing Women's Wisdom of Country through Songlines*. Sydney: Allen and Unwin.

Hamilton, Patrick. 1938. *Gas Light: A Victorian thriller in three acts*. [Play]

Harding, Elizabeth U. 1993. *Kali: The Black Goddess of Dakshineswar*. Berwick: Nicolas-Hays.

Hawthorne, Susan. 2002/2022. *Wild Politics: Feminism, Globalisation and Biodiversity*. North Melbourne and Mission Beach: Spinifex Press.

Hawthorne, Susan. 2014. *Bibliodiversity: A Manifesto for Independent Publishing*. North Melbourne: Spinifex Press.

Hawthorne, Susan. 1976/2019. *In Defence of Separatism*. Mission Beach: Spinifex Press.

Hawthorne, Susan. 2020. *Vortex: The Crisis of Patriarchy*. Mission Beach: Spinifex Press.

Henderson, Carol. 1998. *A Blaze of Colour*. Christchurch: Hazard Press.

Hennessy, Annabel. 2019. 'Right-wing extremists use Minecraft, Grand Theft Auto to "recreate" Holocaust, Christchurch attacks, offer mass shooting "tips."' *The West Australian*. 4 November. <https://thewest.com.au/news/social/right-wing-extremists-use-minecraft-grand-theft-auto-to-recreate-holocaust-christchurch-attacks-offer-mass-shooting-tips-ng-b881371239z>.

Herman, Judith. 1992/2015. *Trauma and Recovery: The Aftermath of Violence – From Domestic Abuse to Political Terror*. New York: Basic Books.

Heldman, Carol. 2013. 'The Sexy Lie'. Ted.com. <https://ed.ted.com/on/GvKYBTag>.

hooks, bell. 1994. *Teaching to Transgress: Education as the Practice of Freedom*. New York: Routledge.

Hughes, Stephani. 2019. 'Male-Pattern Violence, Women's Trauma and the Need for Women's Safe Spaces.' IWD Brisbane. 16 October. Accessed via YouTube.

Jeffreys, Sheila. 1997. *The Idea of Prostitution*. North Melbourne: Spinifex Press.

Jeffreys, Sheila. 2005. *Beauty and Misogyny: Harmful Cultural Practices in the West*. New York: Routledge.

Jeffreys, Sheila. 2012. *Man's Dominion: The Rise of Religion and the Eclipse of Women's Rights*. New York: Routledge.

Jensen, Derrick. 2018. 'Anarchism and the Politics of Violation'. Unpublished manuscript.

Jensen, Derrick. 2022. 'Resistance Radio: Guest Renee Gerlich'. Resistance Radio. 30 January. Accessed via Apple Podcasts.

Jensen, Derrick, Lierre Keith and Max Wilbert. 2021. *Bright Green Lies: How the Environmental Movement Lost Its Way and What We Can Do About It*. New York: Monkfish.

Johnson, Sonia. 1987. *Going Out of Our Minds: The Metaphysics of Liberation*. California: The Crossing Press.

Johnson, Sonia. 1989. *Wildfire: Igniting the She/Volution*. Albuquerque: Wildfire Books.

Johnson, Sonia. 2016. 'Going Farther out of our Minds'. Slamolo. 23 August. Accessed via YouTube.

Kara, Siddharth. 2009. *Sex Trafficking: Inside the Business of Modern Slavery*. New York: Columbia University Press.

Karlis, Nicole. 2019. 'New Zealand Prime Minister Jacinda Ardern and the power of "feminine" leadership'. *Salon*. 25 March. <https://www.salon.com/2019/03/25/new-zealand-prime-minister-jacinda-ardern-and-the-power-of-feminine-leadership/>.

Karim, Sabrina and Mona Krewel. 2019. 'Is there a 'feminine' response to terrorism?' *The Conversation*. 29 April. <https://theconversation.com/is-there-a-feminine-response-to-terrorism-115873>.

Kasl, Charlotte. 1989. *Women, Sex and Addiction: A Search for Love and Power*. San Francisco: Harper and Row.

Keith, Lierre. 2011. 'Liberals and Radicals'. In Aric McBay, Lierre Keith and Derrick Jensen. *Deep Green Resistance: Strategy to Save the Planet*. New York: Seven Stories Press.

Klein, Naomi. 2007. *The Shock Doctrine: The Rise of Disaster Capitalism*. London: Penguin.

Klein, Naomi. 2020. '"Coronavirus Capitalism": Naomi Klein's Case for Transformative Change Amid Coronavirus Pandemic'. Democracy Now! 20 March. Accessed via YouTube.

Klein, Renate. 2017. *Surrogacy: A Human Rights Violation*. Mission Beach: Spinifex Press.

Klein, Renate. 2021. 'Strategies for Stopping International Surrogacy: Beyond the Compassion Trap'. In Marie-Josèphe Devillers and Ana-Luana Stoicea-Deram (eds). *Towards the Abolition of Surrogate Motherhood*. Mission Beach: Spinifex Press.

Kohn, Alfie. 1993. *Punished by Rewards: The Trouble with Gold Stars, Incentive Plans, A's and Other Bribes*. Boston: Houghton Mifflin.

Krishnamurti, J. 1972. *You Are the World*. New York: Harper and Row.

Laursen, Eric. 2021. *The Operating System: An Anarchist Theory of the Modern State*. Edinburgh: AK Press.

Leidholdt, Dorchen and Janice Raymond. (eds). 1990. *The Sexual Liberals and the Attack on Feminism*. New York: Pergamon Press.

LePera, Nicole. 2019. 'Mental Resistance: Why You Feel "Stuck."' *The Holistic Psychologist*. 17 June. Accessed via YouTube.
LePera, Nicole. 2021. *How to Do the Work: Recognise Your Patterns, Heal From Your Past, and Create Your Self*. London: Orion Books.
Lerner, Gerda. 1986. *The Creation of Patriarchy*. Oxford: Oxford University Press.
Lerner, Gerda. 1993. *The Creation of Feminist Consciousness: From the Middle Ages to 1870*. Oxford: Oxford University Press.
Lerner, Harriet. 1989. *The Dance of Anger: A Woman's Guide to Changing the Pattern of Intimate Relationships*. London: Pandora.
Lewis, Oliver. 2018. '"We're not asking to be millionaires": nurses' pay offer vote expected to be close'. *Stuff*. 9 July. <https://www.stuff.co.nz/national/health/105347696/were-not-asking-to-be-millionaires-nurses-pay-offer-vote-expected-to-be-close?rm=m>.
Long, Jessica. 2019. 'Massey University cancels controversial Feminism 2020 event due to "health, safety and wellbeing" concerns'. *stuff.co.nz*. 16 October. <https://www.stuff.co.nz/national/education/116640486/massey-university-cancels-controversial-feminism-2020-event-due-to-health-safety-and-wellbeing-concerns>.
Long, Julia. 2020. 'A Meaningful Transition?' *Uncommon Ground Media*. <http://uncommongroundmedia.com/a-meaningful-transition-julia-long/>.
Lorde, Audre. 1984. *Sister Outsider: Essays and Speeches by Audre Lorde*. New York: The Crossing Press.
Maathai, Wangari. 2008. *Unbowed: One Woman's Story*. New York: Random House.
Mamonova, Tatyana. 1984. *Women and Russia*. Boston: Beacon Press.
Manch, Thomas and Collette Devlin. 2020. 'Policing the pandemic: The "unprecedented" powers deployed to keep Kiwis at home'. stuff.co.nz. 29 March. <https://www.stuff.co.nz/national/health/coronavirus/120646079/policing-the-pandemic-the-unprecedented-powers-deployed-to-keep-kiwis-at-home>.
Mau, Alison. 2018. 'New Zealand needs to shut down its prisons – or blow them up'. Stuff.co.nz. 26 August. <https://www.stuff.co.nz/national/crime/106568275/alison-mau-new-zealand-needs-to-shut-down-its-prisons--or-blow-them-up>.
Maxwell, Joel. 2015. 'Corrections fast-tracks approval to shift trans woman prisoner from Rimutaka'. Stuff.co.nz. 27 August. <https://www.stuff.co.nz/dominion-post/news/71510201/corrections-fast-tracks-approval-to-shift-trans-woman-prisoner-from-rimutaka>.
MacKinnon, Catharine. 2000. 'Points Against Postmodernism'. *Chicago Kent Law Review*. 75:3, pp. 687–712.
McGowan, Rose. 2018. *Brave*. San Francisco: HarperOne.
Ma, Vajra. 2016. *From a Hidden Stream: The Natural Spiritual Authority of Women*. Shakti Moon Publishing.

Martin, Lisa and Ben Smee. 2019. 'What Do We Know About the Christchurch Attack Suspect?' *The Guardian*. 15 March.<https://www.theguardian.com/world/2019/mar/15/rightwing-extremist-wrote-manifesto-before-livestreaming-christchurch-shooting>.

Maté, Gabor. 2013. 'Addictions and Corrections with Gabor Maté'. joy96815. 20 July. Accessed via YouTube.

Maté, Gabor. 2019. *When the Body Says No: The Hidden Cost of Stress*. London: Vermilion.

Media Council. 2018. 'Renée Gerlich against Scoop'. August, <https://www.mediacouncil.org.nz/rulings/renee-gerlich-against-scoop/>.

Miller, Chanel. 2019. *Know My Name*. UK: Penguin Random House.

Millett, Kate. 1969/2000. *Sexual Politics*. Chicago: University of Illinois.

Molisa, Grace. 1987. *Colonised People*. Port Vila: Black Stone.

Moreno, Carolina. 2017. 'Portland Burrito Cart Closes After Owners Are Accused of Cultural Appropriation'. *Huffpost*. <https://www.huffpost.com/entry/portland-burrito-cart-closes-after-owners-are-accused-of-cultural-appropriation_n_5926ef7ee4b062f96a348181>.

Morgan, Robin. 1989. *Demon Lover: On the Sexuality of Terrorism*. London: Methuen.

Morgan, Robin. 2019. 'And Again: The Means of (Re)Production'. robinmorgan.com. 25 March. <https://www.robinmorgan.net/blog/and-again-the-means-of-reproduction/>.

Morningstar, Cory. 2019. 'The Manufacturing of Greta Thunberg – For Consent: The Political Economy of the Non-Profit Industrial Complex [Act I]'. Wrong Kind of Green. 17 January. <https://www.wrongkindofgreen.org/2019/01/17/the-manufacturing-of-greta-thunberg-for-consent-the-political-economy-of-the-non-profit-industrial-complex/>.

Murphy, Meghan. 2016. 'Are we women or are we menstruators?' *Feminist Current*. 7 September. <https://www.feministcurrent.com/2016/09/07/are-we-women-or-are-we-menstruators/>.

Murphy, Meghan. 2017. 'Mary Lou Singleton: "We need to go back to rallying for abortion on demand without apology."' *Feminist Current*. 8 September. <https://www.feministcurrent.com/2017/09/08/mary-lou-singleton-need-go-back-rallying-abortion-demand-without-apology/>.

Murphy, Meghan. 2021. 'It's not a good thing that Trump was banned from Twitter'. 10 January. Accessed via YouTube.

New Zealand Council of Trade Unions. 2003. 'Sex Workers Need Protection Under the Law'. *Scoop*. 24 June. <https://www.scoop.co.nz/stories/PO0306/S00153/sex-workers-need-protection-under-the-law.htm?from-mobile=bottom-link-01>.

New Zealand Herald. 2018. 'Midwives march on Parliament over pay and conditions'. *New Zealand Herald*. 3 May. <https://www.nzherald.co.nz/nz/

midwives-march-on-parliament-over-pay-and-conditions/SM5KS6YKYOLFF264TJ6GIZKNQI/>.

New Zealand Herald. 2019. 'Women in the World summit 2019: Oprah praises Jacinda Ardern's leadership'. *New Zealand Herald*. 11 April. <https://www.nzherald.co.nz/nz/women-in-the-world-summit-2019-oprah-praises-jacinda-arderns-leadership/5NZ6NI7NF7WZYGI5TY234D2EQ4/>.

New Zealand Family Violence Death Review Committee. 2017. 'Fifth Report Data: January 2009 to December 2015'. Wellington: Family Violence Death Review Committee.

New Zealand Police. 2019. 'Police to pilot Armed Response Teams'. *police.govt.nz*. 18 October. <https://www.police.govt.nz/news/release/police-pilot-armed-response-teams>.

Nhat Hanh, Thich. 1966/2000. *Fragrant Palm Leaves: Journals 1962-1966*. London: Random House.

Noah, Trevor and Greta Thunberg. 2019. 'Greta Thunberg – Inspiring Others to Take Stand on Climate Change'. The Daily Show with Trevor Noah. 15 September. Accessed via YouTube.

Noble, Vicki. 1991. *Shakti Woman: Feeling Our Fire, Healing Our World*. San Francisco: Harper and Collins.

No Pride in Prisons. 2016. *Abolitionist Demands: Toward the End of Prisons in Aotearoa*. Auckland: No Pride in Prisons Press.

O'Brien, Ani. 2020. 'Ani O'Brien, Speak Up For Women event'. 26 February. Accessed via YouTube.

Office of the Wet'suwet'en. 2020. 'Wet'suwet'en Hereditary Chiefs Launch Court Challenge to Coastal GasLink Pipeline's Environmental Approval'. wetsuweten.com. 3 February. <wetsuweten.com/files/Media_Release_Feb._6,_2020_-_CGL.pdf>.

Orwell, George. 1949/1989. *Nineteen Eighty-Four*. London: Penguin.

Osho. 2001. *Love, Freedom, Aloneness*. New York: St Martin's Griffin.

Osho. 2002a. *Sex Matters: From Sex to Superconsciousness*. New York: St Martin's Griffin.

Osho. 2002b. *Yoga: The Science of the Soul*. New York: St Martin's Griffin.

Peace Action Wellington. 2015. 'Media Release: NZ Weapons Conference sponsors tied to illegal US drone war'. PAW website. 18 October. <https://peaceactionwellington.wordpress.com/2015/10/18/media-release-nz-weapons-conference-sponsors-tied-to-illegal-us-drone-war/>.

Phillips, Jock. 1987. *A Man's Country?: The Image of the Pakeha Male – A History*. Auckland: Penguin.

Ptacek, James. (ed). 2010. *Restorative Justice and Violence Against Women*. Oxford: Oxford University Press.

Radio New Zealand. 2015. 'TPP protesters arrested in Wellington'. 15 September. <https://www.rnz.co.nz/news/political/284249/tpp-protesters-arrested-in-wellington>.

Radio New Zealand. 2018. 'Kaumātua, kuia tried to lift us out of those dungeons'. 23 August. <https://www.rnz.co.nz/national/programmes/morningreport/audio/2018659345/kaumatua-kuia-tried-to-lift-us-out-of-those-dungeons>.

Radio New Zealand. 2019. 'Grace Millane murder trial: call to stop victim blaming'. 23 November. <https://www.rnz.co.nz/news/national/403931/grace-millane-murder-trial-call-to-stop-victim-blaming>.

Rahera, K. 2019. 'The Fall of Pride: Auckland Pride Parade 2019'. 2 February. Accessed via YouTube.

Raymond, Janice. 1979/1994. *The Transsexual Empire*. London: The Women's Press; New York: Teachers College Press.

Raymond, Janice. 1986/2001. *A Passion for Friends: Towards a Philosophy of Female Affection*. London: The Women's Press; North Melbourne: Spinifex Press.

Raymond, Janice. 1993/2019. *Women as Wombs: Reproductive Technologies and the Battle over Women's Freedoms*. Mission Beach: Spinifex Press.

Read, Herbert. 1967. *Art and Alienation*. New York: The Viking Press.

Reid, Melanie. 2019. 'Don't take my baby'. *Newsroom*. 8 May. <https://www.newsroom.co.nz/2019/05/08/575167/dont-take-my-baby?fbclid=IwAR0FuQXHxIt4Zmda-A7YvPZ3tv7mc2QNF-Bo2h8HCob7woHX-xCmW6bmx_g>.

Rich, Adrienne. 1980/1996. 'Compulsory Heterosexuality and Lesbian Existence'. In Stevi Jackson and Sue Scott. (eds). 1996. *Feminism and Sexuality: A Reader*. Edinburgh: Edinburgh University Press, pp. 130–143.

Rizvi, Jamila. 2019. 'Jacinda Ardern just proved typically 'feminine' behaviour is powerful'. *stuff.co.nz*. 19 March. <https://www.stuff.co.nz/national/christchurch-shooting/111385688/jacinda-ardern-just-proved-typically-feminine-behaviour-is-powerful>.

Root, Elena and Bogdan Melnykov. 2018. 'Malware Displaying Porn Ads Discovered in Game Apps on Google Play'. *Check Point Research*. 12 January. <https://research.checkpoint.com/2018/malware-displaying-porn-ads-discovered-in-game-apps-on-google-play/>.

Ruiz, Don Miguel. 1997. *The Four Agreements: A Toltec Wisdom Book*. California: Amber-Allen Publishing.

Sadhguru. 2016a. *Inner Engineering: A Yogi's Guide to Joy*. New York: Penguin.

Sadhguru. 2016b. 'Samadhi – A Taste of 'That Which is Not'.' Isha Foundation. 13 June. <https://isha.sadhguru.org/us/en/wisdom/article/samadhi-to-go-beyond-existence>.

Sadhguru. 2020. 'Sadhguru Explains the Difference between the Mind and The Brain'. *Mystics of India*. 9 October. Accessed via YouTube.

Sanders, Barry. 2009. *The Green Zone: The Environmental Costs of Militarism*. Oakland: AK Press.

Shakur, Assata. 1998. *Assata: An Autobiography*. London: Zed Books.

Shiva, Vandana. 2009. *Soil Not Oil: Climate Change, Peak Oil and Food Insecurity*. North Melbourne: Spinifex Press.
Shiva, Vandana with Kartikey Shiva. 2018. *Oneness vs. the 1%: Shattering Illusions, Seeding Freedom*. Mission Beach: Spinifex Press.
Sitka, Chris. 2019. 'Sheltering Out in the Open'. In Sand Hall. (ed). *Shelters and Building*. Wollongong: Shall Publishing.
Sjöö, Monica and Barbara Mor. 1987. *The Great Cosmic Mother: Rediscovering the Religion of the Earth*. New York: HarperOne.
Solis, Marie. 2017. 'How the Women's March's "genital-based" feminism isolated the transgender community'. mic.com. <https://www.mic.com/articles/166273/how-the-women-s-march-s-genital-based-feminism-isolated-the-transgender-community>.
Speak Up For Women. 2018. 'Stop Hate Speech ... full recording of MP Louisa Wall's hate speech'. speakupforwomen.nz. 24 November. <https://speakupforwomen.nz/stop-hate-speech/>.
Stewart, Matt. 2018. 'Mother of murdered Christchurch 3-year-old slams Government's criminal justice summit'. stuff.co.nz. 22 August. <https://www.stuff.co.nz/national/crime/106470793/mother-of-murdered-christchurch-3yearold-slams-governments-criminal-justice-summit>.
Stoler Miller, Barbara (translator) and Patanjali. 1998. *Yoga: Discipline of Freedom*. New York: Bantam Books.
Stone, Merlin. 1976. *When God Was a Woman: A Treasury of Goddess and Herione Lore from Around the World*. New York: Dial Press.
Stone, Merlin. 1979. *Ancient Mirrors of Womanhood*. Boston: Beacon Press.
Suu Kyi, Aung San. 1991. *Freedom from Fear*. London: Penguin.
Suu Kyi, Aung San. 1997. *The Voice of Hope*. London: Penguin.
Teen Vogue. 2019. 'Black Lives Matter Co-Founder Patrisse Cullors Talks Prison Abolition, Therapy as Reparations, and Teaming Up With Angela Davis and Yara Shahidi'. <https://www.teenvogue.com/story/black-lives-matter-patrisse-cullors-interview-prison-abolition-angela-davis-yara-shahidi>.
Television New Zealand. 2019. 'The Black Hole'. *Sunday*. 7 April.
The Wireless. 2015. 'Protest Against "Pinkwashing."' 24 February. <https://www.rnz.co.nz/news/the-wireless/372722/protest-against-pinkwashing>.
Thunberg, Greta. 2019. '"Our House is on Fire": Greta Thunberg, 16, urges leaders to act on climate'. *The Guardian*. 25 January. <https://www.theguardian.com/environment/2019/jan/25/our-house-is-on-fire-greta-thunberg16-urges-leaders-to-act-on-climate>.
Tzu, Lao and Stephen Mitchell (translator). 2015. *Tao Te Ching*. London: Frances Lincoln Limited.
Wagner, Sally Roesch. 2001. *Sisters in Spirit: Haudenosaunee (Iroquois) Influence on Early American Feminists*. Tennessee: Native Voices.
Walker, Sophie. 2019. 'Attacks like the Christchurch shooting won't stop until links between toxic masculinity and terror are recognised'. *The Metro*.

18 March. <https://metro.co.uk/2019/03/18/attacks-like-christchurch-shooting-wont-stop-links-toxic-masculinity-terror-recognised-8928030/>.

Waring, Marilyn. 1988. *Counting For Nothing: What Men Value and What Women are Worth*. Sydney: Allen and Unwin.

Wilton, Caren. 2018. *My Body, My Business*. Auckland: Aotearoa Books.

Wolf, Naomi. 1991. *The Beauty Myth*. London: Vintage.

Woolf, Virginia. 2001. *A Room of One's Own and Three Guineas*. London: Vintage.

Zinn, Howard. 1999. *A People's History of the United States*. New York: Harper Collins.

Zuboff, Shoshana. 2019. *The Age of Surveillance Capitalism: The Fight for a Human Future at the New Frontier of Power*. London: Profile Books.

Zukav, Gary. 1990. *The Seat of the Soul: An Inspiring Vision of Humanity's Spiritual Destiny*. London: Rider.

Index

#MeToo, 1, 3, 14, 124, 138, 156

A Woman's Place UK (WPUK), 180–181
abolition, 2, 6, 148, 151
abortion, 105, 150, 154–156, 178, 202
   Abortion Law Reform Association New Zealand (ALRANZ), 155–156
abuse, 85, 126, 139
   abuser, 100, 159
Access Radio, 51
ACT party (New Zealand), 178
Adams, Abigail, 109
Adams, John, 107, 136
addiction, 1, 3, 13, 80–81, 83–84, 88
Al Noor mosque, Christchurch, 167
Aidoo, Ama Ata, 116
alienation, 10, 32, 52, 81–82, 192. *See also* disconnection; helplessness; isolation
Allen, Darren, 205, 210
Allione, Tsultrim, 199, 209
altruism, 111
Amazon, 165–166
Amnesty International, 48, 126
anarchism, 24, 206–208, 210, 213–215
   Catalonian anarchism, 24
   feminist anarchist, 190, 207
anger, 79–80, 97–98, 109, 191, 193, 197–198, 209
anti-fascist/antifa organization, 149, 152
anxiety, 1, 13, 40–41, 46, 79, 90, 97, 159. *See also* depression
Ap, Raki, 165
Aquilina, Rosemarie, 2–3
Arab Spring, 31, 160
Arden, Elizabeth, 61
Armed Offenders Squad, 168, 172
Arps, Philip, 169

Ashman, Thaya, 169
Assata, Shakur, 147
Atwood, Margaret, 164
Auckland High Court, 101
Aung San Suu Kyi, 24–25, 35
authentic power, 66–67, 77, 95–96, 183, 189–192, 195, 198, 200–201, 205–208, 210, 212–215
   external power, 61, 66–67, 71, 74, 95, 99, 102, 135, 143, 180–181, 183, 193, 195–196, 198, 201, 206–207, 215
Awatere, Donna, 143

Babysitters Club, 22
backlash, 55, 138, 161, 177, 183, 214
'banking' education, 32
bargaining, 115, 144, 180, 201
Barry, Kathleen, 83, 142
Beeby, Clarence, 33
bell hooks, 42, 157
Bergdorf, Munroe, 176
Berlin Wall, 120
Bieringa, Luit and Jan, 33
Bilek, Jennifer, 43
Bindel, Julie, 176
biological sex, 44, 73, 94, 130, 134, 138, 153, 174
Black Lives Matter (BLM), 1–3, 7, 148–149, 152, 160, 165, 173
Blackstone, William, 75, 109
Bolsonaro, Jair, 165
Bowles, Nellie, 160, 172
Breivik, Anders, 171
Bright Green Lies, 166
Brookie, Ian, 101
Brown, Brené, 1, 40, 78, 82
Brown, Michael, 148
Buhner, Stephen, 63

231

Bush, Mike, 172
Butler, Josephine, 112
Butler, Judith, 132

Calvinism, 107
Calvin, John, 107
Cameron, Ewen, 121
Canadian National Inquiry on Missing and Murdered Indigenous Women, 165
cannibalism, 12
capitalism, 12, 23, 31, 39, 45, 103–106, 110–112, 118–122, 124, 129, 131, 140, 144
   disaster capitalism, 120, 124
   liberal capitalism, 110. *See also* free market, free marketeers
caregivers, 78
   nurses, 157–158, 170
Carson, Rachel, 63, 166
Cassandra, 185, 189, 191, 195
Catholic Church, 136
Ceallaigh, Mary, 43
Chalker, Rebecca, 202
Challenor, Aimee, 175
Challenor, David, 175
Chávez, Hugo, 24
Chen, Ellen, 68
Cheyne, Brenda, 89
child sexual abuse, 2
Child Youth and Services (CYFS)/ Oranga Tamariki, 158
childhood dependency, 77, 83
Chödrön, Pema, 208
Christ, Carol, 195
Christchurch massacre, 2019, 3, 148
CIA, 121, 143
Clevy, Gerald, 23
climate change, 4, 6, 10, 144, 148, 162–167, 173, 209
   carbon dioxide emissions, 4
   global fossil fuel emissions, 4
   School Strike 4 Climate, 2019, 167
   We Don't Have Time, 166
Climate Reality Project, 166
   Gore, Al, 166
Cline, Sally, 89

Cold War, 126
Colonised People, 116
commodification, 105, 110, 129. *See also* degradation, dehumanisation; objectification
conditioning, 10–11, 40, 77, 89, 92, 94, 96, 99, 135, 176, 213. *See also* gaslight/gaslighting, socialisation,
social conditioning, 11, 40, 77, 94, 96, 135, 176, 213
Connor, Siobhan, 157
consent, 87, 101
conservativism, 102, 209
Contagious Diseases Act (CDA), 112, 125
coronavirus, 1, 173
   COVID-19, 5–6, 8, 170, 173–174
   traffic light system, 5
   government lockdowns, 1
Cosby, Bill, 2
Crothall, Jayne, 152
Cruz, Nikolas, 161
Cullors, Patrisse, 2, 152
cultural appropriation, 7
cultural relativism, 22
Curie, Pierre, 133

Daring Greatly, 40
DARVO – deny, attack, reverse victim and offender, 100, 102
Davis, Angela, 2, 152
degradation, 85, 123. *See also* commodification, dehumanization, objectification
dehumanisation, 59, 65–66. *See also* commodification, degradation, objectification
dehumanised, 34, 100
depression, 1, 13, 40, 79, 90, 159. *See also* anxiety; dissociation; vulnerability
   perinatal depression, 159
Detective Sergeant Paul Gillespie, 3
Dewey, John, 32, 66, 208
Dhavida, Usria, 71
Diallo, Nafissatou, 124
dialogue in academia, 140
Dickey, Brian, 101

Index

Dines, Gail, 84
disconnection, 1, 10, 13, 40–41, 78, 82, 111. *See also* alienation; helplessness; isolation
Dispenza, Joe, 81
dissident, 120, 130
dissociation, 79, 86–87, 94, 121, 127, 129, 132
distortion, 55, 59–62, 71–72, 74, 84–85, 88, 91, 94–97, 129, 139, 206, 208–209, 211
divorce, divorced, 70, 75, 109, 162, 198
Dobrokhotova, Valentina, 117
Documents with Dignity policy, 4
Doe, Emily, 2
Domestic Abuse Intervention Project in Minnesota, 50
domestication, 76, 79, 131
domesticity, 113
double bind, 90–91, 113
Douglas, Roger, 120
Downer, Carol, 202
Doyle, Glennon, 40, 197, 205, 209
DSK affair, 124
  Strauss-Kahn, Dominique, 124
dualism, 66, 71–72, 74, 76, 127
  dualistic morality of patriarchy, 95
  dualistic philosophy, 102
Dunbar-Ortiz, Roxanne, 111, 141
Dunedin Technical College, 33
Dworkin, Andrea, 17, 41, 92, 95, 105, 133, 137, 153, 203
dystopian, 62, 164

Eagleton, Terry, 136
ecstasy, 85
Education Act, New Zealand, 33
Effect, Greta, 164
Ekman, Kajsa Ekis, 127
elite, 105, 108, 124, 140, 145, 180
empathy, 40, 85
enclosure of the commons, 104, 112
Enloe, Cynthia, 41, 110, 113, 124, 170
Enriqueta, Dona, 198
epidemic, 1, 13–14, 86, 94, 120
eros, 57, 59–61, 65–66, 70–71, 76–77, 79, 83–84, 86, 208, 210

eroticism, 60
Evans, Constable Michelle, 169
exploit, 31, 129
exploitation, 66, 102, 105, 111, 117, 127, 190
Export Processing Zones (EPZs), 119

Fahdl, Nancy, 91
Fair Play for Women, 180
Falk, Will, 179
famine, 7–9, 19, 22, 39
  40 Hour Famine, 9, 19, 22
  African famine, 19
Fawzia, Fawzia, 115
FBI's counterintelligence programs (COINTELPRO), 143
Federici, Silvia, 104, 131
female-only spaces, 6, 45, 56
  female-only rape crisis shelters, 46
feminine grooming, 98
'feminine' leadership, 170
  Ardern, Jacinda, 3, 140, 157, 170
feminism, 5, 9, 11, 15, 40–42, 48, 95, 118, 137–138, 148, 153–157, 159, 172, 174, 177, 180, 183–184, 187, 192, 198–199, 201, 204, 206, 209
feminist analysis, 15, 110, 137, 139, 157
feminist blog, 97
feminist literature, 9, 36, 39, 43
feminist theory, 137, 157
Feminist Current, 179
Festival for the Future, 31
feudal Japan, 20–21
First Amendment, of the US Constitution, 177–178
Floyd, George, 4, 148
Follett, Jade, 151
Ford, Ezell, 148
Foster, Judy, 71
Fraser, Peter, 33
free market (capitalism/capitalists), free marketeers, 111, 119–120, 141. *See also* liberal capitalism
free speech, 176–180
Freire, Paulo, 26–27, 42, 97, 132, 140, 189, 205, 214

French, Marilyn, 72, 143
Friedan, Betty, 36
Friedman, Milton, 119
fundamentalist ideologies, 137

Gage, Matilda Joslyn, 73, 199
Garner, Eric, 148
gaslight/gaslighting, 86, 99–100, 102, 121, 136, 183. *See also* conditioning; hijacking; socialization
GAYTMs (ANZ Bank) 148, 154
gender, identity, 6, 10, 39–41, 43–45, 47, 51, 73–74, 79, 83, 92–94, 102, 124, 130–132, 137–139, 149, 151, 155, 159, 164, 174–175, 180, 182, 201, 208
gender norms, 10, 39
Genter, Julie Anne, 5, 51
Geraghty, Lisa, 158
Ghahraman, Golriz, 174
Gibran, Khalil, 183
Gimbutas, Marija, 72
global financial crisis (GFC), 23
Global South, 165
goddess, 19, 69, 72–73. *See also* Great Mother/Mother-goddess
goddess Shakti, 190
Indian goddess Kali, 186
Godfery, Morgan, 169, 173
Goldman, Emma, 205, 207
Gonzalez, Emma, 161
Grand Theft Auto, 84, 169
grassroots solidarity, 31, 183
Graves, Robert, 19
Great Mother/Mother-goddess, 68–69, 74–75. *See also* goddess, patriarchal religions/religious beliefs
Great Cosmic Mother, 68–69, 74–75
Mother Nature, 68, 71, 75–76
Sumerian myths, 72
Tao, 65, 68, 71, 75, 132–133, 189, 210
Greek myths, 19, 40
Green New Deal, 144
Green Party, 4–5, 51, 156, 174–176
gun control, 3, 161
gun owners, 6
gun violence, 1, 10, 161–162
March for Our Lives, 2018, 1, 161

mass shootings, 10, 161–162
National Rifle Association, 161
School Walkout, 161
Gurley, Akai, 148
gynaecology, 106, 202

Hamilton, Dontre, 148
Hamilton, Patrick, 99
Harrison, Kristina Jayne, 181
Haudenosaunee Great Law of Peace, 109
Hawthorne, Susan, 110–111, 189, 203
Hayton, Debbie, 181
healing, 89, 96, 121, 140, 186
Healy, Catherine, 156
Heldman, Caroline, 87
helplessness, 6, 8, 15, 82. *See also* alienation; anxiety; depression; disconnection
Henderson, Carol, 33
Hennessy, Annabel, 169
Herman, Judith, 82
heterosexual, 45, 90, 141, 203–204
hierarchy, 39, 70–72, 103
hijacking, 99, 120–121. *See also* gaslight/gaslighting
hijacked, 86–87
Hite, Shere, 203
Hite Report on female sexuality, 1977, 203
Hitler, Adolf, 147
homo sapiens, 67, 167
hormones, 81
Hughes, Stephanie, 45
Human Rights Commission (HRC), 49
humanisation, 27, 34, 42, 66, 95, 98, 135, 137, 157, 180–181, 189, 205, 210, 216
hominisation, 63, 77
hypervigilance, 7, 78

identification, 5–6, 27, 77, 79, 82, 87, 92–96, 114, 135, 139–141, 144, 153, 159, 179, 194, 203–204, 206, 208–209
incarceration, 148, 150, 152
Indigenous people, 6, 111, 141
Indigenous America, 71

Index

Indigenous Irish, 103
indigenous women, 150, 165, 199
industrial revolution, 113
internalised oppressor, 96
International Labour Organisation (ILO), 125–126
International Monetary Fund (IMF), 119–121, 124
interracial marriage, 108
intersectionality, 156–157
intimacy, 34–35, 40, 58, 85–86, 105, 197
   human intimacy, 35
   intimacy and sex, 34
   intimate, 34–35, 58, 129, 131–132, 151, 197
invisible hands, 111
Invisible Women of Prehistory, 71
Islamic centre, 3, 161, 168
Islamic Women's Council and Muslim Association, 169
isolation, 36, 41–42, 52, 82, 100, 121, 183. *See also* alienation; disconnection

Jefferson, Thomas, 107
Jeffreys, Sheila, 14, 128, 136
Jensen, Derrick, 60, 206
Crawford, John III, 148
Johnson, Sonia, 189–190, 202
Jong, Kim, 160
Jönsson, Kutte, 127
Joyous Birth, 200
   Fraser, Janet, 200

Kara, Siddharth, 112, 124
Kasl, Charlotte, 88
Keith, Lierre, 41, 48
Kempson, Jesse, 101, 169
Kim Jong Un, 160
Klein, Naomi, 85, 118, 120–121, 131, 166
Klein, Renate, 130
Know My Name, 2, 155
Kohn, Alfie, 26
Krishnmurti, Jiddu, 10, 210, 214
Kubark Counterintelligence Interrogation manual, Kubark manual, 1963, 121

Kurdi, Aylan, 160

Labour Party, 153, 182
land privatisation, 123
Lao Tzu, 68, 189. *See also* Tao
Lauder, Estée, 61
leftist activism, 36, 114
legal system, 31, 71, 75
Leigh, Carol, 128
LePera, Nicole, 82, 97
Lépine, Marc, 172
Lerner, Gerda, 69, 183, 198
Lerner, Harriet, 15, 97, 191
lesbian, 45, 47, 50, 98, 104, 131, 149, 176, 199, 203–204
   lesbian feminism, 199, 204. *See also* radical feminist
liberal left, 140–141, 152–154, 157, 175
liberalism, 102, 107, 119, 136, 209
Locke, John, 107
Lockheed Martin, nuclear manufacturer, 37–38
Logie, Jan, 51, 156
Long, Ian David, 162
Long, Julia, 180, 182
Lorde, Audre, 164, 205
Luther, Martin, 103

Ma, Vajra, 55, 198
Maathai, Wangari, 122
Mackenzie, Fiona, 101
MacKinnon, Catharine, 136
male gaze, 96
male sexual entitlement, 129
male/men's dominance, 9, 11, 52, 75, 143
male/men's violence, 9–12, 44, 47, 99, 153, 168
man camps, 12, 164–165
manipulation, 62, 67, 140. *See also* gaslight/gaslighting; hijacking
Māori, 143, 150, 158–159
   Māori Midwives Aotearoa, 158
March for Science campaign, 4
Marjory Stoneman Douglas High School, Parkland, 161
marriage, 58, 73, 90, 108, 113, 141, 199

Martin, Antonio, 148
masculine norms, 10, 40, 143
　masculine system, 110
masculinity, 42, 83–84, 92, 171, 208
mass starvation, 9
Massey University, 184, 186
Maté, Gabor, 3, 15, 90, 152, 208
matriarchal culture, 68–69, 198–199
McCarthyism, 143
McDonald, Laquan, 148
McGill University, 121
McGowan, Rose, 86, 99, 138
McKibben, Bill, 166
men's dominance, 75
men's egos, 89
menstrual cycle, 63, 69
Michael Fowler Centre, Wellington, 186
midwives, 104–105, 157–158
militarism, 12, 14, 36, 95, 162–163
　nuclear arm, threat, button, 37, 118, 160–161
Millane, Grace, 101, 169
Miller, Chanel, 1, 87, 100, 196, 209
Millett, Kate, 9
Ministry of Foreign Affairs and Trade (MFAT), 36–37
misogyny, 52, 98, 154, 156
　misogynistic, 40
Mix, Jonah, 9–10
Molisa, Grace Mera, 116
Molisa, Pala, 36
Montreal Massacre, 172
Mor, Barbara, 62, 67
Morales, Evo, 24
Morgan, Robin, 142, 172
Morse, Valerie, 38
Murdoch, Rupert, 176
Murphy, Meghan, 179

Nassar, Larry, 2
natural birth, 199
natural disaster, 120, 162
neoliberalism, 85, 102, 118–123, 125, 127, 129, 131–132, 136, 138, 140, 164
　neoliberal reforms, 121
NetSafe, 49

New Zealand Defence Industry Association, 37
New Zealand Family Violence Death Review Committee, 150–151
NewsTalk ZB, 169
Noah, Trevor, 163
Noble, Vicki, 186, 190, 209
non-binary, 55
numbing, 13, 20, 62, 81

objectification of women, 88. *See also* commodification, deumanisation, degradation
　media objectification, 11, 129
　sexual objectification, 41.
Occupy movement, 31
　Occupy Wellington, 31, 35
Olowaili, Antje, 71
Organise Aotearoa, 155
Ormsby, Ripeka, 158
Osho, x, 55, 57, 59, 61, 62, 64, 65, 93, 94, 95, 118
Orwell, George, 59, 134, 182

Pagourtzis, Dimitrios, 161
Palestine Liberation Organisation, 115
Palestinian Women and the Revolution, 115
Paley, Nina, 194
Paris Agreement, 162, 167
Parliamentary Services, 167
paternalism, 8, 15
　paternalistic, 141
patriarchal religions/religious beliefs, 61, 71, 102–103
　Judeo-Christian myth, 73–74
　Christianity, 73, 206
　father god, 70, 73
patriarchy, 9–11, 14, 39, 42, 52, 69, 84, 95–96, 102, 129, 137, 143, 164, 184, 189–190, 194, 203, 207, 209, 216
　patriarchal system, 10–11, 69
pauperisation of women, 112
　women's poverty, 113
pay gap, 159
Peace Action Wellington (PAW), 37–38, 49, 142
Penny, Christian, 31

Index

Peterson, Jordan, 174
Pettersen, Thistle, 48
PinkNews, 138
Pinochet, Augusto, 120
Pokémon Go, 48
police brutality, 1, 7, 10
pornography, porn, 11, 13, 21, 39, 60–62, 81, 84–85, 101–102, 106, 118, 129, 139, 176. *See also* sex industry
porn industries, 102
pornographers, 3, 84, 141
postmodernism, 22, 102, 132, 134–137, 139–140, 206
postmodern academics, 23, 135
Power and Control Wheel, 50, 99, 136
Pride Parade, 43, 131, 144, 148, 151, 153, 182, 209
   Auckland Pride programme/Board, 148, 154
   KIWIFIST, 148
   Sh*t Hot People's Politburo, 151
prison abolition, 2, 6, 148, 151
   Justice Summit, 152
   No Pride in Prisons (NPP), 149
   People Against Prisons Aotearoa (PAPA), 149–151, 154
   prison abolitionist, 3, 149, 153–154, 173
   Restorative Justice, 153
private sphere, 14, 39, 44, 70, 102, 115, 177, 192
public sphere, 14, 44, 102, 176
public/private split, 14
prostitution, 11–12, 44, 51, 61, 88, 112–113, 115, 117–118, 123–129, 139, 141, 159, 182. *See also* sex industry
   'harm reduction', 112, 125
   brothel, 123
   legitimisation of prostitution, 126
   Network of Sex Work Projects (NSWP), 125
   New Zealand Prostitutes Collective (NZPC), 49
   prostituted woman, 127–128
   sex trade, lobby, 112, 124–125, 139
   'sex work', 125–126, 139
Prostitution Reform Act, 2003, 126

Protestantism, 103, 107, 136
   Protestants, 107
Ptacek, James, 153
public discourse, 10, 14

queer theory, association, 49, 137–138, 212, 217

racist, 1, 3–4, 6, 147, 150, 165, 173
radical feminist, 36, 48, 131, 180, 212. *See also* lesbian feminism
   TERF (trans exclusionary radical feminists), 48, 153
Rākete, Emmy, 149
rape, 1–2, 6, 10–15, 39, 42, 45–46, 56, 60–61, 65, 74, 85–87, 92, 94–95, 99–102, 112, 115, 118, 121, 126–127, 129, 131, 141, 151–152, 154–155, 159, 171, 176, 179–180, 192, 194–195, 212
   rape culture, 6, 15, 45–46, 56, 60, 87, 129, 176
   rape victims, 1
Rapira, Laura O'Connell, 152
rationalisation, 104–105
rationalism, 111
Raymond, Janice, 204
Read, Herbert, 32, 60, 78
Reid, Jerame, 148
Reid, Melanie, 158
replacement theory, 160–161, 172
repression, 61–62, 79–82, 93–94, 97–98, 118, 181
reproduction, 57, 60, 63, 72, 110
   reproductive autonomy, 199, 202
Repulsion Standard, 178–179
resistance, 96–97, 104, 107, 109, 140, 142, 214
Rice, Tamir, 148
Rich, Adrienne, 203
Richard, Cliff, 206
Rico, Puerto, 162
Right Wing Women, 154
Rodger, Elliot, 171
Ruiz, Don Miguel, 79

Saadawi, El, 93

Sadhguru, 15, 70, 93
safe space, for women, 45, 56, 130
Salient, 139
samadhi, 64, 85
   satori experience, 24
Sanders, Barry, 162
Santa Fe High School, 161
Save the Children Fund, 8
sensitivity, 13, 62–63, 78, 85–86, 215–216
sex denialism, 94
   female erasure (book/phrase), 43, 208, 213
   one-step sex self-identification, 5, 159
   sex self-identification, 5–6, 159
sex discrimination, 91
sex industry, 125, 128
sex repression, 61–62, 118
sex-based system, 10
sexual anatomy, 129
sexual assault, 2, 6–7, 13, 150
sexual fixation, 94
sexual harassment, 21, 115, 185
sexual intimidation, 40
sexual politics, 9, 42, 92
sexual predation, 1
sexual violence, 152
sexually transmitted diseases, 112
Seymour, David, 178
Shanks, David, 169
Shiva, Vandana, 119, 166, 189
Silent Spring, 166
Silicon Valley, 31
Singleton, Mary Lou, 48, 200–202
Sitka, Chris, 204
Sjöö, Monica, 62, 67
slave, 75, 93, 106–108, 177
   enslaved, 85
slave trade, 107
Smith, Adam, 110, 119, 139
social order, 11, 15, 60, 71, 75, 79, 207
socialisation, 13, 40, 88, 94, 194, 208. *See also* conditioning, gaslight/gaslighting
   masculine socialisation, 13
Solis, Marie, 155
Soviet Union, 117

Speak Up For Women (SUFW), 182, 184, 186
Spender, Dale, 89
split self, 127–128, 132, 140
Sprinkle, Annie, 128
Sproule, Linda, 129
Standing Rock Indian Reservation, 165
Stanton, Elizabeth Cady, 211
status quo, 15, 39, 156, 202
stereotypes, 11
Stone, Merlin, 69, 72
structural adjustment, 102, 119–122, 127, 129, 132
Stuff, 47
surrogacy industry, 112, 130, 139
sweatshop workers, 113

Tamini v Howard Johnson Company, Inc, 91
Tanis, Gokmen, 171
Tännsjö, Torbjörn, 127
Tarrant, Brenton, 161, 167
Te Huia, Jean, 158
technology, 9, 31, 166
   digital technology, 31
   GPS trackers, 48
   technological, 106, 166
Teen Vogue, 3
Thatcher, Margaret, 206
The Creation of Feminist Consciousness, 183, 198
the Guardian, 132, 167
The New York Times, 160
Thich Nhat Hanh, 17, 24, 208
thinking-feeling loop, 81
Thunberg, Greta, 163
Tolle, Eckhart, 68
Toronto Sex Crimes Unit, 3
torture, 106, 120, 143, 176
   sadistic tortures, 106
   sexualised torment, 21
Tovey, Gordon, 33
Trans Pacific Partnership Agreement (TPPA), 36
transgenderism, 43–44, 47–48, 55–56, 62, 93, 129–132, 139, 141, 148–149,

Index

151, 154–155, 159, 175, 178,
  180–183, 201, 209
InsideOut, 47, 49
pro-transgender media coverage, 43
RainbowYouth, 47, 49
trans activists, 6, 44
trauma, 1, 3, 10, 14, 44–45, 53, 57,
  59–60, 62, 82, 86, 127, 129, 152–154
trigger, triggering, triggered, 40, 65,
  81, 86, 174
Trump, Donald, 2, 142
Turner, Brock, 1, 100

United States women's national
  gymnastics team, 2
Universal Declaration of Human
  Rights, 1948, 126

vaginally, 85
Vera, Veronica, 128
Victoria University, Wellington, 35–36
Victorian England, 112, 125
Vietnam War, 118
Vinson, Michelle, 91
violence against women, 12, 141, 153
Virgin Mary, 74–75
Vista, Isla, 172
vulnerability, 1, 40, 82, 94. *See also*
  depression; helplessness

Wagner, Sally Roesh, 199
Walker, Sophie, 171
Wall Street, 31
Wall, Louisa, 153, 182
Waring, Marilyn, 110, 123
Weinstein, Harvey, 2, 86
When the Body Says No, 79
white supremacy, 98, 140, 160, 173
White, Karen, 151
WikiLeaks, 175
  Assange, Julian, 175
wild politics, 189, 205, 210, 214–215
Wilkinson, Danni, 158
Williams, Sunil, 94
Winfrey, Oprah, 170
witch, 56, 102, 104, 106, 129–130
  witch hunts, 102, 104, 106

witchcraze, 103, 106, 111, 202
Wolf, Naomi, 61, 91, 113
womanhood, 45, 69, 129, 155
women's experiences, 95, 157
women's freedom, 85
women's lands, 99, 199, 204
Women's Liberation Movement, 98,
  131, 203
Women's Marches, 155–156
Women's Studies, 136–139, 156
women-friendly cultures, 14
Workers' Youth League (AUF), 171
World Bank, 119

yoga, 65
  yogic philosophy, 93–94, 114
YouTube, 178, 181

Zinn, Howard, 108
Zukav, Gary, 66

*If you would like to know more about
Spinifex Press, write to us for a free catalogue, visit our
website or email us for further information
on how to subscribe to our monthly newsletter.*

Spinifex Press
PO Box 105
Mission Beach QLD 4852
Australia

www.spinifexpress.com.au
women@spinifexpress.com.au